SOUTHERN LITERARY STUDIES

SOUTHERN LITERARY STUDIES

Edited by
LOUIS D. RUBIN, JR.

A SEASON OF DREAMS: The Fiction of Eudora Welty
by Alfred Appel, Jr.

A Season of Dreams

A Season of Dreams

THE FICTION
OF EUDORA WELTY

Alfred Appel, Jr.

LOUISIANA STATE UNIVERSITY PRESS | Baton Rouge 1965

Manufactured in the United States of America by
Vail-Ballou Press, Inc., Binghamton, N. Y.
Designed by Jules B. McKee

Published with the assistance of a grant
from the Ford Foundation.

*To my father
and
my grandfather*

ACKNOWLEDGMENTS

I wish to thank Harcourt, Brace, & World for kindly permitting me to quote extensively from the following copyrighted works by Eudora Welty: *The Bride of the Innisfallen; A Curtain of Green and Other Stories; Delta Wedding; The Golden Apples; The Ponder Heart; The Robber Bridegroom; The Wide Net and Other Stories;* and *Selected Stories of Eudora Welty.* Parts of this book appeared in somewhat different form in *Sequoia* and *Short Fiction Studies,* and I wish to thank the editors for permission to include them here.

I am grateful to Professor Thomas C. Moser, Executive Head, Department of English, Stanford University, for the department research grant which helped to defray typing costs. Robert Penn Warren's essay on Miss Welty stimulated my initial researches into her fiction, and Ruth Vande Kieft's sensitive monograph, *Eudora Welty,* also proved suggestive, although a good part of this book was completed before hers appeared. I am indebted to Professors

Robert Gorham Davis, Lewis Leary, and Joseph Ridgely, all of Columbia University, and to Professor Louis D. Rubin, Jr., of Hollins College, who read the manuscript and furnished many valuable suggestions; and especially to my friend and former undergraduate teacher at Columbia University, Professor William A. Owens, whose early encouragement not only led to a book, but, most happily, to a career. My wife's good sense informed every stage of this study; if it is not felt sufficiently in the final stage, it's through no fault of her own. No "acknowledgment" or "dedication" could adequately express my debt to her.

CONTENTS

INTRODUCTION

IF FRANK O'CONNOR is right in stating that the short story is "the art form that deals with the individual when there is no longer a society to absorb him and when he is compelled to exist, as it were, by his own inner light," then Eudora Welty is the quintessential modern short story writer. Like so many American authors, Miss Welty often writes of individuals who are alienated and isolated from the world. Although many of her characters are imprisoned and a few are even destroyed by their isolation, an important distinction should be made: the sense of loneliness is most oppressive in her early stories, whereas in her later work human isolation is no longer necessarily "tragic" and, in fact, may even be beneficent.

Because many of Eudora Welty's characters are small town "isolatoes" and eccentrics, they might at first seem comparable to the seemingly endless number of lonely, thwarted, and victimized characters who people the towns of Edgar Lee Masters' Spoon

River, Sherwood Anderson's Winesburg, and E. A. Robinson's Tilbury Town. But the resemblances are superficial, for in her artistry and her more complex view of existence, Miss Welty transcends the "village" genre. Experience renders *all* of Anderson's characters helpless and, in his word, grotesque. In setting and mood, *Winesburg, Ohio* (1919) is a world restricted to twilight and night. But Eudora Welty varies the tone and atmosphere of her stories, and like the impressionist painter Monet, who again and again painted the same scene but in different seasons and at various times of day, she renders human separateness in many different "lights." The results of isolation in Miss Welty's fiction are multifarious, and her perspectives vary greatly, from the lyrical to the grotesque, from pathos to satire, irony to gay humor, dream to nightmare. It is impossible to categorize Eudora Welty's fiction. The uninformed generalizations about it do not allow for her wide range in fictional modes and character types and fail to notice that her stories are basically concerned with the mystery of personality.

In an essay, "How I Write," Miss Welty comes close to summarizing her abiding concern: "Relationship is a pervading and changing mystery. . . . Brutal or lovely, the mystery waits for people wherever they go, whatever extreme they run to." [1] Whether the modes being employed are "tragic" or "comic"—to use the traditional division—one continually finds her characters probing the mysteries of identity and relationship. Because of their researches into the ineluctable, her characters seem to live in a world apart from ours.

"Whatever happened, it happened in extraordinary times, in a season of dreams," writes Miss Welty in the opening sentence of "First Love." The action of many of her stories takes place in this "season of dreams"—a special world in which events are perceived as if they happened in a dream, where illusion is paramount, and where characters release their fears and enrich their lives through dream and fantasy. "Whatever happened," she writes, thereby telling us that no one is exactly certain what *did* happen, that often there is a confusion experienced by the characters in her stories, and that this confusion may even challenge the reader's sense of reality. "Everybody to their own visioning," says Mrs. Rainey in "Shower of Gold." Even Eudora Welty's most "objective" stories will belong to the "season of dreams" by virtue of a character's state of acute apprehension or crisis. Yet, however dreamlike her stories may be, they are never merely dreams. Her dreamers have a particular personality and history. They react to the everyday world, and Miss Welty plumbs their dreams and fantasies in order to effect a heightened psychological realism.

The "season of dreams" is not a refuge or escape mechanism. Eudora Welty is not defending autistic regression; the deepest needs of her characters can only be fulfilled through communication with others. They turn to the possibilities of the inner life in order to fortify themselves for the "journey without." Although the "season of dreams" is most prominent in *The Wide Net,* the phrase goes far in describing the total impression of Eudora Welty's fiction, her sense of the primacy of the imagination, and her view of reality.

The actualities of life in Eudora Welty's fiction are Southern. She was born in Jackson, Mississippi, on April 13, 1909. Her late father was the president of an insurance company, and she was brought up in Jackson, where she has lived for most of her life. It was here that her family encouraged her interests in painting and photography, which she pursued diligently before she turned seriously to writing. She was educated in the Jackson public schools, at Mississippi State College for Women, the University of Wisconsin, and the Columbia School of Business, and then returned to live and work in Mississippi. The settings of most of her stories are in her home state; the small towns in the Jackson area, the Yazoo Delta country, and the countryside around Natchez in the southwest part of the state. In only a few stories does she venture into the historic past, or out of the South. She writes equally well about the poor whites of the backcountry and the Mississippi River bottoms, the lower- and middle-class town dwellers, the aristocrats *manqué,* and the Negroes.

Several critics have deemed Eudora Welty the outstanding short story writer of her generation. She has received many awards, honors, and grants,[2] and her work has been translated into many languages and frequently anthologized. Her finest stories can be numbered among the masterpieces of short fiction. A survey revealed that in recent years only William Faulkner, James Joyce, and Katherine Mansfield have been better represented in American short story anthologies, while Miss Welty's stories have appeared more frequently than those of Henry James, D. H. Lawrence, and Ernest Hemingway.[3] The wide anthologizing of her stories underlines the need for a full-scale critical study of her seven books, for many readers are acquainted with Miss Welty's work only through her anthologized pieces and are therefore unaware of the breadth of her achievement.

The purpose of this book is to examine Eudora Welty's fiction as completely as possible. The eight chapters will discuss Miss Welty's rendering of the theme of human isolation; the various comic modes which she employs; her use of the grotesque and Gothic modes; her techniques as a writer; her characterization of the Negro; the role of the pastoral-like Natchez Trace in the most pronounced of the "season of dreams" stories; the rich thematic and symbolic organization of *The Golden Apples,* which involves all the main characters in a "search" that is at once personal and universal; the extremely elusive nature of some of her most recent stories; and how, through the years, there has been a definite but almost imperceptible widening of scope in her fiction, concurrent with a shift of emphasis in her comic writing. The importance of the "sense of place" in her fiction will be stressed, and she will be compared to other Southern writers. Several analogies will be drawn with painting and photography in an effort to suggest the possible influences of her earliest artistic ventures, and her use of myth, legend, fairy tales, and folklore will be examined. The readings of individual stories will be close: the "mysteries" Eudora Welty probes are not easily apprehended, and the order of her stories is a poetic order—often the intricate patterning of recurrent themes, symbols, and metaphors must be unraveled to gain a full understanding of the story. Given her methods as a writer, there is no other choice than to quote freely from her prose. Page references to Miss Welty's fiction will be placed in parentheses within the text and, unless otherwise noted, refer to the first editions cited in the bibliography, except for quotations from *A Curtain of Green* and *The Wide Net,* which refer to the Modern Library collation, *Selected Stories of Eudora Welty.* When necessary for clarity, the initials of the book will also be placed in the parenthesis.

A Season of Dreams

1

CURTAINS
OF
GREEN

> He could understand God's giving Separateness first and
> then giving Love to follow and heal in its wonder; but
> God had reversed this, and given Love first and then Sep-
> arateness, as though it did not matter to Him which came
> first.
>
> —EUDORA WELTY, "A Still Moment"

ALTHOUGH THEY VARY greatly in method, mood, and subject matter, the stories in Eudora Welty's first volume, *A Curtain of Green,*
all record the impact of human separateness on the innocent or
defenseless individual. Seven representative stories from that volume merit first consideration: "A Memory," "The Whistle," "A
Piece of News," "The Key," "Flowers for Marjorie," "Old Mr.
Marblehall," and "A Curtain of Green"—stories in which the
characters are trying to cope with a primal loneliness that is
heightened by physical isolation, the vagaries of chance, the indifference of others, and by their own sense of the paradox expressed
in "A Still Moment." Tentative or desperate, their painful efforts
to bridge the distance between love and separateness only lead to
a deeper sense of isolation; turned back upon themselves, they try
to order their lives through dreams and fantasies, a process telescoped in the book's title.

"A Memory" provides an ideal entry into the world of Miss

3

Welty's fiction. It is one of her most important stories because it presents the moment of the discovery of the two poles: innocence and experience, love and knowledge, the dream and the world. The contrast is presented in terms of horror and the issue is left in suspension.[1] In addition to establishing the axis on which Miss Welty's fictional world turns, "A Memory" serves to point out an important quality in her work—what Miss Welty calls the "sense of place."

"A Memory" reproduces the sensibilities of childhood. Told by a first person narrator, it presents the "initiation" of an artist-personality into the world of experience. The story is probably autobiographical because of the narrator's concern with the nature of reality, with what she calls the "mystery deeper than danger" (CG, 151)—a phrase that summarizes Miss Welty's own pre-occupation as a fictionist. The narrator recalls herself as a young girl, lying on the beach of a lake one summer morning. She already has the artist's habit of vigilance, of trying to identify and give form to random discoveries: "Ever since I had begun taking painting lessons, I had made small frames with my fingers, to look out at everything." The girl is looking out at the bright beach scene through this "frame"—exactly as Miss Welty, years later, said that "place, to the writer at work, is seen in a frame. Not an empty frame, a brimming one." [2] The noon heat and the child's introspective mood create an atmosphere in which sensory perceptions overlap one another, sometimes even blending together. The narrator's acute sensitivity prepares one for the ultimate shock later expressed in the story. Every detail is of importance to the girl. She seems to sense intuitively that reality is unpredictable, even terrifying: "When a person, or a happening, seemed to me not in keeping with my opinion, or even my hope or expectation, I was terrified by a vision of abandonment and wildness which tore my heart with a kind of sorrow" (148). Obsessed with "notions about concealment," she has tirelessly lain on the sand all through the summer, peering intently through her squared fingers, trying to understand the nature of reality by isolating the "outward world" in her "frame," concluding from any observation that "a secret of life" has been nearly revealed to her, and wresting from the "smallest gesture of a stranger" what is to her "a communication or a presentiment."

Her state of exaltation is heightened by her secret love of a boy in school, with whom she has never spoken, but whose wrist she had once accidentally brushed. This first love has made her "doubly austere" in her observations. "Through some intensity I had come almost into *a dual life, as observer and dreamer.* I felt a necessity for absolute conformity to my ideas in any happening I witnessed" [italics mine] (149). School routine and the undisturbed perfection of her love hold both the narrator and the boy in their protective focus. But in her "life as observer," this love has sharpened the girl's expectation that reality might at any moment impinge upon the "absolute conformity" of her dream. When the boy has a nosebleed in Latin class, she "recognizes" her intuitive fears and suddenly faints.

The incident has provided the girl with her first insight into human vulnerability, and she recognizes her helplessness before the vicissitudes of reality. She knows nothing about the boy, increasing her constant uneasiness over his welfare. "I felt a mystery deeper than danger which hung about him." But on the beach, the girl is able to forget about the nosebleed, at least for the moment. With her "framing" device she wills order on the scene, "controlling" reality—or whatever comes within her selective gaze. Miss Welty utilizes Proust's perspective: to the girl on the beach, the past (before the nosebleed) is the true reality. She manages to make that memory superior to the recent incident, although the child's remembrance of it is interwoven with her perception of the physical reality of the present: "I would still not care to say which was more real—the dream I could make blossom at will, or the sight of the bathers. I am presenting them, you see, only as simultaneous" (151). Miss Welty is too fine an artist to tell "which was more real." Rather, she sustains the dialectic by contrasting the dream and the "real"—the sight of a family of bathers who confirm, with a vengeance, the existence of the mysterious "dangers" that were suggested to the girl by the nosebleed.

The girl suddenly sees between the frame of her fingers a family of "loud, squirming, ill-assorted people who seemed thrown together only by the most confused accident, and who seemed driven by foolish intent to insult each other" (152). Flabby, clumsy, gross, and brutal, they sprawl on the sand "in leglike confusion" and cavort with a maniacal, animalistic vigor, pinching and kicking each other with great hilarity. They come tumbling into the narrator's "frame" of vision like a carnival of fools out of a painting by Brueghel, Goya, or Ensor. Their impact upon the girl is heightened by her deep state of reverie, which is subtly rendered by the dissociation of her visual and aural perceptions: "A slow, repetitious sound I had been hearing for a long time unconsciously, I identified as a continuous laugh which came through the motionless open pouched mouth of the woman." The bathers represent a release of all the horror, lawlessness, and chaos that the girl guessed to be part of reality. They embody a threat to human love, beauty, and identity; in their grotesque physiognomies and their destructive abuse of each other they seem ready to sink back into inanimate matter and nothingness: the fat which hangs from the woman's arms "like an arrested earthslide on a hill" suggests that her first motion may send her "slid[ing] down upon herself into a terrifying heap" (153).

The ugliness of all their "confusion and vulgarity and hatred" reaches a culmination when the man pours sand inside the woman's bathing suit between her bulbous breasts, making the family laugh. The girl tries to withdraw "her most inner dream, that of touching the wrist of the boy I loved," but the reality of the beach scene is too great; even with her eyes closed, the fond memory does not come to her. It is obliterated in the climactic moment of "initiation," when the fat woman condescendingly pulls down the front of her bathing suit, emptying out the lumps of mashed, folded sand: "I felt a peak of horror, as though her breasts themselves had turned to sand, as though they were of no importance at all and she did not care" (156). The image of a grotesque transformation telescopes the child's reaction to the whole encounter. She has witnessed a complete defilement of beauty—the beauty of both her memory and of the physical world—the breasts of sand suggesting a desecration and reduction of the human body and life itself to a formless, meaningless level. "When finally I emerged again from the protection of my dream, the undefined austerity of my love, I opened my eyes onto the blur of an empty beach" (156) —or a world temporarily without beauty or meaning. The child's "undefined austerity" has been shattered by the horror of the life around her; in its place is her knowledge of the two polar extremes—the dream and the world. She bursts into tears. Sensing from this experience that the chaos of reality conceals oblivion, the girl realizes that she *must* impose order on her vision, for without some kind of "frame," life will become meaningless. She "squares [her] vision" once more, and recovers the dream. Thinking ahead to the coming school year, she imagines the boy, still "solitary and unprotected," pitiable in his innocence.

The reactions of the girl in "A Memory" are validated by the story's strong "sense of place." Her extreme shock is justified not only by her sensitivity and introspection, but by the summer atmosphere which intensifies her mood. The earlier analogy with Monet is again appropriate, for Miss Welty has the impressionist painter's eye for capturing a detail that is concrete as well as atmospheric and the talent for suggesting, with only a few strokes, the play of light on its surface: "The water shone like steel, motionless except for the feathery curl behind a distant swimmer" (147), writes Miss Welty in the story's first paragraph; one senses that perhaps in no other "place" would the family of bathers have had such an overwhelming effect on the girl. The importance of "place" in Miss Welty's fiction should not be minimized, for her best stories seem almost to have grown out of their settings.

In *Place in Fiction,* Miss Welty says, "It is both natural and sensible that the place where we have our roots should become the setting, the first and primary proving ground, of our fiction." This assertion is borne out by Miss Welty's own faithfulness in "rooting" her fiction in home soil. Yet she does not like the descriptive term "regionalism" (which she calls an "outsider's term"). To her, "regional" is a careless and condescending term because it fails to "differentiate between the localized raw material of life and its outcome as art." For Miss Welty, "place has the most delicate control over character"; it defines feeling while validating the fiction:

> Place in fiction is the named, identified, concrete, exact and exacting, and therefore credible, gathering-spot of all that has been felt, is about to be experienced, in the novel's progress. Location pertains to feeling; feeling profoundly pertains to place. . . . Every story would be another story, and unrecognizable as art, if it took up its characters and plot and happened somewhere else. Imagine *Swann's Way* laid in London, or *The Magic Mountain* in Spain.

Her conception of "place" transcends the more limiting definitions of regionalism; "place" ultimately connects us with "the deep and

running vein, eternal and consistent and everywhere purely itself—
that feeds and is fed by the human understanding."

"A Memory" suggests that the child alone can find it possible to
lead "a dual life as observer and dreamer," without any harmful
effects; the child, after all, is not often forced to confront experience. But what of the adult? In its encounters with experience, how
does the self preserve its innocence, or identity, or sanity? One
might say that all of Miss Welty's fiction—if not *all* serious fiction—is written in answer to this question. Miss Welty's characters
depend upon the possibilities of the inner life for their survival and
many of them use their dreams and fantasies to impose order on
a chaotic reality, exactly as the narrator of "A Memory" used her
"framing" device.

In "The Whistle," two impoverished fifty-year-old tomato
farmers, Jason and Sara Morton, have been forced to the extrem-
ities of existence by the brutal realities of their "place." Spring
freezes have year after year stunted or ruined their crops. The
long, slow winter seems never to end, even though the Almanac
says it is spring. Each night they lie trembling with cold. Sometimes
weeks go by without words, for their continual, numbing exhaustion has driven them apart, and the coldness serves as an extended
metaphor for the physical, emotional, and sexual barrenness of
their existence. On the single night in which the story takes place,
the Mortons rebel against their poverty and the literal and figurative
coldness of their lives by burning all their firewood and furniture
in a futile, ritualistic attempt to bring "warmth" into their lives.

The tightly written opening paragraphs of the stories in *A Curtain of Green* and *The Wide Net* immediately render setting and
character and foreshadow the action of the entire story. "The
Whistle" opens in this manner:

Night fell. The darkness was thin, like some sleazy dress that has
been worn and worn for many winters and always lets the cold through
to the bones. Then the moon rose. A farm lay quite visible, like a white
stone in water, among the stretches of deep woods in their colorless
dead leaf. By a closer and more searching eye than the moon's everything belonging to the Mortons might have been seen—even to the
tiny tomato plants in their neat rows close to the house, gray and
featherlike, appalling in their exposed fragility. The moonlight covered
everything, and lay upon the darkest shape of all, the farmhouse where
the lamp had just been blown out (CG, 111).

The paragraph is a model of compression: the action is set at night; the "thin" darkness is metaphorically linked with the coldness which, in turn, is stated in a fine simile; the characters are named and their poverty is immediately sensed; the central importance of the tomatoes as fact and symbol is signified by their placement near the house, and the words describing them foreshadow their fate; the ominous-toned description of the house as "the darkest shape of all" suggests the burdensome nature of the Mortons' lives; and the images of immolation ("a white stone in water," "deep woods"), of death (colorless dead leaves, the fragile, threatened tomatoes), of a lamp's being blown out, and of a worn dress exposing a body to the cold simultaneously describe both the isolated, oppressive setting and the Mortons' emotional and physical exhaustion. The quality of their existence has been skillfully expressed in terms of "place," and throughout the story, setting and character are equated.

In the first part of "The Whistle," the Mortons are lying fully clothed beneath the quilts of a pallet near the fireplace. Sara is awake, staring into the dark, and Jason is sleeping. His spent passion and deep fatigue are subtly echoed in the course of the fire, which "fluttered in the grate, making a drowsy sound now and then, and its exhausted light beat up and down the wall, across the rafters, and over the dark pallet where [they] lay" (112). Later, when the "fire had at last gone out," Sara looks at the remaining "hulk of red log, a still, red, bent shape, like one of Jason's socks thrown down to be darned somehow" (115). As the story progresses and Jason sinks deeper into sleep the fire conversely ebbs lower, as if measuring his descent into a sleep that seems to will oblivion: Jason's "long-spaced, tired breathing" grows "heavy and solemn . . . as the fire grew lower and lower" (113).

While Jason's exhaustion is expressed in the extended image of the dying fire, Sara's hopes for a rebirth of their love and passion are projected in her reverie about the tomato harvest. Lying awake, she takes refuge from the cold in a "season of dreams" that is literally a season: "Like a vain dream, Sara began to have thoughts of the spring and summer" (113). She thinks of the dusty town of Dexter in the shipping season, and then, "in her mind . . . Dexter became a theater for almost legendary festivity, a place of pleasure. On every road leading in, smiling farmers were bringing in wagonloads of the most beautiful tomatoes . . . the May sun was shining." The tomatoes dominate her dream, and, as a natural emblem of ripeness and fecundity, they function as a perfectly integrated symbol: "Train after train of empty freight cars stretched away, waiting and then being filled"—just as Sara's unarticulated needs are waiting to be filled. "Was it possible to have saved out of the threat of the cold so many tomatoes in the world?" (114). In her dream, warmth, abundance, and ripeness are everywhere. "A strong, heady, sweet smell hung over everything." Tanned and stockingless packers all the way from Florida bring with them a sense of sexual vitality, and Sara imagines herself and Jason standing with them, "under the burning sun near the first shed, giving over their own load" of tomatoes—luxuriating in the fecundity that has disappeared from their actual lives. Although Sara's ability to dream has not been destroyed, the harsh reality of their estrangement and their lot as sharecroppers intrudes even on her dream: she "watch[es] their own tomatoes"—her hopes for a sexual regeneration—"shoved into the process, swallowed away—sorted, wrapped, loaded, dispatched in a freight car—all so fast" (115). Their lives, like the annual packing process, have gone "all so fast," leaving them exhausted, "weightless under [their] quilts." She is able to "see the vision of ripe tomatoes only in brief snatches, like the flareup of the little fire" (the analogy foreshadows the story's strange climax); "the rest of the time she thought only of cold, of cold going on before and after."

Blasts from the landowner's powerful whistle are heard, signaling a freeze. They leave the cabin to cover the tomatoes; when some remain uncovered, Sara pulls off her dress and they use that, too. Their isolation assumes its bleakest perspective, and the frozen landscape is seen in a spectral light. The cold grips them "like the teeth of a trap."

Back in the cabin, they quietly attempt to rebel against their entrapment. "Jason did a rare, strange thing": he pours kerosene over the remaining kindling and lights it. They draw together by the fire. Then he brings in another load, including a big log being saved for the very last of winter, and he lights that, too. "The extravagant warmth of the room had sent some kind of agitation over Sara, like her memories of Dexter in the shipping season." With a fervor that is almost sexual, Jason knocks apart a chair and

burns it, "as though for a little time he would conceal or defend
his tiredness. . . . Then the kitchen table. To think that a solid,
steady four-legged table like that, that had stood thirty years in
one place, should be consumed in such a little while! Sara stared
almost greedily at the waving flames" (119). Jason's assertion par-
allels Sara's reverie and is full of wild but unarticulated hopes for
a new life, for a renewal of passion; one recalls how in the first
scene the "exhausted light" of the flame beat against the rafters
and the walls, "like a bird trying to find its way out of the room"
(112). It is as if the physical *fact* of their thirty years of poverty
and loveless isolation were being ritually destroyed, briefly realizing
their love: "The fire . . . the table had made seemed wonderful
to them—as if what they had never said, and what could not be,
had its life, too, after all" (120). But as they sit in the darkness
after the fire goes out, the cold returns, and a frightening sensation
of complete helplessness takes possession of her, for she realizes
that the "fire" is forever gone from their lives; she speaks Jason's
name—the first dialogue of the story. He tells her to "listen," and
the story ends:

> They held very still, as before, with bent heads.
> Outside, as though it would exact something further from their lives,
> the whistle continued to blow.

Any rebellion or attempts at communication can only be futile in
the face of the forces represented by "The Whistle" and the "place."

"The Whistle" is a touching response to the same kind of bleak
existence memorably recorded by James Agee and Walker Evans
in *Let Us Now Praise Famous Men* (1941). Agee's almost overabundant sensibility and the tone of his prose—with its acute
lyricism and intense sense of moral indignation—is very different
from Miss Welty's more restrained tone and her less socially and
politically oriented perspective. Miss Welty is concerned not so
much with the surface events of the sharecroppers' lives or with the
socioeconomic causes behind the system as with the reaction of the
inner life to these conditions; the "revolution" that takes place is
a private one. Certain critics cannot forgive Miss Welty for not
being more "socially conscious," which is like criticizing Emily
Dickinson for not having written more like Walt Whitman. Thus
the comparison with Agee is instructive. Although Miss Welty may

not be interested primarily in the injustices of tenant farming, she nevertheless *does* articulate a condemnation of this system, which is implicit throughout the story: Mr. Perkins, the landowner, stands "in the very center of everything" in Sara's dream, "buying, directing . . . shouting with grand impatience," and he ends the reverie with Sara's vision of him after the tomatoes have been shipped, when he "holds out his hard, quick hand. Shake it fast! How quickly it is all over!"—summarizing their victimization. Miss Welty never has to raise her voice to tell us this; the continual blowing of Mr. Perkins' whistle at the end of the story does this for her. In its own muted way, then, "The Whistle" can be as affecting as Agee's organ voice.

But a more direct resemblance is to be found with Walker Evans' photographs. By using a decisive visual image to fix a character in our minds, Miss Welty reminds us that she devoted herself to painting and photography before she became serious about her writing. Jason "lay under the quilt in a long shape like a bean" (112) and "Sara's body was as weightless as a strip of cane, there was hardly a shape to the quilt under which she was lying" (113). Miss Welty thus demonstrates her ability to capture the entire quality of a life in just a few words: when Sara lies silently awake, staring at the rafters in the darkness, "her eyes seemed opened too wide, the lids strained and limp, like openings which have been stretched shapeless and made of no more use" (112)—a graphic description that may recall our response to an enlargement of a Walter Evans photograph of a woman sharecropper in whose face is etched, like a woodgrain, the strain and worry of a lifetime.

It is fitting that Miss Welty should be compared to Evans. In the mid-1930's, when she worked for three years as a publicist for the Works Progress Administration (W.P.A.) in Mississippi, she photographed W.P.A. projects and many scenes similar to those recorded by Evans. She also wrote newspaper copy, erected booths at county fairs, and interviewed people; the "job let me get about the state and gave me an honorable reason to talk to people in all sorts of jobs," she told an interviewer.[3] Thus, Miss Welty was exposed to the kinds of people and places that most Southern girls of her class and background were not likely to encounter and would certainly not have sought out. These experiences may in part account for the sensitive and sympathetic manner in which she writes about backcountry people in stories such as "The Whistle" and "A Piece of News."

Like Sara and Jason Morton, the couple in "A Piece of News" live in an isolated backcountry region. As the story opens, Ruby Fisher, an almost illiterate married girl, has returned in the rain to her cabin with a new sack of coffee wrapped in a newspaper (given to her by "the coffee man with a Pontiac car" in gratitude for certain services rendered). In order to dry off, Ruby lies down on top of the spread-out newspaper and by chance comes upon a little news item: "Mrs. Ruby Fisher had the misfortune to be shot in the leg by her husband this week" (CG, 23). Although she realizes that it's a "mistake"—for her husband Clyde knows about her infidelities and at most has given her a slap or two—she nevertheless indulges in a daydream in which she imagines that she is that girl and like her namesake has been shot by her husband, in the heart rather than the less-romantic leg. When Clyde returns he interrupts this fantasy, disposes of the newspaper, and the incident seems on the way to being forgotten.

The story is deceptively simple. Some readers may feel that it has little or no "meaning" apart from its humorous commentary on the psychology of primitive folk, for "A Piece of News" is that kind of eminently modern story, after Chekhov's example, in which nothing—and everything—happens. The story's meaning lies in its atmosphere and in the gradual manner in which Miss Welty unfolds Ruby's extended reverie.

Ruby's isolation is imposed by ignorance, poverty, loneliness, and geographic distance. She and Clyde live outside the law because he runs a whisky still; he always carries a rifle, underlining their separation from the world. Ruby is trapped within her isolation: "in her very stillness and pleasure she seemed to be hiding there, all alone." There are erotic overtones in the details describing her idleness: she bends her head forward, "the yellow hair hanging out streaming and tangled"; she shakes her wet hair "like a cat reproaching itself for not knowing better" (21); and when she thinks of a sexual encounter "she stretched her legs tiredly behind her, like a cat." As her mind wanders, "she stretched, growing warmer and warmer, sleepier and sleepier" (25). At the height of her reverie, she tiptoes on "warm feet" (28). Ruby and the scene itself exude a natural warmth that is directly opposite to the pervasive coldness of "The Whistle."

Even though Ruby is divorced from ordinary moral standards she is still childish, even innocent in her unfaithfulness. But she finds her greatest solace in reverie: "She dragged the newspaper by one corner in a dreamy walk across the floor" (22). Ruby exists in a "season of dreams," and she enjoys the mysterious confusions that she encounters there. Although she knows that it was unlike Clyde to shoot her, she wonders what *would* happen "if he were truly angry," if he cared enough to actually shoot her? Her deep-seated needs engage her imagination and it projects a daydream that fills the void in her life with excitement, drama, and romance: "At once she was imagining herself dying. She would have a nightgown to lie in, and a bullet in her heart." Ruby delights herself with visions of her grave, her burial, and of Clyde's inconsolable grief. Her life thus assumes a new importance. But Clyde suddenly returns, and when "he poke[s] at Ruby with the butt of his gun as if she were asleep" the reality principal intrudes on her dream. " 'What's keepin' supper?' he growled" (27).

In spite of Clyde's return she continues to imagine herself in the new role created by the daydream, and she moves through a familiar setting with a new sense of happiness and excitement: "There was some way she began to move her arms that was mysteriously sweet and yet abrupt and tentative, a delicate and vulnerable manner, as though her breasts gave her pain" (28). For the moment, the dream has transformed everyday reality, infusing it with mystery and romance. With her wet, tangled hair, Ruby is a kind of Venus image—a backwoods Botticelli who exudes a dreamy eroticism. She seems a stranger to Clyde; he is stunned and apprehensive as she circles the table. Ruby shows him the news item and he angrily cries, "It's a lie," but as they look at each other in the new perspective afforded by the piece of news and their fantasy roles, they somehow perceive that their isolation, forced to extremes, can make such a "lie" conceivable:

The moment filled full with their helplessness. Slowly they both flushed, as though with a double shame and a double pleasure. It was as though Clyde might really have killed Ruby, and as though Ruby might really have been dead at his hand. Rare and wavering, some possibility stood timidly like a stranger between them and made them hang their heads (30).

The possibility is simultaneously exciting, frightening, and saddening. Then Clyde throws the newspaper on the fire, dismisses the coincidence, and spanks her good-humoredly.

The plot, such as it is, is rendered in terms of the story's atmosphere, which is presented in both Ruby's musings and the natural setting. The atmosphere *is* the story; the "action" could not occur in any place *except* Ruby's imagination. The storm outside the cabin accentuates and increases Ruby's sense of isolation. "The pouring-down rain" is evoked in the story's first sentence, and it continually underscores her loneliness. The storm not only provides a natural background for Ruby's reveries, but, like the coldness in "The Whistle," appears in conjunction with fire imagery, thus supplying the story with an objective correlative that charts the growth of Ruby's daydream as it envelopes the lonely reality of her life. When she recognizes her name in the newspaper, "the fire slipped and suddenly roared in the house already deafening with the rain which beat upon the roof and hung full of lightning and thunder outside" (23). The unexpected verb "hung" vividly defines the atmosphere in the cabin below and, in the sense of Coleridge's famous phrase, suspends our disbelief by highlighting the special nature of Ruby's world; the fire imagery which projects her strong sexuality is exactly opposite to the dying fire in "The Whistle." The storm reaches its apex at the climactic moment of her fantasy when she imagines Clyde at her grave, wild and shouting: the rain splashed at the window, "the way it was to fall on her grave. . . . A whole tree of lightning stood in the sky. She kept looking out the window, suffused with the warmth from her fire and with the pity and beauty and power of her death. The thunder rolled" (27).

Also rendered in terms of the rain is Clyde's outwardly good-humored yet brooding and potentially destructive nature: "dark streams flow[ed] over the floor where he had walked" (27), and "his enormous hands seemed weighted with the rain that fell from him and dripped down the barrel of the gun"; he sits down, making a "little tumult of his rightful wetness and hunger" (28). His wetness is "rightful" because it represents a sense of reality that insists on impinging upon the dream. He destroys the newspaper and the story ends as

> Ruby folded her still trembling hands into her skirt. She stood stooping by the window until everything, outside and in, was quieted before she went to her supper.
> It was dark and vague outside. The storm had rolled away to faintness like a wagon crossing a bridge (31).

Reality and the dream—"outside and in"—have been rendered congruently, demonstrating Miss Welty's skill at investing the details of a story with a significance that is symbolic yet unobtrusive. The inner "storm"—the quiet desperation momentarily stilled by the dream—does not disappear but subsides into "faintness." "Like a wagon," it can still return to reassert itself in ways perhaps unimagined but fleetingly glimpsed in that moment when "some possibility stood . . . like a stranger between them"—reappearing and recrossing the "bridge" between dream and reality—between Ruby and Clyde—the bridge that, metaphorically, Ruby erects to narrow the distance between herself and the world. "A Piece of News" insists on the inviolable separateness of the individual and suggests that even when a sense of isolation is shared the "mysteries of personality" remain constant.

"The Key" is a poignant enlargement of this theme. The story is set in the waiting room of a remote little railroad station. Albert and Ellie Morgan, a deaf-mute farm couple, are tensely awaiting the arrival of their train. They are using all their savings for a trip to Niagara Falls; Ellie has no idea that it is days away. In their silence and isolation from the world and each other they represent a paradigm of all the loneliness experienced by Miss Welty's characters. Ellie's "face worked and broke into strained, hardening lines, as if there had been a death—that too-explicit evidence of agony in the desire to communicate" (CG, 57). Their affliction is not identified until the story's sixth page, when the people in the waiting room see them using sign language. Instead, Miss Welty creates a sense of acute apprehension in the station that suggests the truth about the Morgans and guides one's gradual entry into the silence and secrecy of their lives. Miss Welty prepares the reader for their silence by strengthening the story's "ear," as it were—heightening its auditory sensitivity so that the reader may be able to "hear" actual sounds more intensely and thus be prepared to feel the Morgans' *silence* as well. In the opening paragraph,

It was quiet in the waiting room . . . except for the night sounds of insects. You could hear their embroidering movements in the weeds outside, which somehow gave the effect of some tenuous voice in the night, telling a story. Or you could listen to the fat thudding of the light bugs and the hoarse rushing of their big wings against the wooden ceiling (56).

Because the Morgans cannot hear, their visual faculty is heightened: although the "prickly light" of an overhead light globe seems to have "stung" into silence the faces of the people below it, to the Morgans, the ceiling lights seem to "pulsate like a living and transient force" (59).

Ellie Morgan is larger, older, and stronger than Albert, who looks "homemade, as though his wife had self-consciously knitted or somehow contrived a husband when she sat alone at night" (58). He is "too shy for this world," but he has not been defeated by it; he anticipates some kind of mysterious surprise: for a moment he seems to be sitting there "quite filled with hope."

His nameless hope is provided by the key of the title. A strange red-haired young man who has been watching Ellie and Albert accidentally drops the key. The sense of quiet that has been established so well is literally shattered by the key as it hits the floor, making "a fierce metallic sound like a challenge, a sound of seriousness. It almost made people jump. It was regarded as an insult, a very personal question, in the quiet peaceful room." The key slides across the floor and lands at Albert's feet. He picks it up. The young man looks at him with "a peculiar flash of interest or of something more inscrutable, like resignation, in his lowered eyes" (61). There is a startling, disturbing quality about the young man: his gaze is so wide and intent "that anyone who glanced after him seemed rocked like a small boat in the wake of a large one" (59); he seems burdened by his intuitive powers. With his compassion, strength, detachment, and humor, the young man is an intriguing, almost allegorical figure.

The young man watches Albert examine the key wondrously, "as if it had fallen from the sky" (the image is teasing, for the young man's omniscience is virtually God-like). Albert holds the key in his hand "with an almost incandescent delight"; its shininess stirs a buried memory of a flashing fish he had seen in his childhood, which helps to explain its appeal to him as a harbinger of happiness. The young man intuitively recognizes the key's importance to Albert, whose strange joy "took precedence with him over whatever need he had for the key." He lets Albert keep it and watches them talk through sign language:

On his hands he said to her, "I found it. Now it belongs to me. It is something important! Important! It means something. From now on we will get along better, have more understanding. . . . Maybe when we reach Niagara Falls we will even fall in love, the way other people have done. Maybe our marriage was really for love, after all, not for the other reason—both of us being afflicted in the same way, unable to speak, lonely because of that. Now you can stop being ashamed of me, for being so cautious and slow all my life. . . . You can take hope. Because it was I who found the key. Remember that—I found it." He laughed all at once, quite silently (62).

When he puts the key in his pocket, he is symbolically hoarding his happiness.

Their train noiselessly arrives and departs without them. Ellie looks "resigned for a moment to hopelessness," and then reasserts her domination. But Albert is now cowed: "Never fear Ellie," he says, "I've got it safe in a pocket" (67). Ellie becomes perplexed, then anxious, in the face of Albert's new bravado and sense of security. "The whole story [of the key] began to illuminate them now. . . . There was something lacking in Ellie." The pathetic, sadly funny truth about their marriage is that Ellie is a compulsive "talker." Her hands are "desperate to speak." When they are alone together on the farm and she has the slightest suspicion of some "unhappiness lying between them. . . . She must worry about it, talk about it" (68). Albert can find peace in the farm chores of an uneventful day, but everything is jolted and disturbed by Ellie's manic "talk."

Ellie takes out her little picture of Niagara Falls, and in a touching sequence they talk about their hopes of "hearing" the Falls through the vibrations of the rail. When she was a little girl, Ellie had been told that newlyweds started their happiness at Niagara Falls—"and that came to be where she put her hope, all of it." She broods over her disappointment and, most important, she fears Albert's "secret life." She tries to *deny* their separateness; she cannot bear the idea of Albert's quiet and private joy. On the surface he seems submissive, but he has the key in his pocket. As he touches it, he dreamily reappraises its "symbolism": "Perhaps he had even decided that it was a symbol not of happiness with Ellie, but of something else—something which he could have alone, for only himself, in peace, something strange and unlooked for which would come to him" (73).

But just when Albert is contemplating the possibilities of free- dom—perhaps a life without Ellie?—the omniscient stranger steps in to rescue her—he gives her a key, too, and then he "went out abruptly into the night." They are equal again; perhaps there is still a chance that the future will see a "changing and mixing of their lives together," even if it is not accomplished by a trip to Niagara Falls. But the story does not end on an optimistic note. The young man is too much the realist to entertain any vision of an easy solution. He lights a cigarette on the way out. "As he held the match close he gazed straight ahead, and in his eyes, all at once wild and searching, there was certainly, besides the simple compassion in his regard, a look both restless and weary, very much used to the comic. You could see that he despised and saw the uselessness of the thing he had done" (73). When Albert picked up the first key, the young man looked at him with resig- nation. His gesture to Ellie is useless because he knows that it is impossible to provide someone with a key to any final happiness. He may be omniscient, but he is not omnipotent. He cannot change Ellie's refusal to allow Albert his rightful privacy—"the secret and proper separation that lies between a man and a woman, the thing that makes them what they are in themselves, their secret life, their memory of the past, their childhood, their dreams. This to Ellie was unhappiness" (72). Miss Welty is saying that even if a shared isolation forces or draws them together, people must still be able to keep their secret key—in whatever form it may take.

The silent, motionless onlookers in the waiting room seem to sense that they are witnessing a confrontation that somehow in- volves each of them: "They were embarrassed, vaguely aware of some crisis . . . but unable to interfere; it was as though they were the deaf-mutes and [Albert] the speaker" (63). In their own ways, Albert and Ellie *are* speakers, expressing a basic human truth, its form magnified by their affliction, exactly as the intensity of the young man and of the harshly lit yellow room shocks the onlookers into looking away and closing their eyes, impressing upon each imagination "a shadow of itself" (65).

The mystery of personality is also the central theme of "Flowers for Marjorie," but in this story it takes on decidedly darker tones. Howard and Marjorie, a young, shy, and impoverished married couple from a small Mississippi town, have gone to New York City during the Depression to seek work. Marjorie is pregnant, and Howard's unsuccessful search for a job has left him humiliated and without hope.

Howard's despair has reached numbing proportions: change no longer seems possible and time itself has ceased to exist for him—he lives in a state of flux, no longer even looking for work. Appropriately, a dreamlike atmosphere is paramount in the opening scene, when he sits on a park bench with other unemployed men. The point of view immediately renders his sense of alienation. Even though someone asks him if he is going to join a demonstration, all that Howard—and the reader—perceives of these men are their feet. Howard only notices things on the ground. His eyes follow some pigeons and he lifts his gaze, but "his eyes ached when [the pigeons] whirled all at once, as though a big spoon stirred them in the sunshine" (CG, 193).

When Howard returns to their room, Marjorie is sitting by the window, the wind blowing her soft cut hair. While life has become pointless for Howard, Marjorie can only look forward to a new life—her baby's. In spite of their hunger and poverty, her pregnancy seems to absolve her from suffering, to imbue her with a kind of mystical aura that makes "her never notice the single and lonely life around her" (194), thus separating her from Howard and isolating him even further. When they lie in bed, "her fullness seemed never to have touched his body. Away at his distance, backed against the wall, he regarded her world of sureness and fruitfulness and comfort, grown forever apart, safe and hopeful in pregnancy" (199). Radiant with her knowledge of time and change, she embodies values in direct contrast to Howard's despair, making her seem "faithless and strange, allied to the other forces."

Marjorie has found a bright yellow pansy which she has stuck in the buttonhole of her old coat; looking at the flower, Howard "winced inwardly, as though she had displayed some power of the spirit" (194). The flower symbolizes Marjorie's immunity from despair, and when Howard has a vision in which he destroys the "blazing" flower and then sinks onto the couch, trembling, the story's denouement is deftly foreshadowed. Marjorie's gentle concern for him only heightens his despair, and he desperately shouts at her,

"Just because you're going to have a baby, just because that's a thing that's bound to happen . . . that doesn't mean everything else is going to happen and change! . . . It doesn't mean that we aren't starving to death. . . . You may not know it, but you're the only thing left in the world that hasn't stopped!"

Marjorie, who "hasn't stopped," represents Time to Howard. "Oh, Howard, can't you keep track of the time? Always asking me . . ." (195). As he lies in bed with her, "the ticks of the cheap alarm clock grew louder and louder as he buried his face against her, feeling new desperation every moment in the time-marked softness and the pulse of her sheltering body" (197). She affronts his deep well of aimlessness and alienation: he regards "her world of sureness and comfort . . . as if he thought it strange that this world, too, should not suffer" (199). He must make Marjorie conform to his reality—he must stop time. "His hand went to the shelf as if he were blind." He picks up a butcher knife and gently thrusts it under her breast, killing her instantly. He symbolically completes his murder of time by throwing the clock out the window. He has perfected his despair. Although violence occurs frequently in Southern fiction, the action here is too dreamlike to be really violent at all. Marjorie does not fall over, but rather, with her arm propped against the sill, she retains her balance—and the composure that characterized her in life.

Near hysteria and in a state of shock, Howard leaves the apartment and wanders through the city. The dreamlike action is transformed into a surrealistic nightmare and the city becomes fantastic, hallucinatory. He looks in a window filled with grotesquely incongruous items and then finds himself in a subway tunnel. "All along the tile wall was written, 'God sees me, God sees me, God sees me, God sees me'—four times where he walked by" (202). As Howard moves through the streets he encounters a series of surprises. With "shy joy" he picks up a glass-ball paperweight from a store counter "and in shocked submission and pity saw the landscape [inside] deluged in a small fury of snow" (202). The symbolism is explicit enough. He is then unexpectedly given a dime by a passing stranger. He goes into a bar and uses his last nickel in the slot machine. He hits the jackpot: "The many nickels that poured spurting and clanging out of the hole sickened him; they fell all over his legs, and he backed up against the dusty red curtain" (203). It is as if some inscrutable force were mocking him ("God sees me," it said in the subway). The profusion of nickels is so great that one of the men says, "Fella, you ought not to let all hell loose that way" (203)—an accurate description of what has happened since Howard killed Marjorie. The series of surprises reaches a monstrous climax in a sequence that, in spite of its brevity, deserves favorable comparison with and even antici-pates much longer scenes in Nathanael West, such as the Holly-wood premiere in *The Day of the Locust* (1939), which was published two years after Miss Welty's story. In her story,

> He walked further and further. It was late when he turned into a large arcade, and when he followed someone through a free turnstile, a woman marched up to him and said, "You are the ten millionth per-son to enter Radio City, and you will broadcast over a nationwide red-and-blue network tonight at six o'clock, Eastern standard time. What is your name, address, and phone number? Are you married? Accept these roses and the key to the city."
>
> She gave him a great heavy key and an armful of bright red roses. He tried to give them back to her at first, but she had not waited a moment. A ring of men with hawklike faces aimed cameras at him and all took his picture, to the flashing of lights.
>
> "What is your occupation?"
>
> "Are you married?"
>
> Almost in his face a large woman with feathery furs and a small brown wire over one tooth was listening, and others were waiting be-hind her.
>
> He watched for an opening, and when they were not looking he broke through and ran (205–206).

All hell *is* loose. The surprises combine to play a kind of cosmic joke intended as proof that Howard's continual bad luck was *not* inevitable, that there is no predicting the workings of chance, and that his seemingly successful attempt to conform everything to *his* vision of reality can easily and mysteriously be nullified. The irony is cruel, for his luck has changed too late. It is seen grotesquely. He runs home, "the roses nodding like heads in his arm," and, when he gets there, he tries to unlock the door with the key to the city. He finds that Marjorie's body has slumped over; she is really dead. He has been right about his fate. He finds a policeman, who, when confronted with Howard's confession, "did not seem for a moment to be sure of the time and place they were in, but had to consult his own watch and pocket effects" (208). Howard's presence is significantly unsettling. When the slot machine showered nickels into the bar, "Howard agreed that they should all have drinks around and that his fortune belonged to them all" (203). The implication is that everyone is helpless before the terrifying mysteries of the universe. After Howard passes the "God sees me" inscriptions, he reads the subway signs, "Entrance" and "Exit only," and "where someone had printed 'Nuts!' under both words" (202). The events of the story suggest that existence is meaningless, unregenerate, and absurd in the existential sense of the word.

Some readers may justifiably feel that those subway signs labor the point, for "Flowers for Marjorie" is perhaps the least successful story in *A Curtain of Green*. It is one of the few stories in which Miss Welty has ventured out of Mississippi, a significant fact when we consider that its central weakness can be traced to its "sense of place"—or *lack* of it. Howard and Marjorie have been transplanted to a new place, and it is obvious that what happens to them is in part a result of this dissociation. But the place is not sufficiently felt; one cannot believe in the demonstration that the men mention, and in spite of the talk of starvation and lonely men, a sense of the Depression is not fully rendered. The point of view limits this possibility, although it need not; one has only to compare this story with "The Whistle" or "A Piece of News" to see how the "season of dreams" can be expressed without losing a sense of the two couples' physical isolation and poverty. The act of displacement in "Flowers for Marjorie" is frontal rather than oblique, the strategy too evident; one sees the seams. The overtly symbolic clock-throwing and parts of the hallucinatory sequences are strained, as if Miss Welty were aware that in these city scenes she was not in her element. This is not damning criticism, however, for one would not expect Dreiser, Farrell, or Saul

Bellow—those bards of the city—to fare too well with the Natchez Trace.

"Old Mr. Marblehall" is a brilliantly executed story that could well serve as a touchstone against which to measure the varying degrees of success in Miss Welty's delineations of the inner life. Of all the stories in *A Curtain of Green,* the "season of dreams" is most conspicuous in "Old Mr. Marblehall" and in the volume's title story.

The opening pages of "Old Mr. Marblehall" are rendered objectively. The story is in the third person, and the point of view seems to be omniscient. "Old Mr. Marblehall never did anything," states the first sentence, "never got married until he was sixty." But he and his old wife have managed to have a child, much to everyone's amazement. However odd the Marblehalls may look, the story's surface reality appears to be in order. In "A Memory," the narrator stresses the importance of even the "smallest gesture of a stranger." The portentous naturalistic details in "Old Mr. Marblehall" have this kind of significance. Out walking "very luxuriously," Mr. Marblehall "looks quaintly secretive and prepared for anything," and even though it is summer, he is wearing his thick tweed coat, for "he is cold all the time"—a fact that foreshadows the story's later revelation. Other details prove to be symbolic as the story unfolds. There is "a knocker shaped like a gasping fish" on the black mahogany front door of Mr. Marblehall's ancestral home. "You always look towards [his home] the way you always glance into tunnels and see nothing. The river is after it now, and the little back garden has assuredly crumbled away, but the box maze is there on the edge like a trap, to confound the Mississippi River" (181). As the story later shows, Mr. Marblehall also performs a most precarious balancing act, and, like the teetering back garden, he too has his defensive ploy, his "box maze." Except for these descriptions, all the other details serve to render the drowsy atmosphere of sunny little Natchez. People are bored. They are not interested in Mr. Marblehall: "There has been an old Mr. Marblehall in Natchez ever since the first one arrived back in 1818—with a theatrical presentation of Otway's *Venice,* ending with *A Laughable Combat between Two Blind Fiddlers*—an actor!" (183). But midway in the story, its focus suddenly changes; the surface reality drops out of sight:

"[Mr. Marblehall] is just like other people to them. He could have easily danced with a troupe of angels in Paradise every night, and they wouldn't have guessed. Nobody is likely to find out that he is leading a double life" (184–85).

The seemingly omniscient point of view now reports Mr. Marblehall's fantasy life. He also has an "other wife," an "other child," and, in a poorer neighborhood, an "other house"—complete with a garden of dust-covered zinnias that don't have any smell. The "other wife" thinks Mr. Marblehall's name is Mr. Bird. Unlike the anxious and self-conscious Mrs. Marblehall, who is a member of the Daughters of the American Revolution and the United Daughters of the Confederacy, Mrs. Bird "stands still and screams to the neighbors." And though "not so ugly," she is fatter, shorter, "funnier looking" than Mrs. Marblehall (186). This other wife tells the truth about "insultingly" well-preserved Mr. Marblehall (or Mr. Bird). He spends each night reading *Terror Tales* and *Astonishing Stories*. "He is killing time"—or waiting to die: "And then Mr. Bird—he doesn't even want a shade on the light, this wife moans respectably. He reads under a bulb" (187). In the passage describing the "normal" Mr. Marblehall's house, "everything is draped and hooded and shaded" (182). The bulb symbolizes the terror of his other self: at night, under its stark glare, Mr. Marblehall's inner turmoil becomes apparent and he confronts it in its unshaded rather than hooded form.

His duplicity derives from his sense of idleness and his realization that "nobody gives a hoot about any old Mr. Marblehall" (183). Like the door knocker on his house, a bored and unoccupied Mr. Marblehall is as helpless as a gasping fish out of water—and this feeling is intensified by his fear of death. His name and the detailed descriptions of his ancestral home complement his inner state.[4] "It's like old eyelids, the house with one of its shutters, in careful working order, slowly opening outward" (182). Because Mr. Marblehall's more conventional efforts to open outward prove insufficient—"nobody cares"—he has sought to fill the empty "hall," to enrich his life through fantasy. In its second part, the story itself is like a marble hall in which the sounds of the real world and those of the fantastic invisible world echo and resound, becoming indistinguishable from one another, each world assuming the same identity.

Like the girl in "A Piece of News" and Albert in "The Key," he is sustained by his compensatory imaginings. "Plunging deeper and deeper," Mr. Marblehall attempts to transcend his fears, "speculat[ing] upon some glorious finish, a great explosion of revelations . . . the future" (191). And while he lives his time out, "he dreams that he is a great blazing butterfly stitching up a net; which doesn't make sense" (191). His dream of death—"stitching up a net"—confuses him because *he* is doing the stitching, which is fitting in the terms of his fantasy: since he seems to have created his other life, it is only logical that he should dream of ending it, too, for he is his own Apocalypse—"a great blazing butterfly," preparing for "some glorious . . . revelation." But because he is without recourse to any of the traditional modes in which one finds solace or hope, he depends completely on his dreams and fantasies; he is metaphysically "killing time" by "storing up and multiply[ing] his life by deception."

He can imagine the excitement if his duplicity were to be known. His second child may find out, and write on a fence, "Papa leads a double life." Mr. Marblehall imagines a public confession: "What an astonishing, unbelievable, electrifying confession that would be, and how his two wives would topple over, how his sons would cringe! To say nothing of most men aged sixty-six" (190). And so he leads this double life—and why not? The first Mr. Marblehall was an actor. But the principal "actor" in the story is the narrator.

A full sense of the richness of "Old Mr. Marblehall" depends on our seeing that the story is not told omnisciently after all, but through a narrating consciousness that has a definite personality and urgent needs of its own, and a voice almost as distinctive as the monologuist's in "Why I Live at the P.O." or "Shower of Gold." The seemingly complete omniscience of "Old Mr. Marblehall" is rare to Miss Welty's work; like most modern writers, she tries to show, rather than to tell an action. Even when a story appears to depend on omniscience, there is an attempt to eschew an overtly omniscient point of view. In "The Key," the powers of perception emanate from the young man, and even if the narrating intelligence can read the Morgans' sign language, the accomplishment is at least credible. But what one learns about the Marblehalls strains all credence. In no way does the point of view have any access to the inside view of Mr. Marblehall—and Miss Welty takes care not to give this impression. On the few occasions in her stories when she does enter a character's mind and report on what is there, she does it in a neutral, infallible, and detached authorial voice. Yet the narrative voice in "Old Mr. Marblehall" is congenial, informal, local ("nobody gives a hoot"), and above all, confidential; the reader is on Catherine Street with the narrator, whose voice slides into the second person, present tense as he shows the local sights: "You can see [Mr. Marblehall] out taking a walk. Watch and you'll see . . ." (179). The narrator is intimate with the social scene and seems to resent Mr. Marblehall's position in it. "It's not so wonderfully large," he says of Mr. Marblehall's ancestral home, "it has only four columns." He is full of supercilious concern for the old man. "He ought to have a little black boy to follow around after him. Oh, his precious old health" (184). Although the story is not in the first person and the narrator is not given a name, the special tone of his voice defines a character who is more vivid than Mr. Marblehall and makes it clear that Miss Welty is not trying for authorial omniscience. The narrator views Mr. Marblehall from a distance and gives no hint of the slightest acquaintanceship between them; excepting divine powers, there is no way for him to know what he knows.

Indulging his obsessive concern with concealment, the narrator makes teasing and oblique allusions to his narrative reliability and his privileged access to special knowledge. "It's full of a hollow wind and echo, winding out through the wavery hope of her mouth," he says of the first Mrs. Marblehall's voice. "Do people know of her perpetual amazement?" (181). When he describes one little Marblehall boy confronting the other, he envisions "a moment of strange telepathies" (190). Both boys, he says, "have that look of cunning little jugglers, violently small under some spotlight beam, preoccupied and silent, amusing themselves" (188). When he tells how the second little boy "finds out things you wouldn't find out," and adds, "he is a monkey," he is speaking of himself (189). The interior world is his creation; the story dramatizes the narrator, who is the real "monkey," the juggler and actor and ventriloquist who imagines and performs all the roles.

The narrator knows that people are indifferent because that is *his* attitude: "Why look twice at him? . . . Mr. Marblehall isn't so important"; "you see, it becomes complicated, full of vindictiveness," he says of "everybody's" attitude. It is *he,* and not Mrs. Marblehall, who "has spent [his] life trying to escape from the parlor-like jaws of self-consciousness," who feels "out on the fringe of habitation" (180). "Drive out any of these streets in and under the hills and you find yourself lost. You see those scores of little galleried houses nearly alike," he says after telling us of the "double life," but not mentioning Mr. Marblehall at all. "Nobody ever looks to see who is living in a house like that . . . you hear the radio for the next two hours. It seems to mourn and cry for [the people]. They go to bed early" (185). It is not Mr. Marblehall but the narrator who is self-consoling and who "has finally caught on, he thinks, to what people are supposed to do." This is it: "they endure something inwardly—for a time secretly; they establish a past, a memory; thus they store up life. He has done this, most remarkably" (191), by projecting his own sense of tedium and futility, his own nocturnal terrors and need for recognition, into "Mr. Marblehall"—and the quotation marks refer not to the title, but to the fantasist's construct, the fiction which is a mask for the narrator.

Readers who prefer less-labyrinthian modes may wonder why the story was not told in the first person, or in the third person, like James Thurber's "The Secret Life of Walter Mitty." The story is not about self-enlargement only; it is a resonant comment on the ambiguity of reality, and to tell it directly would be to limit this possibility. The *trompe l'oeil* effects transport us to that mysterious threshold between sleeping and waking, where external life and the internal voice of the imagination seem to merge, where appearance and reality refuse to be defined. The story abounds in interrogatory phrases, and, through direct address, the narrator involves the reader in his inquiries. The verb "see" appears thirteen times; again and again the narrator uses "you see" in an epistemological as well as conversational sense. He says, "You can see how people are taken aback" by the Marblehalls having had a child; "at least, Mr. Marblehall sees them," he quickly adds (182). He imagines Mr. Marblehall shaking his stick at traffic and saying, "Well, look! I've done it, don't you see?" But even what one literally sees in "Old Mr. Marblehall" is negligible, and all that is imagined is surely never to be known ("nobody is likely to find out that he is leading a double life"). The fantasy forms before us. "You always look toward [the Marblehalls' home] the way you always glance into tunnels and see nothing. . . . You have every reason in the world to imagine the inside is dark, with old things about" (181), he says, eliciting the reader's participation as he fills the *tabula rasa*—those marble halls—with wonderfully absurd Gothic furnishings and then a family to match them. A communion between teller and reader has been created; it is as if one had been told of someone else's dream, and then been made to dream it. "La poésie," wrote Sainte-Beuve, "ne consiste pas à tout dire, mais à tout faire rêver."

In its act of creation, the fantasying mind comes close to outdistancing its anxieties. It is no accident that the narrator has Mr. Marblehall reading *Terror Tales* or perceiving his other wife as resembling "a woodcut of a Bavarian witch, forefinger pointing, with scratches in the air all around her" (186), but as the story progresses, he takes abundant delight in Mr. Marblehall's nocturnal terrors, and the humorous tone almost overrides them. When the narrator projects the dream of death—stitching up a net—he stops short, remarking that it "doesn't make sense"; his imagination has outrun his comprehension. In that one instant of bewilderment one sees the intensity and complexity of his need, and in the next moment, as the story ends, he is frenetically projecting into Mr. Marblehall's future: "Old Mr. Marblehall! He may have years ahead yet in which to wake up bolt upright in the bed under the naked bulb, his heart thumping, his old eyes watering and wild, imagining that if people knew about his double life, they'd die" (191). People *would* "die," colloquially speaking, if they knew his—and our—fantasy lives. But "nobody cares" (his "amazing life" notwithstanding), and his "double life," like all double lives, is ultimately comic and impenetrably absurd, performed alone and in the dark—didn't the *first* "Mr. Marblehall" star in a play called *A Laughable Combat Between Two Blind Fiddlers?*—the combat between the public and private selves which we all variously wage, unendingly.

Unlike Thurber, whose Walter Mitty commutes so easily between sharply defined external and internal worlds, Miss Welty refuses to anchor her story in actuality and thereby avoids the "return to reality" ending that would vitiate the story's implicit ontology. If her narrator's inner life is more important to him than his external life—and is, in fact, his "real" life—then it is fitting that the story should end with that "other life." "Isn't he crazy?" the narrator asks of "Mr. Marblehall," no doubt knowing that in terms of the story, any answer would be irrelevant. A strong sense of the extent of human need and possibility is felt in the story and seems to appear even in the penumbra of mystery that surrounds its characters and scenes—a mystery to be accepted rather than solved.[5] "Old Mr. Marblehall" is not solved, just as we do not "solve" the plot of a play by Pirandello or a novel by Nabokov. "Just what Mr. Marblehall is bending over the Zinnias [in his "second" garden] for is a mystery, any way you look at it. But there he is, quite visible, alive and old, leading his double life" (186).

In "A Curtain of Green," a young widow, Mrs. Larkin, faces a terror far greater than that of "Mr. Marblehall." The opening paragraphs underline the special nature of the story's fictional world: "Every day one summer in Larkin's Hill, it rained a little. The rain was a regular thing, and would come about two o'clock in the afternoon." But on this day the sun is still shining as late as five o'clock. "It seemed almost to spin in a tiny groove in the polished sky." The strange regularity of the rainfall and the unexpected image of the sun suggest a sense of oppressiveness and cosmic dread. Since the death of her husband the previous summer, Mrs. Larkin has spent her days working tirelessly in her large, densely grown garden. She had seen him killed, had watched from the front porch as an enormous chinaberry tree toppled over without any warning. She "had spoken in a soft voice to him, never so intimate as at that moment, 'You can't be hurt.' " But the tree had struck his car, crushing him to death. "It was accident that was incredible, when her love for her husband was keeping him safe" (214). The narrator of "A Memory" also tried to order reality, but her experiences with the boy's nosebleed and the bathers were only a prelude to the ultimate form of chaos represented by Mr. Larkin's sudden and inexplicable death. Mrs. Larkin has discovered that the protective powers of love are useless against the terrors of chance. Like Howard in "Flowers for Marjorie," she has found that she is helpless before the arbitrary machinations of the universe. This knowledge has proved devastating. Her eyes have become dull and puckered, and her mouth is a sharp line. "People said she never spoke." Nor does she have any social contact with her neighbors; her garden is her sole concern.

Mrs. Larkin has literally immersed herself in the nature which killed her husband. In an effort to discover the meaning of this monolithic reality, she works day after day, never stopping, submerged among the thick plants, by now perhaps "unable to conceive of any other place" (210). She virtually becomes a part of nature; her stained, man-sized overalls are almost the color of the leaves. Neither the rain nor the hot, "flashing sky" can detain her. She plants everything that she can, rarely cutting or separating the overreaching clumps of vegetation: "she seemed not to seek order, but to allow an over-flowering, as if she consciously ventured forever a little farther, a little deeper, into her life in the garden" (211). By allowing it complete freedom, she hopes that its uncultivated and wild growth will provide her with a refuge and an answer to the meaning of her husband's death. The paradox is expressed in her eyes, "puckered as if from long impatience or bewilderment." She is bewildered because, after having shut out the everyday world and having drawn a self-protective curtain of green around herself and created a fecund world which would seem to exclude all suffering and death, she nevertheless cannot block the memory of her husband's death, which comes to her "as if a curtain had been jerked quite unceremoniously away from a little scene" (213); nor can she keep the finger of an inscrutable "outside force" from parting the hedge and pointing out her misery. And she is "impatient" because the curtain of green, the veil suspended between the finite and infinite, remains impenetrable, separating man from knowledge of the powers which may or may not control him.

Mrs. Larkin is an enigma to her neighbors, for "she certainly never sent [them] a single one of her fine flowers," not even if "they might get sick and die." Even worse, she plants without any concern "as to what constitut[es] an appropriate vista, or an effect of restfulness, or even harmony of color." Restfulness indeed! One smiles at their fatuous, naïve assumptions and at what they don't know about Mrs. Larkin. To them, "it was impossible to enjoy looking at such a place." After Mr. Larkin's death the

neighbors "had called on her with decent frequency. But she had
not appreciated it, they said to one another." Their dutiful but
limited sympathy has hardened into an attitude not unlike the
cosmic indifference which Mrs. Larkin has suffered; as they look
down casually from their windows and find her in the garden, "as
they might have run their fingers toward a city on a map of a
foreign country," her neighbors are as uncaring as the intense
light which "like a tweezers" picks out her figure in the garden.
To the neighbors, her garden is "a sort of jungle, in which the
slight, heedless form of its owner daily lost itself" (212). Theirs
is a just metaphor, for the actual world *is* a jungle to Mrs. Larkin,
and she is indeed lost in it. Her private world is physically realized, and its "growth" is measured in Mrs. Larkin's actual acts of
planting and transplanting, as she extends her garden and plunges
deeper and deeper into its greenness in a desperate attempt to
discover the mystery that is hidden behind the "curtain of green."

Mrs. Larkin has an infrequent assistant, a Negro boy named
Jamey, who is gardening with her on the day of the story. The
garden suddenly assumes a terrible aspect: "The cries of the birds
had hushed. The sun seemed clamped to the side of the sky. Everything had stopped once again," as it seemed to when her husband died (214). She calls Jamey, but her voice does not carry
in the dense garden. "She felt all at once terrified, as though her
loneliness had been pointed out by some outside force whose finger parted the hedge" (215). She approaches his kneeling figure;
he is smiling softly, "lost in some impossible dream of his own."
For a moment his calmness and his delight enthrall her, but then
she is infuriated by the inaccessibility of "the bowed head holding
so obviously and so deadly its ridiculous dream." She is seized by
the need to protest against reality—"to defy the workings of accident, of life and death, of unaccountability" (216)—and somehow
to control them through an assertion of will. While she had been
unable to will life, she can at least will destruction and death. She
raises the hoe above her head and is about to bring it down upon
Jamey's head when suddenly the daily afternoon rain comes, releasing her terrible passions and denying the efficacy of her will;
the cool drops gently touch her and, sighing, she lowers the hoe,
her sense of helplessness confirmed. A chance of nature has saved
Jamey from death—just as it took Mr. Larkin's life.

While the harsh sun illumines the malevolent aspects of nature, the rain reveals the lovely, benign side of the "curtain": the little plants shine, and the pear tree gives a "soft rushing noise, like the wings of a bird alighting" (217). Although the garden now vibrates with life "in the light from the rain, different from sunlight." Mrs. Larkin's isolation seems irrevocable, for "everything appeared to gleam unreflecting from within itself in its quiet arcade of identity." Like Jamey's dream, everything is self-contained, utterly impenetrable. A strange tenderness spins through her sagging body. Completely surrendering to the mysteries lurking behind "a curtain of green," she imagines how "she would lie in bed, her arms tired at her sides and in motionless peace: against that which was inexhaustible, there was no defense" (218), and then in one motion she sinks down into the flowers, fainting. Her rain-streaked face is fully upturned among the plants. She moves slightly, "in the sad adjustment of a sleeper." Her immolation in the flower bed suggests that Mrs. Larkin will discover no answers, will find no solace in a dream world, and that her final release can only come through oblivion—in sleep and, ultimately, death. Jamey seems to sense this. The story ends as he calls her name "in a horrified, piteous, beseeching voice" (219). The story's significance is highlighted by the fact that Miss Welty entitled her first book *A Curtain of Green,* when there were sixteen other stories in the collection that might have provided her with a title. Perhaps she chose this story because it establishes the nadir in her fictional world and suggests the overpowering nature of the reality against which the individual is pitted—"like a tweezers," the sun picks out the clumsy, small figure of Mrs. Larkin. The volume is well named, for the title story rehearses, in its most extreme form, a strategy for survival to which many of Miss Welty's characters subscribe; the needs may differ and the results are various, but each self weaves and uses its own "curtain."

The characters in these representative stories do not look to any divine, shaping force for their emotional sustenance; they find meaning in their lives only through their dreams and fantasies. Thus "A Memory" foreshadows the general pattern of behavior followed by her characters, especially those in her first three books: even though they are not incipient artists, like the narrator of "A Memory," they all seem to impose their dreams on reality in an effort towards self-preservation. But the characters in "Flowers for Marjorie" and "A Curtain of Green" are pushed beyond their limits of endurance. They represent the low point in Miss Welty's vision of human isolation and these stories serve to define one of the basic attitudes in her work—what might be called the "tragic" aspect—for nowhere else does she present so stark, skeptical, and even terrifying a view of man's small and helpless position in a monolithic universe. Yet it would be inaccurate to call Miss Welty a tragic or pessimistic writer, for her work is also brightened by an irrepressible comic spirit.

2

THE
COMIC SPIRIT

HUMOR HAS ALWAYS been conspicuously present in Eudora Welty's fiction—from the gently satiric "Lily Daw and the Three Ladies" (1937) to the exuberant *The Ponder Heart* (1954). Throughout her career, Miss Welty's work has been distinguished by its comic spirit and by the remarkably diverse manifestations which her comedy has taken, ranging from the most ancient to the most modern of comic modes. Although comedy is perhaps the most difficult of all literary modes to analyze, its importance in Miss Welty's work calls for a careful examination of the sources, methods, and techniques used in her comic writing.

Miss Welty's most "modern" type of comedy is found in a story such as "Flowers for Marjorie." Like the creators of Don Quixote and Hamlet and like many twentieth-century writers, Miss Welty seems to feel that the irrational, the inexplicable, and the nonsensical are so inherent in human existence that the traditional distinctions between comedy and tragedy are no longer viable and that the two views of life seem instead to touch one another, to coalesce at the extremes of human experience. Thus in "Flowers for Marjorie," Howard is the victim of a terrifying cosmic joke, and Mrs. Larkin seems to be the plaything of the same inscrutable joker, who can part at will her self-protective curtain of green. At the end of "The Key," the omniscient, God-like young man regards the couple with a look "very much used to the comic," and a sense of the comic absurd is lightly invoked at the conclusion of *The Ponder Heart,* when the townspeople are alienated from Uncle Daniel because of his generosity. Miss Welty articulated her awareness of the interdependence of tragedy and comedy when she reviewed William Faulkner's *Intruder in the Dust* (1949):

> Faulkner's veracity and accuracy about the world around keeps the comic thread from ever being lost or fouled, but that's a simple part of the matter. The complicated and intricate thing is that his stories aren't decked out in humor, but the humor is born in them, as much their blood and bones as the passion and poetry. Put one of his stories into a single factual statement and it's pure outrage—so would life be—too terrifying, too probable and too symbolic too, too funny to bear. There has to be the story, to bear it—wherein that statement, conjured up and implied and demonstrated, not said or the sky would fall on our heads, is yet the living source of his comedy—and a good part of that comedy's adjoining terror, of course.[1]

A sense of the comedy adjoining the terror is most literally present in "A Curtain of Green," with Mrs. Larkin madly gardening on one side of the hedge while her neighbors gossip on the other, and it is implicit in "Old Mr. Marblehall." There is a comical, courageous abandon in his fantastic but futile attempt to "open outward," and his inner life is unfolded with a gay gusto.

This humor of the absurd is but one of Miss Welty's several comic modes and techniques. There is the macabre, bitter satire of "Petrified Man"; the affectionate, tolerant humor of "Lily Daw and the Three Ladies," *Delta Wedding,* "Kin," "The Bride of the Innisfallen," and "Going to Naples"; the comedy that is tinged with pathos and terror in "A Visit of Charity" and "Clytie"; the unique, gay blending of frontier humor and European fairy tales in *The Robber Bridegroom;* the communal involvement in the process of primitive, comic myth-making that takes place in the cafe scene in "Powerhouse," resulting in a kind of group catharsis; the use of the comic monologue in "Why I Live at the P.O.," "Shower of Gold," and *The Ponder Heart,* which culminates Miss Welty's humorous treatment of small-town Southern life; and the re-creation from the most ancient rites of comedy of the free, uncivilized but knowing self—the singer of phallic songs—the unruly self that feels both archaic pleasure and archaic pain which Nietzsche called Dionysian. According to Nietzsche, "the terrible wisdom of Silenus" informs the substratum of art, and it is Silenus, the satyr-god of comedy, who leads the ecstatic "chorus of natural beings who as it were live ineradicably behind every civilization." [2] The mask of Silenus appears, figuratively, in the stories which celebrate the Dionysian self: "Asphodel," "The Wide Net," "Livvie," "Shower of Gold," *Delta Wedding* in the person of Troy Flavin, and throughout *The Golden Apples,* whenever King MacLain appears. Yet King partakes of a comic mythology that is thoroughly American as well as ancient Greek.

Constance Rourke has demonstrated that a distinct tradition of native humor exists, and many of Miss Welty's comic themes and techniques are in this tradition. With their hyperbole and comic vaunting, King MacLain, the Negro jazz musician Powerhouse, the men in "The Wide Net," and Mike Fink in *The Robber Bridegroom* recall the sense of wonder and the rhapsodic speech of western tall talk—the wild, extravagant, improvisatory humor of the frontier. The narrators of Miss Welty's monologues are "quirky," in the nineteenth-century sense of that word—comically idiosyncratic, obstinate, and full of notions—and they remind us of the traditional Yankee peddler, with his oral monologue, his comic lore, his regional ties and lingo, his familiar, homely imagery and his intimate tone, his composure and his wry humor, and his ability to always infuse his reminiscences with an air of improvisation. Miss Welty's faultless ear for the pure sound of native speech and for the nuances peculiar to certain kinds of speech is given its most sustained expression in the comic monologues, but its presence is felt everywhere in her work. She enjoys all kinds of American lingo. "Could you tell me, madam, where a little lady lives in this burg name of Miss Lily Daw?" inquires the carnival musician in "Lily Daw and the Three Ladies." He greets her with, "Hello, Toots. What's up—tricks?" "Well, they emptying buckets," exclaims Powerhouse as he steps into the rain. The itinerant guitar player in "The Hitch-Hikers" listens to a brassy record on a juke box and says, "We had us owls for chickens and fox for yard dogs but we sung true." When Powerhouse's grandiose and violent fantasy seems on the verge of soaring far beyond the credible, one of his enthralled listeners says, "Only, naw, Powerhouse, that ain't true. That sound too *bad*"—and Miss Welty places just enough of the right emphasis on "bad" to invest it with the resonance of meaning that it has in Negro argot: something outrageously marvelous and as indescribable as the ambiguity of the word itself, which can not be "translated," although it is rarely meant as a pejorative. Also in the American grain are the colloquial verbs which are used humorously, especially in the earlier stories, and the homely figures, which exert a very native charm. In "A Worn Path" a dog knocks old Phoenix over into a ditch, "like a little puff of milkweed," and when a hunter asks her what she's doing down there, she says, "Lying on my back like a June-bug waiting to be turned over, mister." In "Powerhouse" the waitress is "taut and apprehensive as a hen" and waits for an order "like a drop"; and, while Powerhouse is playing, "a bubble shoots out on his lip like a plate on a counter."

"Powerhouse" also brings to mind Henri Bergson's definition of the comic in his *Laughter* (1900)—"something mechanical encrusted upon the living." To the audience, Powerhouse appears to be "in motion every moment . . . going all the time, like skating around the skating rink or rowing a boat," and they see him not as a living person but as a performer who promises the inelastic and mechanical actions they have come to expect from him— which Powerhouse, out of self-protection, consistently produces for them. To use Bergson's distinction, the attention of Powerhouse's audience is insensibly fixed on gesture rather than on action, on isolated, disembodied components of his behavior rather than on the entire person engaged in these gestures, on automatism rather than on motivation. Bergson says that there is something explosive in gesture, which suspends our sympathy and prevents us from taking matters seriously, and Powerhouse, the creative dynamo whose "face looks like a big hot stove," literally seems ready to explode, with his "little round piston legs" going all the time and his "inspired remarks" rolling "like smoke" out of his "vast oven mouth." As the sum of his gestures, Powerhouse is a comic grotesque to the audience. But their limited view of him turns ironically, for the reader follows Powerhouse when he leaves the dance hall—a perspective denied the audience—and sees behind his comic mask and perceives that the action, as such, is an inward drama, revealed obliquely through the fantasy which Powerhouse projects. And the irony, exerted at the audience's expense, helps to release Powerhouse from the dehumanizing comic rigidity which they would still seem to be forcing upon him as the story ends.

Irony is one of Miss Welty's most persistent moods in *A Curtain of Green*. In stories such as "Keela, the Outcast Indian Maiden," "A Worn Path," "Lily Daw and the Three Ladies," and "A Visit of Charity," the unfortunate and isolated characters not only withstand but even become ironically superior to their situations and tormentors. In "A Visit of Charity," Marian, a fourteen-year-old Campfire Girl, visits an Old Ladies' Home. The tone is satiric and ironic. "I have to pay a visit to some old lady" (CG, 220), she tells the nurse at the desk. " 'Any of them will do,' Marian stammered. With her free hand she pushed her hair behind her ears, as she did when it was time to study science." She "did not tell [the nurse] that this visit would give her a minimum of only three points in her score," although she has brought a potted plant as a gift; her points would have been doubled if she had brought a Bible to read to the "residents." The nurse "walked ahead down the hall of closed doors to pick out an old lady" (221). However satiric the tone, there are also several forebodings of terror. The Old Ladies' Home is isolated—it is "on the outskirts of town"—and Marian had to "remove her mittens before she could open the heavy door" of the building, "which was of whitewashed brick and reflected the winter sunlight like a block of ice" (220). The nurse "was a woman in a white uniform who looked as if she were cold; she had close-cut hair" (220); "she spoke like a man" (221), and later is seen reading a copy of *Field and Stream*. "There was a smell in the hall like the interior of a clock." The girl hears a "sound like a sheep bleating," which "decides the nurse. Stopping in her tracks, she first extended her arm, bent her elbow, and leaped forward from the hips—all to examine the watch strapped to her wrist . . ." (221). At the end of the story she makes "another triple motion to consult her wrist watch" (229). The portentousness of her gestures suggest, ominously enough, that she is the guardian of "time" in a place where all conceptions of time have become meaningless.

The nurse shoves Marian into a tiny, cluttered room. Hardly realizing what has happened, Marian finds herself closeted with two old women. There is an imperceptible shift in tone as the satiric sense gives way to a realization of the earlier forebodings; nightmare images are now predominant. One old woman has a "terrible, square smile (which was a smile of welcome) stamped on her bony face . . . a strange smile [that] forced her old face dangerously awry" (222). The other old woman, even older, is "lying flat in bed with a cap on and a counterpane drawn up to her chin" (222); she has "a bunchy white forehead and red eyes like a sheep" (224).

Suddenly Marian saw a hand, quick as a bird claw, reach up in the air and pluck the white cap off her head. At the same time, another claw to match drew her all the way into the room, and the next moment the door closed behind her (222). . . . Everything smelled wet—even the bare floor. She held onto the back of the chair, which was wicker and felt soft and damp. Her heart beat more and more slowly, her hands got colder and colder, and she could not hear whether the old women were saying anything or not. She could not see them very clearly. How dark it was! The window shade was down, and the only door was shut. Marian looked at the ceiling. . . . It was like . . . a . . . cave (223).

Marian seems to have entered another world—or, more specifically, an underworld.

Although the story's beautifully controlled irony is its most evident source of appeal, its richest overtones may derive from the myth of the descent to the Underworld and the confrontation of the living with the living dead. Miss Welty seems to have made instinctive, perhaps unconscious, use of this widespread myth; the accounts of Virgil and Dante and the Proserpina story come to mind.[3] Yet the reader can still sense the horror of the Old Ladies' Home and its removal from everyday reality without any knowledge of its possible antecedents in legend and literature. Miss Welty accomplishes this through the story's dream perspective, for Marian loses her sense of reality in the room. Marian's shock is expressed by her sudden inablity to perceive what is happening around her. After giving up the potted plant, she wonders, "What did it look like?" The old woman bleats, "Who—are—you?" and, "to her surprise, Marian could not remember her name." When the old women argue over whether or not they had enjoyed the previous visit of another Campfire Girl, Marian—"without realizing that she had said a word"—blurts out, "We all enjoyed it" (224). Marian's dissociated reactions underline the story's otherworldy atmosphere.

The two old women at first present comic contrasts. One is consistently ingratiating to Marian, while every reaction of the other is hostile. " 'Pretty flowers,' the first old woman insisted" when she saw the potted plant, " 'pretty—pretty. . . .' " But the other "old woman in bed cleared her throat and spoke. 'They are not pretty . . . ,' " adding, a moment later, " ' Stinkweeds' " (223). But the comic perspective shifts quickly as the second old woman gives vent to her despair, protesting against her lack of privacy, her roommate's intolerable presence, and the indignities and terrifying loneliness of their lives in the dark confines of the home:

"Hush!" said the sick woman [to the first old woman]. "You never went to school. You never came and you never went. You never were anything—only here. You never were born! You don't know anything. Your head is empty, your heart and hands and your old black purse are all empty, even that little old box that you brought with you you brought empty—you showed it to me. And yet you talk, talk, talk, talk, talk all the time until I think I'm losing my mind! Who are you? You're a stranger—a perfect stranger! Don't you know you're a stranger? Is it possible that they have actually done a thing like this to anyone— sent them in a stranger to talk, and rock, and tell away her whole long rigamarole? Do they seriously suppose that I'll be able to keep it up, day in, day out, night in, night out, living in the same room with a terrible old woman—forever?" (227)

This passage justifies the allusion to Dante; like the sinners in the Inferno, the two women seem ready to endure this horror forever; to use Sartre's title, there is "No Exit" from the hell they inflict upon each other. When Marian entered the home, the nurse looked at the plant, " 'You have a nice *multiflora cineraria* there', she remarked" (221); similarly, the old women have been coldly "classified" and filed away, seemingly for all time.

Rather than an understanding of the reality of the shut-in's world, the insensitive and point-seeking Campfire Girl has brought with her a sense of the callous indifference and unconscious cruelty with which the young too often treat the aged. But when the first old woman tells Marian "what's the matter with" the second— "Why, she's mad because it's her birthday!" (228)—Marian trembles, and perhaps for the first time in her life shows a genuine interest in another human being:

> "How old are you?" Marian breathed. Now she could see the old woman in bed very closely and plainly, and very abruptly, from all sides, as in dreams. She wondered about her—she wondered for a moment as though there was nothing else in the world to wonder about. It was the first time such a thing had happened to Marian.
> "I won't tell!" (228)

The old woman begins to cry softly and Marian, her face burning, flees from her confrontation of human misery. Struggling out of the clutching "claws" of the first old woman, who begs for a penny, Marian runs out of the room, down the hall and past the nurse, and pushing the heavy door open, she runs out of the "underworld" and into the cold air and bright sunlight of the "real" world. She retrieves a red apple she had hidden by the prickly shrub, and the story ends as she hails a bus.

> "Wait for me!" she shouted. As though at an imperial command, the bus ground to a stop.
> She jumped on and took a big bite out of the apple (230).

Her composure has returned; the egoism of the child reasserts itself. She is once again "protected" against human involvement. The isolated old women are ironically superior to the girl because of her total inability to cope with the situation. The story's controlling irony is implicit in its title; Marian's visit is not in the least "charitable," and the home—supposedly a haven—is rather a hell. "A Visit of Charity" is remarkable for the way in which its comic, satiric, and grotesque effects all contribute to a deeply felt sense of pathos.

The charitable impulse is also examined in "Lily Daw and the Three Ladies," a story in which the inner lives of the ladies are revealed ironically. The setting is the small town of Victory, Mississippi. Mrs. Carson, the Baptist preacher's wife, Mrs. Watts, who wears widow's black—"the least thing made her hot"—and Aimee Slocum, the spinster postmistress who has a bad complexion, have all taken a humanitarian interest in the affairs of Lily Daw, a retarded girl. In the first scene the three ladies and several other unnamed Baptist ladies (who feel "a little left out") are at the post office when an eagerly awaited letter arrives: Lily Daw has been accepted at the Ellisville Institute for the Feeble-Minded of Mississippi. The three ladies are paying her way. The story's lightly satiric tone asserts itself at once:

"What will Lily say," beamed Mrs. Carson at last, "when we tell her we're sending her to Ellisville!"
"She'll be tickled to death," said Mrs. Watts, and added in a gutteral voice to a deaf lady, "Lily Daw's getting in at Ellisville!" (CG, 3)

The dialogue may recall the gossipy bustle of a Helen Hokinson women's club cartoon, but "Lily Daw and the Three Ladies" is not just a simple story about three banal and prying women. Miss Welty's satire immediately questions the motives of these "do-gooders." There is something vaguely frenetic about their concern for Lily. When they read the letter from the institute, "Mrs. Watts held it taut . . . and Mrs. Carson underscored each line slowly with her thimbled finger." Miss Welty's sense of moral realism probes beneath the surface of the humorous action: "Don't you all dare go off and tell Lily without me!" calls Aimee Slocum (4). The Baptist ladies' false solicitousness barely conceals their fascination over Lily's possible sex life:

"Lily lets people walk over her so," said another.
"Last night at the tent show—" said another, and then popped her hand over her mouth.
"Don't mind me, I know there are such things in the world," said Mrs. Carson, looking down and fingering the tape measure which hung over her bosom.
"Oh, Mrs. Carson . . ." (4).

The three ladies go in search of Lily. They find her at home, wearing a petticoat for a dress, holding a zinnia in her mouth, and kneeling over an old trunk—she later calls it her hope chest—packing her trousseau: "It was empty except for two bars of soap and a green washcloth, which Lily was now trying to arrange in the bottom." But Lily's isolation is ironic, for Lily, seemingly lost in the dream world which is her feeblemindedness, sees the ladies, in her own limited way, more clearly than *they* see *her*.

"Go on and tell us what you're doing, Lily," said Aimee Slocum.
"Packing, silly," said Lily.

"Where are you going?"

"Going to get married, and I bet you wish you was me now," said Lily. But shyness overcame her suddenly, and she popped the zinnia back into her mouth (9).

The ladies' veiled interest in Lily's sex life becomes suddenly explicit. They ask her whom she is going to marry, and, when with comical naïveté she implicates a carnival musician, the three women gasp and stagger variously. Aimee rises up with a scream and a threat: "Oh I think I'm going to faint." Their own sexual preoccupations are now clear: they identify vicariously with Lily's experience.

"All right! We'll bring him back!" cried Mrs. Watts [the musician has supposedly left town]. "He can't get away from *me!*"

"Hush," said Mrs. Carson. . . . "It's better in the long run for him to be gone out of *our* lives for good and all. That kind of man. He was after Lily's body alone and he wouldn't ever in this world make the poor little thing happy . . ." [italics mine] (12).

The pronoun references suggest that Lily's encounter has become theirs. And when Lily agrees to go to Ellisville,

She cocked her head and spoke out in a proud imitation of someone— someone utterly unknown.

"O.K.—Toots!"

The ladies had been nodding and smiling and backing away toward the door.

"I think I'd better stay," said Mrs. Carson, stopping in her tracks. "Where—where could she have learned that terrible expression?"

"Pack up," said Mrs. Watts (14).

Of course Mrs. Carson knows where Lily learned the expression, and she is hoping that the musician will return. The minds of the three ladies are never explored and their fantasy lives are never specifically articulated. Instead, their straightforward actions and reactions suggest their own private worlds.

Lily's departure for the institute brings the whole town, including the Victory Civic Band, to the station to see her off. But when her "fiance" does indeed turn up, arriving at the station with intentions of marrying Lily, the ladies change their plans abruptly and drag Lily off the train to get her married, in spite of poor Lily's whispered protestations. "Just as they climbed down the steps at the back end of the train the band went into 'Independence

March' " (19). The "march" provides an ironic correlative, for Lily is anything but free.

Before the musician is reunited with Lily, Aimee Slocum tells him that Lily's gone to Ellisville. He pulls out a notebook, makes a notation, and says, "Women!—Well, if we play anywheres near Ellisville, Miss., in the future I may look her up and I may not . . ." (18). It is clear that he is not prime husband material, but then, Lily's welfare is not really the ladies' concern. Miss Welty subtly shows how the three ladies distract themselves from their deepest problems—and perhaps project them—by engaging in "good works"; in the process they not only patronize Lily and fail to understand her real needs, but manipulate her in a way that denies her humanity. She has become the vessel into which all of their sexual repressions are channeled, and the story is ultimately about the pathology of goodness—the ugly private motivations that may lurk behind the charitable impulse.

But as gentle and pathetic as she is, Lily Daw is *not* essentially a figure of pathos. The story's light tone forbids Lily from becoming a Wordsworthian idiot girl. Miss Welty's gaiety, especially in the farewell scene at the station, subdues one's response to Lily's plight: the train is puffing, the members of the Civic Band are scattered through the crowd, the leader giving false signals to play, and "a crate full of baby chickens got loose on the platform. Everybody wanted to see Lily all dressed up" (15). The action reminds one that Lily does not really know what's happening to her. The satiric tone is in control throughout the story. At the train, Aimee Slocum—"tears shaking from her eyes" because "she was the one who felt things"—says, "Good-bye, Lily," and Lily answers, "Good-bye, silly"—which is what Miss Welty herself would probably call anyone who took Lily too seriously and reacted sentimentally to the story.

"Lily Daw and the Three Ladies" is focused finally on the ladies. Aimee Slocum "looked back and saw the train moving slowly away. . . . 'Oh, the hope chest!' Aimee cried in a stricken voice." Although it is Lily's trunk that has been forgotten on the train, Aimee's voice is "stricken" because of her subconscious identification with Lily's experience. One recalls the pathetic contents of the almost empty hope chest. It symbolizes for Aimee and the other two ladies the emptiness of their lives, and, as the train carries away the hope chest, their own unfulfilled "hopes" symbolically disappear with it. The story ends as "the band went on playing. Some of the people thought Lily was on the train, and some swore she wasn't. Everybody cheered, though, and a straw hat was thrown into the telephone wires" (20). The closing note of mystification suggests that it is irrelevant whether or not Lily *is* on the train, for she is an ironic foil whose own isolation has served to expose the inner lives of the three ladies. As in "A Visit of Charity" and in "Keela, the Outcast Indian Maiden," conventional patterns are reversed, and seemingly defenseless characters become superior to the tangibly superior characters, who are now revealed to be truly unfortunate, due to a more basic failure or deficiency within themselves. One recalls the town's name; the "victory," however ironic, is Lily Daw's.

Like "Old Mr. Marblehall," "Why I Live at the P.O." is another revelation of a private terror, but realized on a grim comic level. Divided in two sections, the story is told by a first person narrator (known only as "Sister"), who is postmistress of China Grove, "the next to smallest P.O. in the entire state of Mississippi" (CG, 92). Her uninterrupted monolgue is delivered in a vulgar, colloquial style and resembles the traditional oral story, for rather than something to read, it long since seems to have become something to tell to at least a listener, if not to an audience. In the long opening section, the narrator relates to her imaginary "listener[s]" a series of events which occurred on the Fourth of July. In "How to Tell a Story," Mark Twain remarked that "the humorous story is told gravely; the teller does his best to conceal the fact that he even dimly suspects that there is anything funny about it." Herein lies the wonderful, grim humor of Miss Welty's story. As far as Sister is concerned, she is blameless and reports the events of her story with the utmost honesty. But in her opening sentences Sister inadvertently exposes her grossness:

I was getting along fine with Mama, Papa-Daddy and Uncle Rondo until my sister Stella-Rondo just separated from her husband and came back home again. Mr. Whitaker! Of course I went with Mr. Whitaker first, when he first appeared here in China Grove, taking "Pose Yourself" photos, and Stella-Rondo broke us up. Told him I was one-sided. Bigger on one side than the other, which is a deliberate, calculated falsehood: I'm the same.

Sister is quick to inform us that as soon as Stella-Rondo "got married and moved away from home the first thing she did was separate! . . . Came home . . . and to our complete surprise brought this child of two" (90). Stella-Rondo told her family the child was adopted, and throughout the story the family comically insists on maintaining this illusion, although Sister takes advantage of every opportunity to remind them otherwise; Stella-Rondo retaliates by telling Papa-Daddy that Sister called his beard a bird's nest, precipitating the first family crisis in a chain of extravagant incidents.

"Why I Live at the P.O." demonstrates Miss Welty's sharp ear for barbarisms and her ability to capture various speech idioms and their odd inflections. Sister is adept at formulating comically succinct descriptions of her family: "Papa-Daddy's Mama's papa and sulks" (90); "You ought to see Mama, she weighs two hundred pounds and has real tiny feet" (98). Miss Welty recognizes the satiric power inherent in a few well-chosen details. She has her narrator mention details that serve to heighten the vulgar level. Stella-Rondo's room is dominated by an icon-like picture of Nelson Eddy, and Stella-Rondo's "adopted child" is called Shirley T. (T. for Temple); the child may be illegitimate, but at least she can tap dance! Stella-Rondo also owns a flesh-colored kimono. After drinking a bottle of "prescription," Uncle Rondo begins his annual Fourth of July rampage by donning the kimono for the day, disrupting the household. The narrator hates the uncle because he threw firecrackers into her room as revenge for questioning him— "Do you think it wise to disport with ketchup in Stella-Rondo's kimono?"—and, moreover, for saying behind his back that he looked like a fool in it (the incongruous and unexpectedly high-toned verb, "disport," adds to the comedy). The uncle has had his troubles, too: "Once Stella-Rondo did something perfectly horrible to him—broke a chain letter from Flanders Field—and he took the radio back he had given her and gave it to me" (100).

Miss Welty uses brand names in the same spirit: they drink Ne-Hi; Shirley T. gobbles Milky Way bars; the narrator despises her tweezers bought at Kress', yet begrudges Stella-Rondo her "gorgeous Add-a-Pearl" necklace. The family's intellectual capacity is mirrored by their favorite card games—Casino and Old Maid. As in "Petrified Man," Miss Welty uses details as an oblique comment upon her characters.

As the narrator continues her straightforward account, the reader becomes aware of penetrating inconsistencies. Miss Welty subtly allows the reader to see beneath the comic surface of Sister's narration in a manner reminiscent of Ring Lardner. The reader becomes aware of Sister's meanness, alienation, sense of persecution, and—in the terminology of our time—"sibling rivalry":

Stella-Rondo is exactly twelve months to the day younger than I am and for that reason she's spoiled.
She's always had anything in the world she wanted . . . (89).

. . . . . .

Papa-Daddy . . . tried to turn Uncle Rondo against me. I heard every word he said. Oh, he told [him] I didn't learn to read till I was eight . . . and he didn't see how in the world I ever got the mail put up at the P.O., much less read it all. . . . And he said on the other hand he thought Stella-Rondo had a brilliant mind . . . (94).

. . . . . .

Stella-Rondo hadn't done a thing but turn [Mama] against me from upstairs while I stood there helpless over the hot stove (100).

One recognizes the dichotomy between events as they really happened and as they are perceived and related by Sister. As in so many of Lardner's oral narratives and "letters," Sister's self-revelation becomes ironic. There are also secondary ironies within her narrative. When Sister points out that the child has never spoken and may be retarded, Stella-Rondo rises to the challenge and gets Shirley T. to speak her first words:

And in a minute the loudest Yankee voice I ever heard in my life yells out, "OE'm Pop'OE the Sailor-r-r-r Ma-a-an!" and then somebody jumps up and down in the upstairs hall.
"Not only talks, she can tap-dance!" calls Stella-Rondo. "Which is more than some people I won't name can do."
"Why, the little precious darling thing!" Mama says, so surprised. "Just as smart as she can be!" . . . Then she turns on me. "Sister, you ought to be thoroughly ashamed! Run upstairs this instant and apologize to Stella-Rondo and Shirley-T."
"Apologize for what?" I says. "I merely wondered if the child was normal, that's all. Now that she's proved she is, why, I have nothing further to say" (100–101).

The irony obviously turns on the question of "normalcy." The sequence is a grotesque parody of that familiar genre scene cherished by almost every family—Baby's First Words.
The growth of Sister's estrangement is measured in comic terms.

Uncle Rondo's firecrackers prove too much for her ("I couldn't eat!"), and she decides to move to the post office and begins to withdraw all her belongings from the family home:

> The first thing they knew, I marched in where they were all playing Old Maid and pulled the electric oscillating fan out by the plug, and everything got real hot. Next I snatched the pillow I'd done the needle-point on right off the davenport from behind Papa-Daddy. He went "Ugh!" (103)
>
> . . . . . .
>
> I marched in and got that radio, and they could of all bit a nail in two. . . . And I very politely took the sewing-machine motor I helped pay the most on to give Mama for Christmas back in 1929, and a good big calendar, with the first-aid remedies on it. . . . I stood on the step-ladder and got all my watermelon-rind preserves and every fruit and vegetable I'd put up, every jar. Then I began to pull the tacks out of the bluebird wall vases on the archway to the dining room.
> "Who told you you could have those, Miss Priss?" says Mama. . . .
> "I bought 'em and I'll keep track of 'em," I says. . . (105).

Her family bids her good riddance, vowing never to use the P.O. again, and Sister departs.

If there is such a thing as the stage Southerner, then "Why I Live at the P.O." is aimed at this Southern caricature. On one level, the story is a farcical treatment of the often obsessive Southern concern with "kin"—a subject which Miss Welty takes seriously elsewhere. In "Why I Live at the P.O.," the traditionally hallowed network of family ties is extravagantly and comically destructive; with Sister as a catalyst, everyone is at odds; the family might have come out of a W. C. Fields movie. But although there is a gaiety in the telling reminiscent of "Lily Daw and the Three Ladies," one must not forget the obvious difference—unlike Lily, Sister is narrating her own story, and her narration ironically sustains a tension between its comic surface and her troubled inner state. Sister's description of her exodus is humorous, but the thoroughness of her vindictiveness is also frightening and suggests a state of mind that is anything but a joke.

Miss Welty reveals the full extent of Sister's alienation in the brief second part of the story. Sister says, "I like it here. It's ideal. . . . You see, I've got everything catercornered, the way I like it. Hear the radio? All the war news. Radio, sewing machine, book ends, ironing board . . . peace" (109). It is clear that she plans to stay there. The title—"Why I Live at the P.O."—is self-explanatory: her narration has been an intense justification. Behind the gay gusto there lurks the groan, for it is also a story about exasperation and frustration, loneliness and near-madness. Living at the P.O., Sister is completely estranged from her family and most of the town. More terrifying than her self-imposed isolation is the dementia praecox which cuts her off from humanity,[4] and the irony produced by her statement, "I want the world to know I'm happy" (110). The world? One recognizes that there is no world for Sister; she has rejected its inhabitants and does not realize the fact of her alienation. Through Miss Welty's sure handling of the story's point of view, the reader becomes aware of the contrast between the comedy of Sister's domestic squabbles and the pathos of her situation.

Yet there is in Sister a certain mad sense of independence—"As I tell everybody, I draw my own conclusions" (109); dementia praecox or not, there is something indomitable about her: "If I have anything at all, I have pride" (103). When her family swears never to write another letter or use the P.O., Sister correctly observes, "Cutting off your nose to spite your face, then" (107). Perhaps she succeeds in convincing us that she *is* better off in the P.O. There is something within Sister that exults, balancing or modulating the pathos, allowing her to transcend her furious need to feel imposed upon and enabling her to rise out of her despair. Thus, Sister pauses for a moment while removing her fern from the garden; she is in the midst of what some would call a complete mental collapse.

"Even you, Mama, can't stand there and deny that I'm the one watered that fern. And I happen to know where I can send in a box top and get a packet of one thousand mixed seeds, no two the same kind, free."

"Oh, where?" Mama wants to know.

But I says, "Too late. You 'tend to your house, and I'll 'tend to mine. You hear things like that all the time if you know how to listen to the radio. Perfectly marvelous offers. Get anything you want free" (104–105).

Sister does indeed exult, and this unexpected dimension points to one of the most affecting qualities in Eudora Welty's fiction: the way in which put-upon characters will suddenly assert, in spite of all circumstances, some joy or pleasure in life. "Why I Live at the

P.O." is one of the finest pieces of American humor because the laughter generated by the action is qualified by a tolerance and sympathy that is generous yet unsentimental.

"Shower of Gold" (from *The Golden Apples*) and *The Ponder Heart* are also presented as comic monologues. They both define a change that has taken place in the comic spirit of the fiction written since *A Curtain of Green*. The comedy in her first book is often satiric and frequently allied with pathos or—as in "Petrified Man"—with the grotesque. In "Petrified Man" the humor is blistering, almost Swiftian in its outraged response to vulgarity and cruelty. But starting with Miss Welty's second book, *The Robber Bridegroom,* her high spirits begin to find expression in more exuberant, joyful, and "open" forms of comedy—a freer laughter asserting itself in comic modes seldom qualified by irony.

"Shower of Gold" and *The Ponder Heart* are narrated, respectively, by Katie Rainey and Edna Earle Ponder, two garrulous women who speak with the assurance of town historians. Mrs. Rainey churns butter by the main road and Edna Earle runs the only hotel in the town of Clay; "I don't run the Beulah Hotel for nothing: I size people up: I'm sizing you up right now," she tells her "listener" (PH, 11). From their strategic positions, these two women have managed to amass a storehouse of community and family lore—stories, legends, gossip, and an awareness of local class distinctions, prejudices, and opinions on every conceivable subject, which they delight in interjecting into their monologues at comically inappropriate moments ("It's always taken a lot out of me, being smart," says Edna Earle [10]). They tell their stories to strangers who happen by and who, naturally, know nothing about the community and must therefore be told *everything*. In "Shower of Gold," Mrs. Rainey tells her "listener" that she could only bring herself to talk about Snowdie and King MacLain to a stranger—"to a passerby, that will never see her again, or me either. Sure I can churn and talk" (GA, 3). Edna Earle's monologue is delivered to a guest who has just arrived at the Beulah Hotel: "And listen: if you read, you'll put your eyes out. Let's just talk" (11).

Mrs. Rainey and Edna Earle tell stories about fabulous local heroes who are laughable because they have an excess of one "humor" in their disposition, establishing them as comic types.

King MacLain's particular "humor" is his outrageous but good-humored promiscuity; Uncle Daniel's, in *The Ponder Heart,* is one of blind generosity; their "humors" involve them both in one comic situation after another.

Edna Earle unfolds the story of her Uncle Daniel Ponder, who is "rich as Croesus"; he has white hair, wears a white suit, and, although "he's up in his fifties," he is "still the sweetest, most unspoiled thing in the world" (10). However, he has one weakness: "He loves society and gets carried away" (7). This weakness compels him to give things away—a pick-up truck, a field of clover, banana ice cream cones to all the girls in the County Fair burlesque show, and "even his own cemetery lot, but they wouldn't accept it" (8). The Beulah Hotel had once been Uncle Daniel's, but he gave it to Edna Earle fifteen years ago. She says, "you couldn't any more stop Uncle Daniel from giving away than you could stop a bird from flying" (146). Edna Earle seems to have spent most of her life seeing her family through the many crises caused by Uncle Daniel—"I'm the last one, isn't that a scream? The last Ponder" (146). All the incongruities and improbabilities in *The Ponder Heart* are made credible by the authority with which Edna Earle relates them. She succeeds in convincing us that not only did the outlandish events take place, but she has participated in them to the fullest possible extent: "I'm the go-between, that's what I am, between my family and the world. I hardly ever get a word in for myself" (120). Of course, she does manage to get in a good many words for herself, and *The Ponder Heart* is, among other things, a comic portrait of an indefatigable talker. In choosing a name for her narrator, Miss Welty slyly alludes to Edna Earle, the beautiful and pious heroine of Augusta Jane Evans' egregiously sentimental best seller, *St. Elmo* (1867), which provided several generations of Southerners with a name for a daughter.

The first half of Edna Earle's narration describes the comic events leading up to Uncle Daniel's trial for murder. One day, Grandpa Ponder decided Uncle Daniel needed a wife. They visit the Baptist church on Sunday, and, when the strong-voiced widow Miss Teacake Magee rises from the choir for her solo in "Work, for the Night is Coming," Uncle Daniel immediately chooses her for a wife. The marriage, however, does not last long. But its failure does not sour Uncle Daniel on matrimony. In the meantime, a little seventeen-year-old "poor white" country girl named Bonnie Dee Peacock had "traipsed" into town. When Uncle Daniel sees her for the first time behind the counter in the ten cent store, he proposes to her: "I've got a great big house standing empty, and my father's Studebaker. Come on—marry me" (30). They are married within two hours, but Bonnie Dee considers it a trial marriage.

Edna Earle observes that "the Peacocks are the kind of people keep the mirror outside on the front porch, and go out and pick railroad lilies to bring inside the house, and wave at trains till the day they die" (29). But she is not disturbed by the social gap which separates Uncle Daniel and his in-laws. She has no respect for such "child-foolishness"; she holds the "commotion" in check and soothingly tells Judge Tip Clanahan that "people get married beneath them every day, and I don't see any sign of the world coming to an end. Don't be so small-town" (37). But the excitement is too much for Grandpa Ponder; he dies, leaving a fortune to Uncle Daniel, whose second marriage seems a success. However, after five years and six months with Uncle Daniel, Bonnie Dee ends the "trial" period by walking out on him, leaving behind six years worth of *True Love Story* and *Movie Mirror* stacked all over the big house.

Edna Earle gets Bonnie Dee back by running an advertisement in a Memphis newspaper in the form of a twelve-line poem. Bonnie Dee returns, only to run Uncle Daniel out of the house. Edna Earle suddenly informs us that Bonnie Dee is dead, and, without pausing to give any further information, she begins to describe the crowded funeral, which was held out in the country at the Peacock house. The Peacock family is numberless. "Mrs. Peacock was big and fat as a row of pigs, and wore tennis shoes to her daughter's funeral—I guess she couldn't help it. I saw right there at the funeral that Bonnie Dee had been the pick" (76–77). The chickens are underfoot, and in her coffin Bonnie Dee is holding a magnolia a little too big for her size: "They had her in a Sunday-go-to-meeting dress, old-timey looking and too big for her—never washed or worn, just saved," topped with a big, shiny

new sash and bow. Uncle Daniel rushes to compliment the bereaved mother:

> He had Mrs. Peacock by the hand in no time. He said, "Mrs. Peacock,
> let me tell you something. Your daughter's pretty as a doll."
>   And Mrs. Peacock says, "Well sir, that's just the way I used to look,
> but never cared to brag" (77).

Two big rawboned Baptist preachers—"both red-headed"—are in
attendance, one on each side of Bonnie Dee; Edna Earle, a Pres-
byterian, notes cryptically that they had one preacher "to get up
and say look what gold and riches brought you to, and at such an
early age," and the other "to get started praying and not be able
to stop" (78). When Edna Earle gets home she discovers that the
Peacocks have charged Uncle Daniel with Bonnie Dee's murder.

The second half of *The Ponder Heart* is devoted to Uncle Daniel's trial, and the story becomes a "murder mystery" of sorts.
Edna Earle's withholding of any information about the cause and
circumstances of Bonnie Dee's death turns her narrative into a
burlesque of the "who-dunit" story, and the action which she
describes is, in turn, another burlesque—this of trial procedure.
The ensuing scene of courtroom bedlam is a celebration of small-
town anarchy that deserves a place beside similar scenes in Twain
and in Faulkner's "Spotted Horses."

The courtroom is "jam-packed," the motley Peacock clan taking up the first two rows: "Old lady Peacock wagged in first, big
as a house, in new bedroom slippers this time, with pompons on
the toes," followed by her numerous children and grandchildren
(87). The prosecuting lawyer is Dorris R. Gladney, who looks
like the stock villain in a silent film melodrama (88). Uncle Daniel's lawyer decides not to allow Daniel to talk, and the trial begins.

Gladney calls a string of comical witnesses who give testimony
which is at best uncertain. Mr. Truex Bodkin, the blind coroner,
is succeeded on the witness stand by an eccentric old Negro whose
addlepated testimony is made to seem incriminating. The questioning of Miss Teacake Magee is unexpectedly interrupted by
the Judge, who wants a show of hands indicating the number of
people Edna Earle can expect at the hotel for lunch (94). The
fourth witness is Narciss, the Ponders' long-time maid, who was
in the house at the time of Bonnie Dee's death. She describes the
terrible storm that had taken place: a bolt of lightning that had

taken the form of a ball of fire had entered the house through the chimney and had gone through the parlor and then streaked out the back.

Edna Earle herself is the next witness. Gladney thinks Bonnie Dee's heart failure was caused by suffocation, but Edna Earle blames it on the fright brought on by the ball of fire. She testifies to Bonnie Dee's extreme frailness—one time she "tried to cut up a leg of his Sunday pants to make herself a skirt out of" (110)— and reduces most of the spectators to tears with her description of the death scene.

Uncle Daniel cannot resist joining the proceedings and insists on taking the witness stand. When he threatens to tell the court what really happened, Edna Earle leaps up and interrupts Gladney's cross-examination. Then she confides to her "listener" that Uncle Daniel had tickled Bonnie Dee to death with a tassel at the reunion which Edna Earle had arranged for them. The growing mystery is solved: she was the victim of a game of "creep-mousie" intended to assuage her fear of the storm, but her heart gave out from laughter. Edna Earle then describes how Uncle Daniel suddenly stepped down from the witness chair and began to hand out fistfulls of money—his entire inheritance—to everyone in the courtroom: "He made every row, like he was taking up collection in church, but doing the very opposite" (144). Over the tumult an argument develops between Edna Earle and Miss Missionary Sistrunk, who accuses the Ponders of having made their money by "not burn[ing] their cotton when Sherman came, and this is their judgment" (147). The jury is charged and, "hating to miss anything," comes right back with a verdict of not guilty. The courtroom empties; all of Uncle Daniel's money is gone. After his acquittal, he moved into Edna Earle's hotel. In the three days that have elapsed since the trial, no one has ventured near the hotel; "You're the first!" Edna Earle tells her "listener" (155).

The narration abounds in delightful incongruities, descriptions, offhanded remarks, and random grotesqueries, many of which have little or no bearing on the main "plot." Each reader will have his favorite comic scenes or moments. They might include the Peacock clan's behavior during the trial; the way Bonnie Dee took over the big, lightning-rod encrusted Ponder house, bought all sorts of expensive clothes with her charge account, but belied any change in her status by keeping her washing machine on the front porch, "just like any Peacock would be bound to do" (68); Edna Earle's delineation of the differences between Baptists and Presbyterians; or Edna Earle's quirky pastimes, such as her idea of relaxation, which is to read through "a good quiet set of directions" on the application of furniture polish or the removal of corns.

Although Uncle Daniel's eccentricities provide the central action, *The Ponder Heart* is as much Edna Earle's story as his. She communicates a vivid sense of her own personality—her humanity and tolerance, her resiliency, her own Ponder eccentricities, and her hypersensitivity about seeming too "small-town." When Johnnie Ree Peacock wants to stop her testimony to tell the court all about the movie *Quo Vadis,* which she saw in Memphis, Edna Earle comments coldly, "as if it had never been to Clay" (123). But most of all, she does not want to be thought of as an old maid: "I was certainly on the side of love—that's well known and not worth denying" (112); she has for many years kept company with Ovid Springer, a traveling salesman. Edna Earle meets her state of spinsterhood head on, becoming a kind of bachelor matriarch.

Much of the comedy is inherent in Edna Earle's delivery, its special idiom and tone—"He loved happiness like I love tea," she says of Uncle Daniel—and in her skill at reproducing the unintentionally funny dialogue of other characters, such as Judge Waite's attempt to quiet the courtroom: " 'Si-lence! . . . Let the public please to remember where they are at. I have never, in all my jurisprudence, seen more disrespectful behavior and greater commotion and goings-on at a trial. Put that right in the record, Birdie Nell' " (150). Fabled Southern rhetoric breaks down into fractured syntax and *non sequitur,* and Edna Earle is especially adept at capturing the comic oscillations between formal and informal tone. Thus Gladney examines Narciss on the witness stand: "Mr. Daniel Ponder, like Othello of old, Narciss, he entered yonder and went to his lady's couch and he suffocated to death that beautiful, young, innocent, ninety-eight-pound bride of his, out of a fit of pure-D jealousy from the well-springs of his aging heart" (98). But when Edna Earle herself tries to gild the trivial and prosaic, the results are sometimes nothing less than mock-heroic: "And my other grandma was the second-to-longest-living Sunday School teacher they've ever had, very highly regarded" (21). Edna Earle is a veritable anthology of platitudes, most of them regional: "I hope I'm not speaking of kin of present company," she says; Uncle Daniel "dresses fit to kill"; she congratulates herself "every night of the world" for not having married Ovid Springer hastily; she says of Grandpa, "we were all running and flying to do his bidding, everything under the sun he said"; and Bonnie Dee is "no bigger than a minute."

Lower-class lingo is savored in "Petrified Man" and "Why I Live at the P.O." (Sister triumphantly says that she left home without any formal words of farewell, even "without saying 'Kiss my foot' or anything.") In *The Ponder Heart,* however, Miss Welty uses her perfectly tuned ear to render the speech patterns— idiom, syntax, rhythm, and image—of small-town, middle-class Mississippi life. To use Grandpa Ponder's verb for discovering a wife for Uncle Daniel, one could "fork up" enough representative regional idioms in *The Ponder Heart* to inform a section of H. L. Mencken's *American Language* or to provide material for a scholarly article in *American Speech.* But Miss Welty is not so much concerned with "transcribing" the surface patterns of speech as she is with suggesting a sense of the shared culture that is projected through these verbalizations. The exaggerations, euphemisms, and platitudes are not offered as just so many humorous abuses upon the language, but rather as the means by which people can delight in their own absurdities and readily communicate and exchange the humor, tenderness, sympathy, and gossip— and bad feeling—that characterize a true community.

Edna Earle's tolerance of the Peacock family also suggests the shift of emphasis in Miss Welty's humor. The antics of the Peacocks may recall the cavorting bathers of "A Memory," and Bonnie Dee has much in common with the beauty parlor women in "Petrified Man," which was written fourteen years before *The Ponder Heart.* But Miss Welty's reaction to their vulgarity is no longer one of disgust: the satiric mode gives way to a sense of comedy that does not deny their vulgarity, but seems almost to relish it, preferring to see it as funny rather than as grotesque, human instead of monstrous.

The Ponder Heart was well received and won its author the William Dean Howells Medal of the Academy of Arts and Letters, yet most of its commentators have been content to appreciate it as a humorous *tour de force,* while overlooking its less apprehendable qualities. There are reasons for this. Humor never yields easily to analysis, and as for genre, *The Ponder Heart* avoids categorization. One hesitates in calling it a novel, in spite of its one hundred and fifty-six pages, because Uncle Daniel is drawn with the caricaturist's pen and ink rather than with the full palette with which a novelist renders character; nor is Edna Earle's self-revelation novelistic. Uncle Daniel is "flat," he does not develop or change much, but this should not deter analysis, since the same can be said of the greatest comic characters.

Early in her monologue, Edna Earle says that Grandpa had put Uncle Daniel in the asylum for awhile. The main reason he "got more vacations than anybody else down there" was because "they couldn't find anything the matter with him" (15). One time Grandpa Ponder brought Uncle Daniel home to vote, and when he took him back to the asylum they put *Grandpa* away—"Uncle Daniel was far and away the best dressed and most cheerful of the two, of course" (18). Edna Earle concludes, "There's more than one moral to be drawn there . . . about straying too far from where you're known and all—having too wide a territory. . . . By the time you have to *prove* who you are when you get there, it may be too late when you get back. *Think* about Grandpa Ponder having to call for witnesses the minute he gets fifty miles off in one direction. I think that helped put him in his grave" (20). The irony underlines a theme constant in Miss Welty's fiction: that "reality" is an illusory, shifting, relative phenomenon, and to assume ever that it is an absolute—by "straying too far from where you're known," by judging on the sanity of others—is to beg the question, to court a sense of the absurd, the *real* chaos and madness of having your identity usurped. But the everyday world—and Gladney, the prosecutor, is its representative in *The Ponder Heart*—pretends to deal in unwavering absolutes, not paradoxes, which is why the Gladneys succeed. Edna Earle knows this; after the verdict is delivered, "that old Gladney cringed. I hoped he was done for, but I expect he's not—he's probably going straight ahead from here and will end up Governor of

Mississippi" (151). She can lie to Gladney easily because she knows that he is committed to *not* believing her and Uncle Daniel. Gladney wants everything clear-cut; Edna Earle knows that there are no absolutes—"I'm sure Bonnie Dee and Uncle Daniel were as happy together as most married people" (156). And through his generosity, Uncle Daniel proves that things are not as they seem.

Uncle Daniel is love's fool. Lacking in moral intelligence, he is all heart: "Love! There's always somebody wants it. Uncle Daniel knew that. He's smart in a way you aren't, child" (70). But the "banked-up" love in his "ponderous" heart ironically leads to his own isolation at the story's end. This irony may dissuade the literal-minded from simply calling Uncle Daniel insane, for his "insanity" illuminates the essential nature of the townspeople. When Edna Earle is arguing with the Sistrunk family about how the Ponders made their money, "Uncle Daniel just then got to [Mr. Sistrunk] and gave him a single hundred-dollar bill, and shuts him up. You know, I think people have lost the power to be ashamed of themselves" (147). After the trial, "Eva Sistrunk had the nerve to tell me that everybody felt so bad about Uncle Daniel at the moment that if he hadn't been so prominent and who he was, they would have taken up a collection for him" (151). But their alienation from Uncle Daniel at the story's conclusion suggests that they have not entirely lost "the power to be ashamed"; his act of love has inadvertently made them see their own short-comings: "You see, that money has come between the Ponders and everybody else in town. There it still is, on their hands" (155). They cannot forgive him—just as none of us wants to face those to whom, in an unguarded moment, we have shown our deepest inadequacies. The Ponder heart has cast a shadow on the town: the generosity of one harmlessly "insane" man has established the selfishness, hypocrisy, and greed of a "normal" community. As Edna Earle says, "Maybe what's hard to believe about the truth is who it happens to" (143). But true to her nature, Edna Earle will not subscribe to absolutes: "it may be anybody's heart would quail, trying to keep up with Uncle Daniel's" (156). She has to admit, "you know, Bonnie Dee Peacock, ordinary as she was and trial as she was to put up with—she's the kind of person you do miss. I don't know why—deliver me from giving you the *reason*"

(156). However lighthearted her presentation, Edna Earle is acknowledging that experience or behavior *is* paradoxical; its "reasons" have to be left unsaid. Edna Earle's comic monologue can be seen in the same context as Miss Welty's "serious" work, for even in his simple-minded innocence, Uncle Daniel, at the end of *The Ponder Heart,* is as isolated as the most "tragic" of Miss Welty's characters.

"Shower of Gold," the first of the seven interrelated stories in *The Golden Apples,* is a comic monologue that represents another type of comedy appearing in Miss Welty's fiction—a revival in spirit, if not in form, of the most ancient sources of comedy, the Dionysiac revels. The masks of the satyrs, Pan, or Silenus are "worn" or embodied in the person of Cash McCord in "Livvie" (a story which ends in the manner of a fertility rite), Mr. Don McInnis and the romping goats in "Asphodel," William Wallace and his river dragging entourage in "The Wide Net," who enact a humorous re-creation of the primitive Seasonal Pantomine and Ritual Combat (*agōn*), and King MacLain in *The Golden Apples.*

In "Shower of Gold," Katie Rainey unfolds the story of gay, generous, "willful and outrageous" King MacLain. King had married Snowdie, an albino—"some said King figured out that if the babies started coming, he had a chance for a nestful of little albinos, and that swayed him. No, I don't say it. I say he was just willful" (3). As with any first-rate provincial gossip, Mrs. Rainey's claims to objectivity make her interpolations comic, and, like Edna Earle, she seems ready to talk forever.

One day King disappeared from town. Like Mr. Don in "Asphodel," the amoral and pagan King MacLain is the natural enemy of the Apollonian forces of order, restraint, and decorum. He has returned home several times over the years, but his sudden arrivals and departures are always unannounced. But "sweet and gentle" Snowdie waits patiently for him, and the townspeople treat the subject with discretion. King always brings gifts on his surprise visits and often leaves behind a substantial reminder of his unexpected return—"children of his growing up in the County Orphan's, so say several, and children known and unknown, scattered-like" (4). He wears "the stiffest-starched white suit" ever seen, which "looked fierce too—the lapels as alert as ears" (223)—Satyr's ears!

Reports of his presence in other places filter back to town: "the most outrageous was the time my husband went up to Jackson. He saw a man that was the spit image of King in the parade, my husband told me in his good time, the inauguration of Governor Vardaman. He was right up with the big ones and astride a fine animal. . . . But King MacLain could steal anyone's glory, so he thought" (9). Mrs. Rainey digresses to recall her vehement hopes for King MacLain's comeuppance, perhaps because his unruly abandon sets a dangerous example for more domesticated males: "When I asked the way [King] looked, I couldn't get a thing out of my husband, except he lifted his feet across the kitchen floor like a horse and man in one [now the Centaur], and I went after him with my broom." Through the years, the rumors of King's whereabouts—of his even being "two places at once"—have invested him with a legendary quality. The large amount of hearsay included in Mrs. Rainey's narrative creates a state of half-belief or disbelief that helps to sustain the story's mythic quality. King has as his counterpart in myth the greatest philanderer of them all, Zeus; fittingly, King's life-giving powers are like a "shower of gold." But in spite of his cuckolding and seducing, which are effected in a courtly way, he and Snowdie get along fine, and she has borne him twin sons.

Mrs. Rainey delights in retelling how King's official heirs inadvertently achieved a comic reversal at their father's expense. King chose to pay a surprise visit home on Hallowe'en. Snowdie has made costumes for the twins—who have never seen King— and they have bought frightening masks. It has been a frustrating day for the twins, for they have had almost nobody to scare (except for "the Y. & M.V. train whistling through at two-fifteen, they scared that"). Wearing tennis shoes, King stealthily approached his front porch. Mrs. Rainey is outraged by King's "Come-kiss-me" attitude—at the idea of a man making "a little shadow knock, like trying to see how it would look," and then knocking on his own front door (13). Their outlandish costumes flapping, the masked twins charged out on roller skates—screaming and waving their arms like "cannibals." Making a tremendous uproar with their skates, they get King "in their ring-around-a-rosy and he couldn't get out." They skate wildly around him: "after they went around high, they crouched down and went around low, about his knees." Thoroughly confused and shaken, King finally gets "aloose and up and out like the Devil was after him—or in him—finally." As he goes, "right up over the bannister and the ferns, and down the yard and over the ditch and gone," disappearing "into the rough toward the Big Black" (14), he joins company with a long line of characters from American humor— the trickster tricked, a traditional figure who recurs in the work of the Southwestern humorists, in Twain, Lardner, and Faulkner. No one knows where King went after the twins scared him, but Mrs. Rainey closes her monologue with a bit of conjecture which reminds us that her "reportage" has not been entirely free from editorial comment: "But I bet my little Jersey calf King tarried long enough to get him a child somewhere. What makes me say a thing like that? I wouldn't say it to my husband, you mind you forget it" (17). The comic quality of her monologue is underlined by her failure to conceal the fact that even *she* may have been visited by King MacLain.

Throughout *The Golden Apples,* King MacLain represents the triumph of Eros over Thanatos. This is especially felt in "The Wanderers," the final story in *The Golden Apples.* Now an old man, King has returned home once again. Mrs. Rainey has died, and he attends her funeral. The story focuses on her daughter Virgie Rainey, who watches King MacLain as he helps himself to ham while the funeral is still in progress and then makes "a hideous face at Virgie, like a silent yell . . . at everything, including death," which leaves Virgie feeling refreshed (227). Later, Virgie's meditations are filled with death; standing in the rain, she suddenly remembers King: "She smiled once, seeing before her . . . the hideous and delectable face Mr. King MacLain had made at the funeral, and when they all knew he was next—even he" (244). The Dionysiac King exults in the face of death not so much out of irreverence but rather in the pure joy of being alive. As Virgie thinks of him she hears through the falling rain the sounds of life, "the world beating in [her] ear," and *The Golden Apples* comes to an end.

"The Wide Net," which won first prize in the O. Henry Memorial Award Contest of 1942, is another of Miss Welty's celebrations of life. It is set in the countryside around the Natchez Trace—

Pearl River area and is the best example of how Miss Welty can lightly evoke the spirit of the ancient rites of comedy, of folk ceremonies and fertility rites, of Dionysiac feasts and birth and marriage celebrations.[5] The story's opening sentences announce that the action occurs at an appropriate time of change in the lives of the characters and in the season: "William Wallace Jamieson's wife Hazel was going to have a baby. But this was October, and it was six months away, and she acted exactly as though it would be tomorrow" (WN, 34). When they walk through the deep, "cool and secret" woods, the character named Doc intones, "We're walking along in the changing-time. . . . Any day now the change will come. It's going to turn from hot to cold." He concludes, " 'Only today . . . today, in October sun, it's all gold —sky and tree and water. Everything just before it changes looks to be made of gold' " (48). Hazel, who is very much in the process of change, is "a golden-haired girl" (47), and when William Wallace thinks of her she is "like a piece of pure gold, too precious to touch." The wide net which figures so prominently in the action is significantly "so old and so long-used, it too looked golden, strung and tied with golden threads" (49).

Hazel's pregnancy has filled her with a sense of mystery, making her hypersensitive and unpredictable. When William Wallace tries to ease the strain by going out with the boys one night he only aggravates the situation: he gets drunk and stays out all night. When he returns in the morning Hazel has vanished. She has left a letter which says "that she would not put up with him after that and was going to the river to drown herself" (35). William Wallace and his friend Virgil Thomas decide to drag the Pearl River for Hazel.

Although the story concerns a possible suicide, its tone is humorous. William Wallace seems most worried about what his mother-in-law will say, and, when he comments on Hazel's fear of water and wonders "how she brought herself to jump," Virgil has the logical answer: "Jumped backwards. . . . Didn't look" (39).

The river dragging provides the story with its appropriate "ritual action." William Wallace is like the heroes from myth and legend whose strength must be tested in ritual encounters with elemental and evil forces. He is the "hero" or "king"—or, finally, "river-god"—in Miss Welty's humorous re-creation of the archetypal "hero with a thousand faces" who must encounter and survive his *agōn*—a series of conflicts or "tests"—and whose ritual death and rebirth is celebrated by his tribe or clan. William Wallace engages in the necessary "quest." It is not only a quest for Hazel, his wife, but for an insight into the causes of her strange behavior—"the real, the true trouble that Hazel has fallen into, about which words in a letter could not speak" (56)— a search for self-knowledge, for a full realization of his new role as a father, and for the meaning of life itself.

The sense of ritual is developed lightly. "It's a pretty *day* for it," says William Wallace, who immediately establishes his superior powers:

> A descent of energy came down on him in the thick of the woods and he ran at a rabbit and caught it in his hands.
> "Rabbit . . . Rabbit . . ." He acted as if he wanted to take it off and hold it up and talk to it (40).

He sets the rabbit down, but it does not try to move. "Let her go," says Virgil. "She can go if she wants to, but she don't want to," William Wallace answers proudly (41). When they look "critically" over the countryside to gather a party to dredge the river, William Wallace warns that these others "would have to watch out. . . . This is my day with the net" (41). They recruit the services of "the six Doyles and their dogs"; the "scary" Malone family—"eight giants with great long black eyelashes . . . already stamping the ground and pawing each other, ready to go" (43); two Negro boys, Sam and Robbie Bell; and Grady and Brucie Rippen—"solemn little towheads" whose "papa was drowned in the Pearl River" (42).

They gather together like a convening tribe or clan—the Malones coming from one direction, the Doyles from the other. "Everybody went up together to see Doc. Old Doc owned the wide net. He had a house on top of the hill and he sat and looked out from a rocker on the front porch" (43). Garrulous Doc is the "tribal elder"; when he sees them approaching "he began to intone across the valley" (44). If William Wallace is the clan's "hero"—when they went through the woods, "they walked in silence around William Wallace, not letting him carry anything, [even though] the net dragged heavily" (47)—then Doc is their "leader" (" 'the smartest man around,' said William Wallace" [45]). He supervises the river dragging ritual from a boat, "sitting up tall with his hat on . . . he went along without even touching water and without ever taking his eyes off the net" (51), making appropriate "philosophical" comments at various turns in the action. He is Miss Welty's version of the Wise Old Man of the myths and fairy tales who gives verbal assistance to the hero throughout the trials of his adventure.[6] His authority is proclaimed by ownership of the net. He wants the river dragging to maintain a ritual-like pace; "things are moving in too great a rush," he says at one point in the action (55).

As the others are slowly drawn into the world of the river they too become imbued with a sense of ceremony and celebration. When they notice a strange little man following them on the other side of the river, Virgil yells, "Who invited you?" and then he swims across to the other bank to send him away. William Wallace becomes so taken up by an intuitive sense of his mission that when they arrive at the river,

all of a sudden William Wallace . . . spoke up in a voice of surprise. "What is the name of this river?"
They looked at him as if he were crazy not to know the name of the river he had fished in all his life. But a deep frown was on his forehead, as if he were compelled to wonder what people had come to call this river, or to think there was a mystery in the name of a river they all knew so well, the same as if it were some great far torrent of waves that dashed through the mountains somewhere, and almost as if it were a river in some dream, for they could not give him the name of that (49).

To apprehend these deep, hidden mysteries William Wallace enters the river world: "most of the time he was out of sight, swimming about under water or diving, and he had nothing to say any more." Here the "hero" undergoes his first "tests." "Everytime William Wallace took hold of a big eel that slipped the net, the Malones all yelled, 'Rassle with him, son!' " (51). While "all day William Wallace kept diving to the bottom" (56), the others shouted and jumped along the banks and on sandbars, the river dragging turning into a saturnalian revel. They catch count-less fish, numerous shoes, a string of beads—which Sam wears around his head—and the Malones, who "swam like fiends," snare an alligator and plan on taking him home. " 'The Malones are in it for the fish,' said Virgil" (54). Just when it looks as if poor Hazel were completely forgotten, William Wallace undergoes his most arduous "test," which is described in a long passage that provides this humorous story with its serious center. Diving "down and down into . . . the dark clear world of deepness," where "it was so still that nothing stirred, not even a fish," he has a revelation of Hazel's mysterious trouble:

He was gone such a long time that the others stared hard at the surface of the water, through which the bubbles came from below. So far down and all alone, had he found Hazel? Had he suspected down there, like some secret, the real, the true trouble that Hazel had fallen into, about which words in a letter could not speak . . . how (who knew?) she had been filled to the brim with that elation that they all remembered, like their own secret, the elation that comes of great hopes and changes, sometimes simply of the harvest time, that comes with a little course of its own like a tune to run in the head, and there was nothing she could do about it—they knew—and so it had turned into this? It could be nothing but the old trouble that William Wallace was finding out, reaching and turning in the gloom of such depths (56–57).

"The old trouble" is an excess of elation that cannot be communi-cated to another. When such "secrets" are compounded by other emotions—underlining the fundamental separateness which exists between two people—the resulting trouble may send them towards the river, as in "The Wide Net," or find them seated side by side, but totally alone (as in "The Key," "Flowers for Marjorie," and "The Whistle").

While William Wallace is swimming in the depths of the Pearl River, Grady and Brucie peer into the water. When Grady sees William Wallace, ·

the image in the river seemed to be his father, the drowned man—with arms open, eyes open, mouth open. . . . Grady stared and blinked, again something wrinkled up his face.

And when William Wallace came up it was in an agony from sub-mersion. . . .

"What did you bring up," somebody called—was it Virgil?
One of his hands was holding fast to a little green ribbon of plant,
root and all. He was surprised, and let it go (57–58).

William Wallace's emergence from his "trial by water," his bringing forth of the symbol of new life, and Grady's identification of
him with his drowned father all recall the equivalent primal ritual
of the death and rebirth of a hero. But Miss Welty does not force
these allusions, which are delicate and loose; the mythic level
works so well precisely for this reason. Except for one incident,
all the action occurs on a realistic level; the many correspondences
from myth work quietly, allowing the humor its play.

William Wallace's reappearance is the signal for a bacchanalian
feast: "All half-naked except Doc" (58), they eat fish until they
are stupefied—groaning, stretched out on their faces, and, finally,
asleep. But suddenly the clan's "hero" leaps up in celebration of
his triumphal "rebirth," and hooking a big catfish to his belt,
William Wallace does a wild dance, until "the tears of laughter
stream down his face" (59). They have all lost themselves in the
river world, in the pagan spirit of their ritual, and have submerged
themselves in the devouring life flux, the undefined force that is
the river. It is man who has the definition, but when he plunges
into the river he may lose it.[7] If Hazel has been forgotten, it is
because the forces of life—the river and its endless, random
enticements—have a way of distracting one from making the
necessary "definitions": as William Wallace dances Doc says,
"The excursion is the same when you go looking for your sorrow
as when you go looking for your joy" (59).

Just as William Wallace finishes his dance the "old hoary head"
and undulating body of his next "test" rises out of the river. "The
King of the Snakes," intones Doc (60). By confronting and staring
down this fabulous creature, the hero proves his ability to face
the evil powers in life and to protect his growing family from harm.

The clan must next endure a trial by storm and fire: "all color
left the world, the goldenness of everything was like a memory . . . a wind touched each man on the forehead" (61). Nature attacks ferociously: heavy rain, wind, thunder, and lightning—"a huge tail seemed to lash through the air and the river
broke in a wound of silver." The storm seems momentarily to
transfigure the huddled little company:

A great curtain of wet leaves was borne along before a blast of wind, and every human being was covered.

"Now us got scales," wailed Sam. "Us is the fishes."

"Hush up, little-old colored children," said Virgil (63).

They endure the storm and William Wallace's "ordeal" is over. A hero should bear the mark of his struggle, and William Wallace does: "We've come all the way. William Wallace, you have walked on a sharp rock and cut your foot open" (64). They enter the town in a final triumphal procession that echoes the joyful *komos* of the archaic rituals (66).

The ritual comes to a comical conclusion. William Wallace infuriates the Malones by selling all the fish for only three dollars, but when Virgil regrets not having caught Hazel, Old Doc in turn infuriates William Wallace by saying that she was never there to be caught. His skepticism proves well-founded. But two more trials still await William Wallace, both of them unfolded humorously. On their way home, Virgil briefly assumes the traditional role of the Imposter (or *alazon*)—the boaster who overvalues his part in the victory. Virgil says, "You couldn't have drug the river a foot without me" (69)—which is another challenge to William Wallace to prove himself hero of the day:

"What are you talking about! Without who!" cried William Wallace. "This wasn't your river-dragging! It wasn't your wife!" He jumped on Virgil and they began to fight.

"Let me up." Virgil was breathing heavily.

"Say it was my wife. Say it was my river-dragging."

"Yours!" Virgil was on the ground with William Wallace's hand putting dirt in his mouth.

"Say it was my net."

"Your net!"

"Get up then."

They walked along getting their breath, and smelling the honeysuckle in the evening (69–70).

When he arrives home he finds Hazel; she had been hiding in the closet while he read her suicide note. His last trial is to accomplish a reunion with Hazel—but this proves to be no trial at all. After a scolding and a spanking, "she lay smiling in the crook of his arm. It was the same as any other chase in the end" (72); the ritual is finally over.

While Hazel's possible drowning is never to be taken too seriously, William Wallace's discovery about "the old trouble" *is* to be taken seriously (although it is accepted with comparative gaiety, since the knowledge of human separateness leads to despair in so many of Miss Welty's other stories). The wide net in which they had hoped to catch Hazel—"the net that was being drawn out, so old and so long-used" (49)—is a metaphor for experience. But the "net" is unselective and ensnares anything in its path; it is for individual men to define, question, and search out the meanings inherent in random experience. What William Wallace catches in his own wide net when he plunges deep into the Pearl River is a revelation of the hidden mysteries of life, and now for the first time he is ready to try and share Hazel's secret elation, ready to take into account any of her sudden needs, however inexplicable they may be; when she "rose up and looked out . . . across their yard . . . into the dark fields. . . . He climbed to his feet too and stood beside her, with the frown on his face, trying to look where she looked." He *has* experienced a kind of rebirth and, as the story ends, Hazel senses their new relationship, and her new ascendancy in it: "after a few minutes she took him by the hand and led him into the house, smiling as if she were smiling down on him" (72).

Reviewing Isak Dinesen's *Last Tales* (1957), Miss Welty described a method of composition that has often been her own, as in "The Wide Net" and, even more so, in *The Robber Bridegroom:* her stories begin in "the fables, the fairy tales, stories from the Bible and the Arabian Nights and ancient Greece and Rome." [8] *The Robber Bridegroom* is a joyful wedding of European fairy tales and the lore of the American frontier—its legends, tall tales, and actual history. Miss Welty delights in her special mode, relishing the imaginative freedom that has been traditionally available to the writers of romance. Just before its publication, Miss Welty told an interviewer that the book contained "a lifetime of fairy-tale reading. Everything in it is something I've liked as long as I can remember and have just now put down." [9] The action occurs during pioneer days in the Mississippi forests along the Natchez Trace. The character types are drawn from Grimms's *Fairy Tales:* Rosamond Musgrove is the story's beautiful and fair-haired "princess"; her father Clement, "an innocent planter," is the "king"; his ugly second wife Salome is the necessary "evil step-mother"; Jamie

Lockhart, the robber bridegroom who abducts Rosamond, is Miss Welty's version of the "prince" who has a secret that must not be pried into (he is both a gentleman and a bandit leader); and the story's "giant" is the legendary Mike Fink, the greatest of the roistering river flatboatmen.

The implausible central action is narrated in a matter-of-fact manner. Several of the familiar fairy tale situations are burlesqued, and the dry humor of the narrative is enriched throughout by a gently welling poetry of pleasure. When a Rumpelstiltskinesque creature named Goat discovers Rosamond tied up, he says,

"Good evening, why are you crying?"

"Oh, I have lost my husband, and he has lost me, and we are both tied up to be killed in the morning," she cried.

"Then cry on," said Goat, "for I never expect to hear a better reason" (150).

Thus Miss Welty lightheartedly satirizes the myths of her childhood—and our own.

Miss Welty is steeped in the violent history of the Natchez Trace. In *The Robber Bridegroom* she re-creates the infamous outlaw brothers, Big and Little Harpe. Big Harpe once tomahawked a man who snored too loudly, and the Harpes were driven out of their Ohio River territory by other robbers who abhorred their savagery. "The Terrible Harpes" were thereafter active in Kentucky, Tennessee, and along the Natchez Trace (1795–1804). After being felled by a bullet that paralyzed him, Big Harpe was decapitated; as the decapitation began, Big Harpe is reported to have said, "You're a God Damned rough butcher, but cut on and be damned." His head was nailed to a post as a warning to other outlaws. Miss Welty reimagines the horrible details to suit her purposes. Her Little Harp [she drops the *e*] is an elf-like character who comments pragmatically, "Oh, the way to get ahead is to cut a head off" (145). His older brother's head has been relegated to a trunk, from which—in the standard fairy tale manner—it complains and pleads to be left out. Jamie Lockhart tells Little Harp to "get out of the country . . . for I have heard of the Harps, that ran about leaving dead bodies over the countryside as thick as flies on the dumpling" (112). Little Harp forgets his trunk.

Goat was leaving, but just then a voice said, "Let me out!" And there was the trunk that the Little Harp left.

"What did you say?" asked Goat, bending down to put his ear to the top. "Repeat it please, for I am a little hard of hearing when there is conversation through a trunk."

"Let me out!" said the voice, a bit louder.

So Goat lifted up the lid. And there sat the head of Big Harp, Little Harp's brother, all wrapped up in the blue mud, and just as it came down off the pole in Rodney.

"Will you look what was doing the talking!" cried Goat, and pulled the head out by the hair . . . admiring it from all directions.

Poor Rosamond, after one look, fainted again. . . .

Setting the head atop his own head, he skipped off. . . (139–40).

Whereas the Harpes are transformed into fairy tale creatures, her re-creation of Mike Fink remains close to its folklore sources. In the book's first scene, Jamie Lockhart, Clement Musgrove, and Mike Fink share a night's lodging at an inn. Mike Fink tries to convince them of his identity by emitting several of the colossal boasts and battle cries associated with the great brawling rivermen:

"I can pick up a grown man by the neck in each hand and hold him out at arm's length, and often do, too," yelled the flatboatman. "I eat a whole cow at one time, and follow her up with a live sheep if it's Sunday. . . ."

"I'm an alligator!" [he] yelled, and began to flail his mighty arms through the air. "I'm a he-bull and a he-rattlesnake and a he-alligator all in one! . . ." And he chanted Mike Fink's song: "I can outrun, outhop, outjump, throw down, drag out, and lick any man in the country!"

"Go down to the corner and buy yourself a new jug," said [Jamie, falling asleep]. "You're still nothing but an old buffalo" (9–10).

Miss Welty captures the full spirit of frontier humor. Many of the Mike Fink stories relate to his prowess as a brutal practical joker. In *The Robber Bridegroom,* he becomes the trickster tricked. Anticipating that Fink will try to murder and rob them, Jamie Lockhart stuffs their beds with cane sacks and the men hide. Fink rips up a board from the floor and aims several "fatal" blows at the sacks. Then he takes their gold and goes to sleep. The next morning Fink examines the gold and their beds: " 'Nothing left of the two of them but the juice,' said he" (17). Jamie and Musgrove then make an appearance; "Bogeys!" he cries, but manages to ask if they slept well:

"Yes indeed," said Jamie, "except for some rats which slapped me with their tails once or twice in the night. Did you notice it, Mr. Musgrove?"

"Yes," said Clement, by the plan, "now that I think of it. . . ."

And at that the flatboatman cried "Bogeys!" for the last time, and jumped out the window. There he had left three sacks of gold behind him [including] his own (18).

Fink is so humilated by the experience that when Rosamond encounters him near the end of the book, he has assumed a disguise; he tells her he is "an anonymous mail rider" (169). But his gift for hyperbole has not deserted him: he gives his version of how he made Jamie Lockhart into a ghost:

"Oh, we had a terrible battle, Jamie Lockhart and I," said he. "It lasted through three nights running, and when we were through they had to get the floor and the roof switched back to their places, for we had turned the house inside out. Dozens and dozens of seagulls were dead, that had flown in off the river and got caught in the whirlwind of the fight. Hundreds of people were watching, and got their noses sliced off too, for standing too close" (175).

When Rosamond tells Fink that she's looking for Jamie because she is pregnant by him, he answers, "Ghosts are getting more powerful every day in these parts." While they are riding along, some bandits rush upon them. Fink commands the bandits to "Pass on!" for "this lady is soon to become a mother." The bandits politely lift up their black hats to Rosamond and ride on up the Trace (178). Writing out of a joy in the epoch she has re-created, Miss Welty succeeds in capturing the lost fabulous innocence of the American frontier, its poetry and comedy.

Miss Welty's comic spirit thus asserts itself in modes varying from the fairy tale to the tall tale, from the most ancient rites of comedy to the most contemporary kind of "absurd" humor. Her comedies of terror are a reminder of the importance of the grotesque in her writing.

3

THE
GROTESQUE
AND THE
GOTHIC

THE GROTESQUE AND Gothic have always been major modes in American fiction and popular culture, from Brockden Brown to Paul Bowles, from frontier humor to W. C. Fields. Perhaps the grotesque is so persistent an American genre because of the peculiarly American belief that happiness is the *norm* of existence— a belief that is accompanied by an almost fanatical resistance to any suggestions to the contrary. It is not surprising that many American writers have felt the need to use the grotesque or Gothic, as though only through distortion and exaggeration could they begin to suggest the complexity of reality—and its tragicomic implications—to an audience thoroughly committed to the "optimistic." As Flannery O'Connor said in *The Living Novel* (1957), "to the hard of hearing you shout, and for the almost blind you draw large and startling figures."

The Gothic and the grotesque may be congruent in a single work, but in recent years the terms have often been used interchangeably, which has proved confusing. Some distinctions should be made.[1] The term "Gothic" originally referred to the prose genre that was popular in Europe in the eighteenth and nineteenth centuries. Heralding the imminent shift of sensibility to Romanticism, the Gothic writers in Germany and England concerned themselves with things inexplicable, violent, grotesque, horrifying, and supernatural. The setting was often in the medieval past, in a dark forest, castle, convent, or tomb; enchantments, ghosts, hauntings, mirrors that gave back unexpected reflections, and paintings and statues that smiled or shed tears were standard Gothic fare. Despite its tendency toward horror pornography, European Gothicism sometimes managed to suggest, however crudely, the irrational aspects of life, the mysteries of the unconscious, and the destructive potential of the sex drive. But often the Gothic writers do not convince us that they are dealing with models of significant reality, and the Gothic effects remain gratuitous. Edgar Allan Poe popularized the Gothic genre in America, where it has been utilized by writers far superior to their European precursors.[2]

The grotesque is characterized by the distortion of the external world, by the description of human beings in nonhuman terms, and by the displacement we associate with dreams. The infinite possibilities of the dream inform the grotesque at every turn, suspending the laws of proportion and symmetry; our deepest promptings are projected into the details of the scene—inscape as landscape. Because the grotesque replaces supernaturalism with hallucination, it expresses the reality of the unconscious life—the formative source which the Gothic writer, in his romantic flights, may never tap. The grotesque is a heightened realism, reminiscent of caricature, but going beyond it to create a fantastic realism or realistic fantasy that evokes pathos and terror, and what Marlow, in Conrad's *Heart of Darkness* (1898), calls "that commingling of absurdity, surprise, and bewilderment in a tremor of struggling revolt, that notion of being captured by the incredible which is the very essence of dreams"—and of the grotesque. Characters seen grotesquely may be "flat"—not likely to develop or change much during the course of the action—but because they have been pushed to extremes, they become representative, objectifying the complex fears and compulsions that constrict the heart. In grotesque comedy one confronts these fears, and through laughter is released from them.

If artists and writers of the grotesque often render human beings in animal-like form or, like Kafka, *as* animals or insects, it is because too often our status seems subhuman, our lives shaped by dehumanizing forces beyond our control. It is the animal's eye view of things to look up and see the world looming above, menacing, dreadful, and confusing; thus writers of the grotesque often use the point of view of a child, animal, or dwarf, or the "lowest" perspective of all, a view from "underground." Although it has flourished in other ages, the grotesque is most compatible with the modern sensibility; perhaps the grotesque vision *is* the modern world view. Joyce, Proust, Mann, and Conrad all employ the grotesque intermittently; it is central to the aesthetic of Kafka, Faulkner, West, Nabokov, John Hawkes and Eudora Welty. These writers rarely invoke the traditional Gothic trappings; [3] instead, they use the technique of the grotesque, which involves the fusion of incongruous forms drawn from *external* reality (this point will be developed later). The impact of the grotesque depends on a sense of the familiar, for what Nathanael West called the "truly monstrous" resides not in the supernatural and the bizarre, but in our ordinary, everyday lives; "Gothic" is a term to be reserved for "special effects."

The prevalence of the grotesque in Miss Welty's fiction became immediately apparent with the publication of *A Curtain of Green.* Louise Bogan's enthusiastic review in the *Nation* was misleadingly entitled "The Gothic South," because only one story, "Clytie," could properly be called Gothic.[4] Clinically minded *Time* noted that "of seventeen pieces . . . only two report states of experience which could be called normal," [5] and Miss Welty was accused of showing "too great a preoccupation with the abnormal and grotesque." [6] But her use of the grotesque and Gothic can be justified, for the meaning of a story never lies solely in its horror or violence; the distortions intensify the pathos of a situation and express psychological and moral truths. Miss Welty herself has provided a rejoinder to such charges by stating in *Place in Fiction* that "life *is* strange. Stories hardly make it more so; with all they are able to tell and surmise, they make it more believably, more inevitably so."

Whereas Miss Welty often employs the grotesque, the Gothic appears in only three stories, "The Purple Hat," "Clytie," and "The Burning," and none of these is as horrifying as Faulkner's "A Rose for Emily," Tennessee Williams' "Desire and the Black Masseur," or almost any one of Paul Bowles's stories. Yet in spite of these distinctions, Miss Welty is often thought of as a Gothic writer. This misconception is the result of a kind of guilt by association, for it has become a critical commonplace to characterize all Southern writers as Gothic.[7] Many reviewers and readers will group Miss Welty with any Southern writer who may come to mind, thus denying her work its virtues. The critics who force such comparisons do not distinguish between the Gothic and grotesque, nor between those writers who have used the two modes with artistic distinction and those who have exploited them. The atmosphere and symbolism in Truman Capote's fiction ultimately seem nearer to the methods of Edgar Allan Poe than to the accuracy of specification of either Faulkner or Miss Welty. Capote's South and Paul Bowles's North Africa represent a romantic symbolism in which the symbols rarely yield more than their own uniqueness. Moreover, Carson McCullers, Williams, Capote, and Flannery O'Connor far exceed Miss Welty in regard to the amount of perversion, violence, and Gothicism in their writing—and none of them has quite Miss Welty's variegated comic spirit. Unlike hers, their humor is almost always allied with horror. And in Mrs. McCullers' work, the loneliness is never relieved by any other mood.

The Gothic elements in "Clytie" and "The Purple Hat" are not a romantic symbolism, for they communicate a sense of social and individual distortion. "The Purple Hat," however, poses several problems, and to a lesser extent, so does "Clytie." "The Purple Hat" is Miss Welty's most obscure story. Here she closely approaches the traditional Gothic mode—with its violent, supernatural, and inexplicable happenings. The setting is a New Orleans bar, "a quiet little hole in the wall. It was four o'clock in the afternoon" and raining outside (WN, 141). An affable fat man tells a story to the bartender and to a thin, unshaven young alcoholic with shaking hands. There is some kind of significance in the way the scene is "staged": "the two customers had chosen very particularly the knobs [seats] they would sit on. They had come in separately out of the wet, and had each chosen an end stool, and now sat with the length of the little bar between them" (141). The intense young man is somehow involved in the story that is to be unfolded.

The fat man is the armed guard who patrols the little catwalk beneath the dome of a huge New Orleans gambling casino, "The Palace of Pleasure." His little hands, "really helpless looking . . . for so large a man," are emblematic of his combination of weakness and impassive cruelty. From his unique position as the "man that everyone knows to be watching, at all they do" (145), he has been able to observe the strange activities of a certain woman:

"In thirty years she has not changed," said the fat man. "Neither has she changed her hat. Dear God, how the moths must have hungered for that hat. But she has kept it in full bloom on her head, that monstrosity—purple, too, as if she were beautiful in the bargain. She has not aged, but keeps her middle-age" (144).

Using her "outrageous hat" as a lure, she has for thirty years picked up a different young man "at the dice table every afternoon, rain or shine, at five o'clock, and gambles till midnight and tells him goodbye" (144). She not only leads them on to no purpose, but also engages them in a strange sexual ritual. Late in the evening she takes off her hat, which the young man watches hungrily.

He is enamoured of her ancient, battered, outrageous hat with the awful plush flowers. She lays it down below the level of the table there, on her shabby old lap, and he caresses it. . . . Well, I suppose in this town there are stranger forms of love than that, and who are any of us to say what ways people may not find to love? She seems perfectly satisfied with it (147–48).

Noticeable only from above or when she takes off the hat is

a little glass vial with a plunger [which] helps decorate the crown . . . [when] she . . . lays [the hat] carefully in her lap, under the table . . . you might notice the little vial, and be attracted to it and wish to take it out and examine it at your pleasure off in the washroom —to admire the handle, for instance, which is red glass, like the petal of an artificial flower (148–49).

There is also a ten- or twelve-inch long jeweled hat pin; the bartender purses his lips as the fat man describes how "she sticks the pin back through" after taking off the hat. But these suggestively obscene details are not to be taken too literally. The fat man announces that the woman is a ghost because "to my belief she has been murdered twice" (146): the first time she had been shot by one of her pick-ups; the second time another "young lover" killed her with the symbol of her lurking, criminal passions; "no one saw it done . . . except for me, naturally." Yet she returned to the casino within a month after each "murder" and resumed her activities.

The hat's grotesque phallic overtones are obvious; their meaning, however, is not. The "flashing needle" piercing the "great, wide deep hat" (147) and the little "vial" that is best examined in the washroom have unpleasant enough symbolic connotations, suggesting that the story told by the fat man is some kind of terrible onanistic fantasy; it is *his* fantasy, after all—or is it? We can't be sure. Although the events narrated by the fat man are fantastic, Miss Welty has been careful to give the story a realistic frame; "fantasy itself must touch ground with at least one toe, and ghost stories must have one foot, so to speak, in the grave," she says in *Place in Fiction*. Thus, the story about the purple hat is more than believable to the young man: the fat man says that "New Orleans . . . is the birthplace of ready-made victims," and the young man, who has been listening with fascination—"as if there were something hypnotic and irresistible" about the fat man (148)—seems to have been already victimized by "this old and disgusting creature in her purple hat" (146). At five o'clock—the woman's hour of arrival—the young man had suddenly disappeared. The fat man gets up and pays for all the drinks, including the young man's. "Is she a real ghost?" the bartender asks confidentially, "in a real whisper." "I'll let you know tomorrow," answers the fat man. She is to be murdered for the third time that very night, and the young man is going to do it. Both he and the fat man have seemingly known it all along. At the beginning of the story the fat man said, "almost dreamily," but without taking his eyes from the young man, " 'Oh, the hat she wears is a creation,' . . . It was strange that he did not once regard the bartender, who after all had done him the courtesy of asking a polite qustion or two" (143). Later, the fat man cried, " 'I can never finish telling you about the hat!' . . . and there was a little sigh somewhere in the room, very young, like a child's" (150). The story thus has a very definite realistic level; the above mentioned "toe" is placed solidly on the ground.

In spite of the Gothicism, the woman is a recognizable type—a fantastic version of "one of those thousands of middle-aged women who come every day to the Palace, would not be kept away by anything on earth" (143). Her loneliness has assumed a terrible form.

One might say—as Poe did in the Preface to *Tales of the Grotesque and Arabesque* (1840)—that the story's "terror is not of Germany but of the soul." Yet the story's admixture of realism and fantasy creates a *trompe l'oeil* effect, making its meaning extremely—if not excessively—obscure. The confusion arises from Miss Welty's relatively unsuccesssful application of the methods by which she achieves her finest stories.

"The Purple Hat" can be read as a loosely allegorical story. Trying to escape boredom and find some exotic and secret pleasure, young men are drawn to the fantasy world of the "Palace of Pleasure." Once there they fall in love with the tawdry image of beauty, the hat, and especially with the mysterious vial in its crown. But the young men are left frustrated—their dreams are as empty as the vial. They try to destroy the temptress but she eludes them, for, as Ruth Vande Kieft suggests, she is "as deathless as is man's pursuit of pleasure." [8]

The fat man shows off his ruby ring and says that from up above, the casino's red carpet "changes and gives off light between the worn criss-crossing of the aisles like the facets of a well-cut ruby" (145). As a miniature of the "Palace," the ring symbolizes his singular position on the catwalk, and the ominpotence which affords him so clear a view of the most terrible aspects of the human comedy.

"Life in the ruby. And yet somehow all that people do is clear and lucid and authentic there, as if it were magnified in the red lens, not made smaller. I can see everything in the world from my catwalk. You mustn't think I brag. . . ." He looked all at once from his ring straight at the young man's face, which was as drained and white as ever (146).

What he "sees" is expressed in the "allegory" of the woman with the purple hat. He has a first-hand knowledge and understanding of the darkest of human aberrations, in the way that a prostitute might: " 'But I can never finish telling you about the hat!' the fat man cried" (150). He is a grotesque version of the compassionate young man in "The Key," who intuitively understood the plight of the deaf and dumb couple and did what he could to help them. But the fat man's sense of power—"up on the catwalk you get the feeling now and then that you could put out your finger and make a change in the universe" (152)—is unaccompanied by any sense of sympathy. Since he somehow knows that the pathetic young alcoholic has succumbed to the lures of "The Purple Hat," his telling of the story becomes cruel. In spite of his superior knowledge he doesn't care what happens to the young man—or to anyone. He even enjoys the spectacle provided by his plight and that of all the others who pass beneath him in their futile pursuit of pleasure.

But even in his heightened awareness, he is not unlike others. After describing the second "murder," he tells the bartender, "If you had ever been to the Palace of Pleasure, you'd know it all went completely as usual—people at the tables never turn around" (151). The fat man luxuriates in his intuitive powers, "lifting his little finger like a pianist" (143), gazing fondly at his ring, but he will never lift that finger to help another, even though he is by profession a guard. His impassive and perverse curiosity is all too familiar; the terror in the story is produced not so much by the supernatural happenings as by our recognition that the fat man's passivity may well be our own.

The problem in "Clytie" is not one of obscurity but of a surfeit of Gothicism and a literary influence that is all too apparent. Clytie Farr is an old maid who lives in Farr's Gin, a tiny town named after her once-prominent family. All her life she has been isolated from others because of a family pride ("the Farrs were too good to associate with other people" [CG, 159]) that is now pathetic and ironic; she spends all her time taking care of her blind and paralyzed father, half-crazed sister, and drunken brother (whose wife left him shortly after their marriage because "he had threatened time and again to shoot her . . . he had pointed the gun against her breast. She had not understood" [167]). Another brother has committed suicide. Even Miss Welty's most ardent admirers must feel uneasy about the Farrs, who together form a virtual museum of Southern Gothic. Inside the Farrs' house,

it was very dark and bare. The only light was falling on the white sheet which covered the solitary piece of furniture, an organ. The red curtains over the parlor door, held back by ivory hands, were still as tree trunks in the airless house. Every window was closed, and every shade was down, though behind them the rain could still be heard.

Clytie took a match and advanced to the stair post, where the bronze cast of Hermes was holding up a gas fixture; and at once above this, lighted up, but quite still, like one of the unmovable relics of the house, Octavia [her sister] stood waiting on the stairs (160–61).

This kind of musty, Gothic interior is almost academic in Southern writing; Miss Welty makes fun of it in "Old Mr. Marblehall" and "Asphodel." Clytie's mansion recalls Sutpen's Hundred in Faulkner's *Absalom, Absalom!* or Miss Emily's house in "A Rose for Emily," whereas the drunken brooding of Clytie's brother may remind one of Bayard Sartoris in *Sartoris*. But as the story unfolds, the resemblances to Faulkner become less important, and, whenever the focus shifts from the setting to Clytie herself, the story assumes a life of its own. And it is told with a tenderness and compassion that is absent from "A Rose for Emily." Miss Welty writes, "on some level all stories are stories of search . . . when Miss Brill [in Katherine Mansfield's story of that name] sits in the park we feel an old key try at an old lock again—she too is looking. Our most ancient dreams help to convince us that her timid Sunday afternoon is the adventure of her life, and measure for us her defeat." [9] The emphasis in "Clytie" falls not on the grotesque facts of her life but on her search for love.

As the story opens, it is raining in Farr's Gin. Everyone has gone under cover, except for Miss Clytie Farr, who stands still in the middle of the road, "peering ahead in her near-sighted way, as wet as the little birds" which are scurrying across her path. She finally clenches her hands and draws them "up under her armpits, and sticking out her elbows like hen wings," she runs out of the street.

When the scene shifts indoors the perspective changes: the reader enters Clytie's mind and discovers that, mad or not, there is purpose in her grotesque antics; the nature of her search is revealed:

In the street she had been thinking about the face of a child she had just seen . . . [who] had looked at her with such an open, serene, trusting expression as she passed by! With this small, peaceful face still in her mind . . . like an inspiration which drives all other thoughts away, Clytie had forgotten herself (162).

Obsessed with the mystery of identity, Clytie has for a long time been inspecting the faces of people on the street; she has a deep, almost religious respect for the uniqueness, the inviolability of others: "The most profound, the most moving sight in the whole world must be a face. Was it possible to comprehend the eyes and the mouths of other people, which concealed she knew not what, and secretly asked for still another unknown thing?" She tries desperately to escape from her inner world; her reservoir of tenderness and wonder transforms reality. Even the idiot who calls himself "Mr. Tom Bate's Boy" seems fabulous to her: she observes grains of sand in his old eyes; "he might have come out of a desert, like an Egyptian" (163).

Clytie is searching for a specific face. "It was purely for a resemblance to a vision that she examined the secret, mysterious, unrepeated faces she met in the street of Farr's Gin." She had seen that face long ago, but "now it was hard to remember the way it looked, or the time when she had seen it first. It must have been when she was young. Yes, in a sort of arbor, hadn't she laughed, leaned forward . . . and that vision of a face—which was a little like all the other faces . . . and yet different . . . this face had been very close to hers, almost familiar, almost accessible." But her terrifying family situation separates her from this vision. "Their faces came between her face and another. It was their faces which had come pushing in between, long ago, to hide some face that had looked back at her" (168). Like the beauty that she saw in the face of the trusting child, this face is beyond Clytie's "reach." But another face comes within distance of her actual reach.

Mr. Bobo, the nervous town barber who "was short and had never been anything but proud of it, until he had started coming to this house once a week," and who is frightened of all the Farrs, comes into the old house to shave Clytie's bedridden father. Clytie looks at "his pitiful, greedy, small face—how very mournful it was. . . . What was it that this greedy little thing was so desperately needing?" (175). All of her desperation and loneliness erupt, and "with breathtaking gentleness" she touches his face.

> Then both of them uttered a despairing cry. Mr. Bobo turned and fled. . . . Clytie, pale as a ghost, stumbled against the railing . . . the horrible moist scratch of an invisible beard, the dense, popping green eyes—what had she got hold of with her hand! She could hardly bear it—the thought of that face (176).

She runs out to the old rain barrel. She "suddenly felt that this object, now, was her friend, just in time, and her arms almost circled it with impatient gratitude." As she looks into the water, she sees a face: "It was the face she had been looking for, and from which she had been separated." It is ugly and distended, and "everything about [it] frightened and shocked her with its signs of waiting, of suffering. . . . Too late, she recognized the face. She stood there completely sick at heart, as though the poor, half-remembered vision had finally betrayed her" (177). Clytie is devastated by the realization that the face she had been looking for all along had been her own and that this lost self can never be recaptured. In that one instant, she recognizes the contrast between the vision of the laughing child of the past and the mirror image of the ugly and maddened adult of the present. Clytie submits to the terrible knowledge that the only kind of love possible for her is narcissistic love and that life for her has therefore become a living death. She "did the only thing she could think of to do." She thrust her body and head down

into the barrel, under the water, through its glittering surface into the kind, featureless depth, and held it there.

When Old Lethy found her, she had fallen forward into the barrel, with her poor ladylike black-stockinged legs up-ended and hung apart like a pair of tongs (178).

The final image of her legs complements the inanimate, almost antiseptic quality of a lonely and loveless existence. The grotesque image expresses all the horror of Clytie Farr's unbearable discovery.

By virtue of its genuine pathos and psychological incisiveness, "Clytie" manages to transcend its Gothicism and resemblance to "A Rose for Emily." But it should not be surprising if Faulkner has exerted an influence on his fellow Mississippian; Miss Welty has called him "the most astonishingly powered and passionate writer we have." [10] When Miss Welty began her career, Faulkner had already completed the best work in his "parable or legend of all the Deep South." If the young Southern writer chooses to write about his region, he must inevitably face the question of how to avoid rewriting Faulkner. With the possible exceptions of "Clytie" and "The Burning," Miss Welty has solved this problem.

In *Love and Death in the American Novel* (1960), Leslie Fiedler deprecatingly refers to Miss Welty as one of the "feminizing Faulknerians," yet the sounds of Faulkner's rhetoric are much more audible throughout the fiction of such "masculine Faulknerians" as Robert Penn Warren, William Styron, and Andrew Lytle. Excerpts from their work might be intermingled with passages from

Faulkner and many readers would be hard put to tell them apart. Except for some passages from the first version of "The Burning" and one from "Moon Lake" (GA, 100), this could not be done with Miss Welty's fiction because the qualities of her language and style are her own. Faulkner's emblem of the Southern experience informs Miss Welty's sense of her region's history and his example helped her to discover the raw materials of her own art. But the influence of his specific works is negligible, for Miss Welty's fiction abounds in characters, settings, and speech rhythms which only she could have created.

"Asphodel" is one of those stories which only Miss Welty could have written. Three old maids—Cora, Phoebe, and Irene—go on a picnic the day after the funeral of a certain Miss Sabina. They climb a hill and picnic near the ruins of Asphodel, an old mansion that had belonged to Miss Sabina's husband, Mr. Don McInnis. One of the old maids says that "he is dead too." Although "her funeral was yesterday, and we've cried our eyes dry," Miss Sabina's death seems a welcomed event: after dipping "their narrow maiden feet" in a stream, they laugh "freely all at once" (97), and then unpack a lavish lunch.

In the first part of the story, they reminisce about Miss Sabina, reconstructing the events of her life. Robert Penn Warren, otherwise one of Miss Welty's most sympathetic critics, describes the story as a "failure," deploring its "hocus-pocus" and "strain for atmosphere." [11] Perhaps it should not be dismissed so quickly. It is an unusual, if sometimes puzzling, combination of disparate elements, including fantasy, mythology, and parody. Its success depends on how the reader reacts to Miss Sabina's history, which is grotesque and highly melodramatic. In the fashion of a Greek chorus, the old maids "tell over Miss Sabina's story, their voices serene and alike: how she looked, the legend of her beauty when she was young" (98), her house, her family, her marriage to Mr. Don, his infidelities, his immense popularity, their three children (all of whom died), how "she drove Mr. Don out of the house . . . with a whip, in the broad daylight" (103) and then "gratified" herself by burning Asphodel, how "she laid down the law that the name of Don McInnis and . . . of Asphodel were not to cross our lips again" (104), how in her madness she ruled the town, and how she died grotesquely in the post office. The reader is unable to accept these events as literal because the "plot" constructed by the old maids is a cataloging of the kind of clichés rampant in Southern romance fiction. I find it hard to believe that Miss Welty intended us to take them all seriously. For example, Phoebe related her part of the narration, the deaths of Miss Sabina's children, as follows:

There was Minerva and she was drowned—before her wedding day. There was Theo, coming out from the university in his gown of the law, and killed in a fall off the wild horse he was bound to ride. And there was Lucian the youngest, shooting himself publicly on the courthouse steps, drunk in the broad daylight.
     "Who can tell what will happen in this world!" said Phoebe, and she looked placidly up into the featured sky overhead (101).

But these events did not discourage Miss Sabina: "she was born grand, with a will to impose" (101). "Asphodel" may be seen as Miss Welty's oblique attack on the old ruling class and the ineffectuality of its descendants—a parody of the romantic view of Southern gentility as perpetrated by Margaret Mitchell's *Gone With the Wind* (1936) and a hundred other novels. Several passages suggest this. Cora talks about Miss Sabina's house and her wedding:

"Inside, the house was all wood . . . carved and fluted . . . even mahogany roses in the ceilings. . . . The house was a labyrinth set with statues—Venus, Hermes, Demeter, and with singing ocean shells on draped pedestals.
     "Miss Sabina's father came bringing Mr. Don McInnis home, and proposed the marriage to him. She was no longer young for suitors. . . . We were there. The presents were vases of gold, gold cups, statues of Diana. . . . It was spring, the flowers in the basket were purple hyacinths and white lilies that wilted in the heat and showed their blue veins. Ladies fainted from the scent . . ." (98–99).

Irene continues the description of Mr. Don. Her narration is delivered in a style parodying cheap fiction:

"A great, profane man like all the McInnis men of Asphodel, Mr. Don McInnis. He was the last of his own, just as she was the last of hers. The hope was in him, and he knew it. He had a sudden way of laughter, like a rage. . . . That night he stood astride . . . astride the the rooms, the guests, the flowers, the tapers, the bride and her father with his purple face. . . . He was a McInnis, a man that would be like a torch carried into a house" (100).

The exaggeration and hyperbole of these passages are certainly suggestive of parody. In its extravagance the mansion becomes absurd, the legendary Southern "gentlemen were without exception drunk," and the usually dashing hero is animalistic—"profane." The beautiful, desirable heroine of Southern romance fiction is transformed into Miss Sabina, and courting procedures are reversed: her father proposes to her suitor and "she was instructed to submit"—she is an *anti*heroine. Miss Welty seems to level Scarlett O'Hara, Rhett Butler, and the mansion of Tara with a few well-chosen words. Perhaps it is no coincidence that the sharpest, most insensitive, and surprisingly personal attack upon Miss Welty's work is found in a review by the late Margaret Mitchell.[12]

Miss Sabina and Mr. Don are thus parodied versions of those staple, stock characters in historical fiction, the tempestuous Southern lovers. But Miss Welty's couple also represent basic contrasting forces. The story told by the old maids was "like an old song they carried in their memory, the story of the two houses separated by a long, winding, difficult, untravelled road—a curve of the old Natchez Trace—but actually situated almost back to back on the ring of hills, while completely hidden from each other, like the reliefs on the opposite sides of a vase" (98). The "two houses" are literally Asphodel and Miss Sabina's house, which are contrasted symbolically by Asphodel's "mounds of wild roses" and "the mahogany roses in the ceilings" of Sabina's house—just as Mr. Don represents the sensual, pagan, life-giving force, and Miss Sabina is a manifestation of the opposing and ultimately destructive urge to control and suppress others. The two "houses" finally suggest Eros and Thanatos.

After she has driven Mr. Don away and he has supposedly died, "all her will was turned upon the population" (104).

"Her law was laid over us, her riches were distributed upon us . . . [she] set the times of weddings and funerals, even for births . . . named the children [and] moved people from one place to another in town, brought them together or drove them apart, with the mystical and rigorous devotion of a priestess in a story; and she prophesied all the things beforehand. She foretold disaster. . ." (105).

One cannot take this literally. The details of Miss Sabina's life become increasingly fantastic and grotesque. Her downfall can be read as a kind of allegory of the decline of the old South. Miss Sabina represents the survivors of the "old order," with their manic attempts to maintain control and to guard against change, and their hostility to all spontaneity: "At the May Festival when she passed by, all the maypoles become hopelessly tangled, one by one" (105).

The end results of Miss Sabina's efforts to sustain an illusion are ludicrous, grotesque, and psychically crippling: she staggers along under the weight of a large black wig and heavy brocades, and suffers a terrible death in the post office—the "one door where Miss Sabina had never entered." Because it is the element of modern life beyond her control, "she acted as if the post office had no existence in the world," and "all the hate she had left in her when she was old went out to [the] little four-posted white-washed building. . . . For there we might still be apart in a dream, and she did not know what it was" (106). But in the end, she enters the post office: " 'It was as if the place of the smallest and the longest-permitted indulgence, the little common green, were to be invaded when the time came for the tyrant to die,' said Phoebe" (107). In a horrifying sequence she first demands her letters—although she never got any—and then attacks the post office "with her bare hands," ripping everything apart.

"She was possessed . . . she raged. She rocked from side to side, she danced. Miss Sabina's arms moved like a harvester's in the field, to destroy all that was in the little room. In her frenzy she tore all the letters to pieces, and even put bits in her mouth and appeared to eat them.

"Then she stood still in the little room. She had finished. We had not yet moved when she lay toppled on the floor, her wig fallen from her head and *her face awry like a mask* [italics mine].

" 'A stroke.' That is what we said, because we did not know how to put a name to the end of her life. . ." (108).

Since it is impossible to regulate *every* aspect of life, the fanatic's will to control is finally self-destructive: Miss Sabina is her own victim, and death reveals her impotency—the wig has fallen from her head. Miss Sabina's story is over, but the story about the three old maids is not.

They present a contrast to the violent and grotesque scene which they have just recalled, considering it happened only a few days before:

Here in the bright sun where the three old maids sat beside their little feast, Miss Sabina's was an old story, closed and complete. . . . Now they lay stretched on their sides on the ground, their summer dresses spread out, *little smiles forming on their mouths, their eyes half-closed. . . . Above them like a dream rested the bright columns of Asphodel, a dream like the other side of their lamentations* [italics mine] (109).

Their idyllic repose is suddenly interrupted by a bearded and naked Pan-like figure who steps out from the vines growing up among the columns and stares at the three spinsters. Terrified, they make "a soft little chorus of screams," and flee from the scene (109).

"Southern summer is nostalgic," Miss Welty once wrote, "because even when it happens it's dream-like. Find the shade of the biggest tree; in it your hammock is dreaming already, like a boat on the stream." [13] The summer atmosphere and the story's opening images of the surrealistic ruins place the action deep within a "season of dreams." With the completion of the story-within-a-story, the controlling image returns, "above them like a dream." They "did not know how to put a name" to her death, and, after narrating the children's death, Phoebe—who is undoubtedly named after Phoebus, the god of prophecy—looks "into the featureless sky" and exclaims: "Who can tell what will happen in this world!" Their narration has a decided improvisatory quality. It seems almost to be part of their consciousness—"an old song they carried in their memory." The "narrative was only part of memory now, and its beginning and ending might seem mingled and freed in the blue air of the hill" (100). They recall the day Miss Sabina drove Mr. Don from home: "It was a day like this, in summer—I remember the magnolias that made the air so heavy and full of sleep. It was just after dinner time and all the population came out and stood helpless to see, as if in a dream" (103). The old maids have related Miss Sabina's story as "in some intoxication of the time and the place," suggesting that most of the events which they have described may *never* have happened and that the three old maids, lost in their fantasy world—heightened and encouraged by the heat—choose to render Miss Sabina's life in the terms of Southern romance fiction, a set of fantasies equivalent to the unreality of their own lives. The elements of allegory and parody in their narration are thus presented in a psychological context, embodied in the characterizations of the three old maids. The parody is not forced upon the story, but grows organically out of its form: "The grapes they held upon their palms were transparent in the light, so that the little black seeds showed within" (107); this describes how Miss Sabina's story reveals the nature of the spinsters' lives. The powerful Miss Sabina was undoubtedly a real enough town eccentric, but her "story" has probably been manufactured by the old maids over a period of years as a legend in keeping with the extravagance of Miss Sabina's actual eccentricities and as a fantasy-projection of their own retreat from reality ("a dream like the other side of their lamentations"). Miss Sabina's highly grotesque death may be the only "real" event of her story. Its violence may symbolize their own suppressed anguish. Unlike Clytie Farr, they are not destroyed by their obsessions. By re-creating Miss Sabina's "life" and grotesque death—her virtual rape of the post office—they may be said to be activating and releasing their own inhibitions: Miss Sabina's story finished, "they lay stretched on their sides . . . little smiles forming on their mouths . . . eyes half-closed." Their contentment is short-lived.

In "Asphodel," Miss Welty uses the grotesque as both a tragic and a comic mask. When Miss Sabina died, "her wig [had] fallen . . . and her face [was] awry like a mask." But the real "masks" in the story belong to Phoebe, Cora, and Irene. What is pathetic, if not tragic, in "Asphodel" is not Miss Sabina's story, but what her "story" has revealed about the three old maids. The full extent of their condition is not apparent until the appearance of the naked man. He represents the first intrusion of reality into the story. After "escaping" from him they stop. The bearded man has not moved. "That was Mr. Don McInnis," says Cora. "It was not," Irene says. "It was a vine in the wind" (110). In that one sentence of dialogue Miss Welty shows the depth of the dream world in which the old maid has immersed herself. It is one of those moments, frequent in her fiction, when she manages to squeeze meaning from the detail which, in ordinary realistic fiction, might be passed over. The reader may wonder, *is* it Mr. Don, or not? It doesn't matter; what is important is that it is a *man,* and how the three react to him.

"He was buck-naked," said Cora. "He was as naked as an old goat. He must be as old as the hills."

"I didn't look," declared Phoebe. But there at one side she stood bowed and trembling as if from a fateful encounter.

"No need to cry about it, Phoebe," said Cora (110).

Miss Welty may be reversing the Freudian method by projecting in broad daylight sexual nightmares that are in reality social symbols. The fantasy-like quality of the spinsters' lives in "Asphodel" is Miss Welty's expression of their tragic refusal to face the present and the failure of their minds to function in terms other than those of the past. Moreover, in creating a "past" for Miss Sabina, they spin fantasies out of clichés; Miss Welty thereby parodies the whole myth about that past, unmasking the myth, just as Sabina herself was unmasked at her death.

In "Asphodel," Miss Welty has maintained a tough-minded and detached attitude toward the *idea* of the South, in spite of her attachment to her Mississippi "place." This is in part due to the fact that Miss Welty is a first generation Mississippian whose parents did not come from the deep South; her mother is from West Virginia, and her father was from Ohio; they moved to Jackson in 1904, five years before Miss Welty's birth. She has humorously said that she did not suffer as a child, "except from my father's being . . . a Yankee" [14]—and her lack of antebellum ancestors has undoubtedly contributed to her sense of perspective and her independent view of Southern tradition. She has never belonged to a literary or political group, and, although many of her early stories appeared in the *Southern Review,* she never involved herself in regionalist theorizing. Unlike several Southern writers, she does not entertain any nostalgia for the grace and innocence of past Confederate days. Nor does she rail against the defilement of the "old order" by the new, commercial order; one cannot imagine Miss Welty as a contributor to *I'll Take My Stand* (1930). She offers no defense of the Old South, a fact made evident by "Asphodel," "The Burning," and the stories about the descendants of the Southern aristocracy. In "A Curtain of Green," the town is named after Mrs. Larkin's father-in-law; the town in "Clytie" is also named for the family; and much is made of old Mr. Marblehall's descent from an old family. The lives of these well-born characters are more circumscribed by fantasy than any of Miss Welty's other characters, suggesting a critical view of the old families' abilities to cope with the vagaries of reality on both a personal and social level.

Suggestions of meaning are multiplied by consideration of the title of the story. The dictionary defines "asphodel" as "any of a genus of plants of the lily family." The present-day ruins of Asphodel hardly suggest any such beauty and the past was no better; at Miss Sabina's wedding the "lilies wilted and showed their blue veins. Ladies fainted from the scent." The three old maids, casting their dreams in Asphodel's shadow, are "wilted" women, existing as "weeds" in an emotional wasteland. The lily is the flower of mourning and, as such, it is an appropriate emblem for the three ladies. The ruins of Asphodel symbolize their physical and imaginative sterility.

The asphodel is also the traditional flower of immortality. In the *Odyssey,* it covers the meadows in the Elysian fields when Ulysses meets the great dead.[15] Miss Welty makes uncommon use of her mythic material. Contemporary writers often utilize mythology in a solemn and pretentious way, but in "Asphodel" the classical correspondences are grotesque, humorous, and ironic. In the figures of Miss Sabina and Mr. Don, Miss Welty light-heartedly invokes Nietzsche's distinction between the Apollonian and Dionysian forces; the naked and bearded Mr. Don is her most explicitly Dionysian character: he steps out from among vines, looks like an "old goat," and is remembered as having "had the wildness we all worshipped" (101). Throughout the story, Miss Welty has fun at the expense of the Old South's identification with a Golden Age; the ruins of "Asphodel" point to that grand anachronism in the history of American style, "the classic revival." At Sabina's wedding, "the presents were vases of gold, gold cups, statues of Diana." She later wielded a "stick mounted with the gold head of a lion," and, when Mr. Don appears before the spinsters, he was "golden as a lion." At the end of the story, Phoebe calls it a "golden day." But instead of the immortal dead, one meets the three old maids and hears about Miss Sabina. She is a Southern Sabine who, though taken against her will, did *not* submit to her "conqueror," the Dionysian Mr. Don. Her children include "Minerva" and "Lucian the youngest." The spinsters serve as a Greek chorus; Cassandra-like, they were the first to inform

Sabina of Mr. Don's unfaithfulness: Cora says, "We told the news.
. . . We went in a body up the hill and into the house, weeping
and wailing, hardly daring to name the name or the deed" (101).
The old maids describe Asphodel as a Greek temple and recall
that Miss Sabina's house had statues of the Seasons and of the
gods—Venus, Hermes, and Demeter. Miss Welty keynotes the
absurdity of the spinsters' "dream" by juxtaposing comical, almost
slapstick action against the "classical" setting. Near the end of
the story, as they gaze at the ruins of Asphodel, "a number of
goats appeared between the columns . . . and with a little leap
started down the hill." It is fitting that the satyr-like Mr. Don
should be living among goats. As if at his command, the goats
pour out of Asphodel—like comic versions of the Eumenides
emerging from a debased temple of Dionysus—and chase the
women: "Into the buggy!" screams one of the ladies. "Tails up,
the goats leapt the fence as if there was nothing they would rather
do. . . . There were billy-goats and nanny-goats, old goats and
young, a whole thriving herd. Their little beards all blew playfully
to the side in the wind of their advancement" (111). The ladies
throw biscuits to the closely pursuing goats to appease them, but
it does not stop them. Miss Welty utilizes her mythology in the
spirit of Mack Sennett rather than Sir James Frazer. "Cora was
standing up in the open buggy, driving it like a chariot. 'Give
them the little baked hen, then,' she said, and they threw it. . . .
The little goats stopped . . . and then their horns met over the
prize" (112). Routing the forces of order and control which Miss
Sabina had exemplified, the chasing goats mock the old maids
and their absurd "tender dreams" of the past.

    After making their escape, Irene and Cora give thanks that
"Miss Sabina did not live to see us then." But in a surprise turn,
Phoebe laughed aloud. As the story ends, "her voice was soft,
and she seemed to be still in a tender dream and an unconscious
celebration—as though the picnic were not already set rudely in
the past, but were the enduring and intoxicating present . . . the
golden day" (113). Phoebe seems to have enjoyed the triumph
of the goats and Mr. Don, thus belying her namesake Phoebus
Apollo. Perhaps all along she was secretly on the side of the
Dionysian rather than Apollonian forces. With its elements of
humor, fantasy, and grotesquery, "Asphodel" is a story about the

South that could not have been written by any Southerner *except* Eudora Welty.

Miss Welty's most brilliant use of the grotesque occurs in "Petrified Man." It seems to be her most popular story, for it has been reprinted more often than any other (fourteen times). It is a tightly controlled, ruthlessly objective study of vulgarity of spirit, a vulgarity so absolute that it appears chemically pure, exposed in its final subhuman form. The characters in "Petrified Man" are the ultimate spiritual embodiments of the grotesque bathers of "A Memory," and the story is Miss Welty's "Waste Land."

"Petrified Man" is set in a cheap beauty parlor. Its setting and manner resemble Ring Lardner's "Haircut," although Miss Welty treats human callousness and meanness in a more complicated way than Lardner. She does not allow the reader and the writer just behind the persona such an easy sense of moral superiority.

"Petrified Man" is unfolded in two scenes, each one week apart, in which Leota, the beauty parlor attendant, and Mrs. Fletcher, her customer, converse at great length. The story's impact is almost completely dependent upon Miss Welty's ear, her gift for rendering all kinds of dialogue. Leota serves as an effaced narrator. She tells Mrs. Fletcher about her adventures with a friend from New Orleans, Mrs. Pike, thereby providing the story with its main theme. Their dialogue exposes their bitterness, rancor, self-pity, and baseness. Miss Welty's satire cuts through these levels of human weakness with unfailing sharpness.

Although there are few descriptive passages in "Petrified Man," Miss Welty selects details which add to the story's scalding humor. Like Gogol, Miss Welty opens the doors and observes the setting, describing it closely, but never cataloging; each detail increases the story's sense of an overwhelming vulgarity. The setting itself affords an ironic comment; the intense revelation of vulgarity occurs in a place whose purpose is to "beautify" at least the exterior of the female. Instead, the *inner* ugliness of the women is revealed in a "den of curling fluid and henna packs" (32), where apparatus—wave pinchers, dryers, permanent wave machines, cold wet towels, and thick fluids—is utilized with a brutal vigor suggestive of a torture chamber: customers get "yanked up by the back locks" and thick wave fluid drips down their necks and into their eyes; "you cooked me fourteen minutes," complains a customer, and Leota, with her "strong red-nailed fingers," digs both hands into Mrs. Fletcher's scalp (33). Miss Welty utilizes her painter's eye: the beauty parlor—and every implement therein, including the combs—is lavender, a particularly vulgar color. There are rows of Coca-Cola bottles along the mirror. A drugstore rental book, *Life Is Like That, Screen Secrets,* and *Startling G-Man Tales* provide the customers and the beauticians with reading material. The story begins and ends with a handful of stale peanuts ("goobers"). As for sanitary conditions, Billy Boy, Mrs. Pike's child, plays on the beauty parlor floor, "making tents with aluminum wave pinchers . . . under the sink" (36). Then there are the women themselves: Mrs. Fletcher looked "expectantly at the black part in Leota's yellow curls as she bent"; Leota "flicked an ash into the basket of dirty towels." Leota runs a comb through Mrs. Fletcher's hair, and the "hair floated out of the lavender teeth like a small storm-cloud" (33). When Mrs. Fletcher asks, "Is it any dandruff in it?" she frowns, her "hair-line eyebrows diving down toward her nose, and her wrinkled, beady-lashed eyelids batting with concentration" (34). The mention of brand names contributes to the tone. The pregnant Mrs. Fletcher talks about buying "Stork-A-Lure" maternity clothes, and the chauvinistic Leota says she drinks only "Jax Beer" because "that's the beer that Mrs. Pike says is made right in N.O." (37). These small details combine to project a grotesque image of humanity.

The dialogue between Leota and Mrs. Fletcher abounds in phrases and passages intended to chill the reader by virtue of their grotesque insensitivity. Too stingy to send Billy Boy to a nursery, Mrs. Pike deposits him with Leota each day. "Only three years old," Leota says, "and already nuts about the beauty-parlor business" (36). Because Mrs. Fletcher does not like children she finds her pregnancy disgusting and is trying to keep it a secret. She hasn't told her husband yet because she is contemplating an abortion. Leota tells Mrs. Fletcher about Mrs. Montjoy of the Trojan Garden Club, a customer who, already in labor, stopped at the shop on the way to the maternity ward because she "wanted to look pretty while she was havin' her baby, is all" (48). And of the woman's labor pains, Leota says, "Yeah man! She was a-yellin'. Just like when I give her a perm'net" (48). The grotesque incongruities embody the baseness of the beauty-parlor women.

The grim comedy reaches its most horrifying level when Leota tells Mrs. Fletcher about the traveling freak show which she and Mrs. Pike visited. "Well, honey," says Leota, "talkin' about bein' pregnant an' all, you ought to see those twins in a bottle, you really owe it to yourself" (39).

> "Born joined plumb together—dead a course." Leota dropped her voice into a soft lyrical hum. "They was about this long—pardon—must of been full time, all right, wouldn't you say?—an' they had these two heads an' two faces an' four arms an' four legs, all kind of joined *here*. See, this face looked this-a-way, over their shoulder, see. Kinda pathetic."

From the bottled Siamese twins, Leota moves on to describe the pygmies:

> "You know, the teeniest men in the universe? Well, honey, they can just rest back on their little bohunkus an' roll around an' you can't hardly tell if they're sittin' or standin'. . . . They're about forty-two years old. Just suppose it was your husband!"
> "Well, Mr. Fletcher is five foot nine and one half," said Mrs. Fletcher quickly (40).

Though the pygmies "are not bad-lookin' for what they are," Leota and Mrs. Pike preferred another "freak"—the petrified man: "ever-thing ever since he was nine years old, when it goes through his digestion, see, somehow Mrs. Pike says it goes to his joints and has been turning to stone" (41). The women not only show no compassion for the petrified man, but, by continuing to talk about themselves and the "freaks" in the same breath, they ironically fail to distinguish between "freaks" and supposedly "normal" people. Leota says,

> "He's turnin' to stone. How'd you like to be married to a guy like that? All he can do, he can move his head just a quarter of an inch. A course he *looks* just *terrible*."
> "I should think he would," said Mrs. Fletcher frostily. "Mr. Fletcher takes bending exercises every night of the world. I make him. . . ."
> "Did Mrs. Pike like the petrified man?" asked Mrs. Fletcher.
> "Not as much as she did the others," said Leota deprecatingly. "And then she likes a man to be a good dresser, and all that."
> "Is Mr. Pike a good dresser?" asked Mrs. Fletcher sceptically (42).

After dropping the petrified man from their conversation, Leota and Mrs. Fletcher discuss love and marriage. In "Petrified Man," life between the sexes is repugnant, to put it mildly: "Dandruff, dandruff. I couldn't of caught a thing like that from Mr. Fletcher, could I?" (34). Mrs. Pike married a man fourteen years her senior. She has always sought advice from fortune tellers; "She ast Lady Evangeline about him" (42). The fortune teller advised Mrs. Pike to marry because Mr. Pike was due an inheritance, and Leota admits, "me an' Fred, we met in a rumble seat eight months ago and we was practically on what you might call the way to the altar inside of half an hour" (45).

In the second scene, a week later, Leota no longer considers Mrs. Pike a "friend." Mrs. Pike had recognized the petrified man's photo in Leota's copy of *Startling G-Man Tales*—he was wanted for raping four women in California. "Did it under his real name— Mr. Petrie" [a logical name] (53). He had lived in the apartment next to the Pikes's in New Orleans for six weeks. The reward was five hundred dollars, which Mrs. Pike collected after the police had arrested the no-longer petrified man. Leota is virtually sick over losing the reward, begrudges Mrs. Pike the money—"it was my magazine"—and says, regarding the rape victims: "Four women. I guess those women didn't have the faintest notion at the time they'd be worth a hundred an' twenty-five bucks a piece some day to Mrs. Pike" (54).

The story ends on a savage note: the two women take out their wrath on Mrs. Pike's child and spank Billy Boy viciously. It is no coincidence that Billy Boy is the only male physically present in the story. At the beginning of "Petrified Man," when Leota says, "So we rented [our extra room] to Mrs. Pike. And Mr. Pike," she inaugurates a theme that is dominant throughout the story (33): like all the other men mentioned in the story, Mr. Pike is reduced to a subordinate position. In the passages concerning pregnancy the women deny their own femininity as well as attack their husbands' sexuality. Their attitude toward the men is exemplified in Leota's first remark to Billy Boy, "Billy Boy, hon, mustn't bother nice ladies" (36). Men must know and keep their place in the world of Leota, Mrs. Pike, and Mrs. Fletcher. "Fred's five foot ten," says Leota, "but I tell him he's still a shrimp, account of I'm so tall" (41). Mrs. Fletcher says that if her husband "so much as raises his voice against me, he knows good and well I'll have one of my sick headaches, and then I'm just not fit to live with" (37). Mr. Montjoy, whose wife stopped by the beauty parlor during her labor, waited in their car but "kep' comin' in here, scared-like, but couldn't do nothin' with her a course" (47). As for his wife's yelling, Mrs. Fletcher thinks that

"Her husband ought to make her behave. Don't it seem that way to you? . . . He ought to put his foot down."
"Ha," said Leota. "A lot he could do. Maybe some women is soft."
"Oh, you mistake me, I don't mean for her to get soft—far from it! Women have to stand up for themselves, or there's just no telling" (48).

It is no wonder that at best, Leota's husband Fred can "lay around the house an' bull . . . with that good-for-nothin' Mr. Pike. He says if he goes who'll cook" (49). Mr. Pike has been unemployed for six months, and Fred is virtually immobile.

The men seem to be well on their way to being figuratively "petrified" by the debilitating effects of their wives' domination; Leota suggests as much with a vivid juxtaposition: " 'All Fred does is lay around the house like a rug. I wouldn't be surprised if he woke up some day and couldn't move. The petrified man just sat there moving his quarter of an inch though,' said Leota reminiscently" (42). Significantly, Mr. Pike does not want to call the police about Mr. Petrie—"Said he kinda liked that ole bird and said he was real nice. . . . But Mrs. Pike simply tole him he could just go to hell" (53); perhaps he recognized a kindred soul in the petrified man. He may have raped four women, but Mrs. Pike, who several times served him breakfast in bed, went unharmed. She either did not appeal to him—or else frightened him. Miss Welty is not morally interested in the rapes. Although the petrified man is sexually warped, he still *acts* and asserts himself—whereas the other men have been unsexed—"Mr. Fletcher can't do a thing with me" (37). They are at the complete mercy of their wives: "Mr. Fletcher takes bending exercises every night of the world. I make him" (42), and Leota has her husband work in Vicksburg because the fortune teller suggested it ("Said my lover was goin' to work in Vicksburg, so I don't know who she could mean, unless she meant Fred" [49]).

With the arrest of the petrified man the women seem to have succeeded in subjugating the only free man in the story—but not quite, for Billy Boy remains to be vanquished. He has been told to "behave" at intervals throughout the story. When they catch him eating the last of the stale peanuts, his simple boyish act is

seen as a major gesture of male defiance. " 'You come here to
me!' screamed Leota, recklessly flinging down the comb, which
scattered a whole ashtray full of bobby pins and knocked down
a row of Coca-Cola bottles. 'This is the last straw!' " Mrs. Fletcher
holds him while Leota paddles him with the brush, the scene becoming a communal rite of female vengeance: "From everywhere
ladies began to gather round to watch the paddling" (55). As the
three-year-old leaves the beauty parlor he yells, "If you're so
smart, why ain't you rich?" Although he remains unconquered,
he is as gross as the adults. But his taunting question is well taken,
for as materialistic as they are, the women have nothing *except*
their vulgarity and viciousness. Miss Welty succeeds in combining
elements of the grotesque that are simultaneously comic and saddening. As Ratliff says of Snopesism in Faulkner's *The Town*
(1957), "soon as you set down to laugh at it, you find out it
aint funny a-tall."

The petrified man symbolizes all the ultimately destructive possibilities of a life between the sexes that has been distorted by
grossness of spirit. He symbolizes the hypocrisy, pettiness, and
sexual barrenness in the lives of the three women and, though less
directly, in the lives of their men as well—lives that can only find
"fulfillment" in vicious, idle gossiping or in somnolent loafing.
The petrified man had pretended to be turning to stone and was
ultimately exposed as "alive." The three women, however, are the
real "pretenders" in the story because they are the ones who, figuratively, are turning to stone. That stone is their death-in-life.
While their husbands have been "petrified" by female domination,
the women are "petrified" because they are incapable of any
human feeling; symbolically, they are as dead as the bottled Siamese twins which enthralled Leota.[16] Mrs. Pike, Leota, and Mrs.
Fletcher belong to Petrified Man—that vast family whose numberless members share a similar corruption of spirit and who are, in
their condition, isolated from the human race. Significantly, Miss
Welty dropped the article when she entitled her story, "Petrified
Man." The meaning thus moves from the particular to the general.

The elements of the grotesque and Gothic in Miss Welty's
stories are artistically justifiable, for unlike Poe, she has never
conjured up scenes of horror for their own sake. As Katherine
Anne Porter says, in writing of "Petrified Man," "her use of this

material raises the quite awfully sordid . . . tale to a level above its natural habitat, and its realism seems almost to have the quality of caricature, as complete realism so often does. Yet, as painters of the grotesque make only detailed reports of actual living types observed more keenly than the average eye is capable of observing, so Miss Welty's little human monsters are not really caricatures at all, but individuals exactly and clearly presented." [17]

As Miss Porter implies, there is a community of feeling shared by artists and writers of the grotesque. The overrun garden in "A Curtain of Green" points to the origin of the word *grotesque* in late fifteenth-century Italy. It initially referred to a style of ornamental wall painting comprised of monstrous and convoluted foliage.[18] The disquieting jungles in the paintings of the surrealist Max Ernst are the nearest modern equivalent to the ornamental grotesque. When Miss Welty "clamps" the sun on one side of the "polished sky" in "A Curtain of Green," she is echoing Ernst's series on the "Sun and Forest" motif. His paintings "The Joy of Living" and "A Moment of Calm" are remarkably accurate visual analogues to Mrs. Larkin's garden.[19]

Miss Welty's techniques recall the works of artists of the grotesque ranging from Bosch to Goya to Leonard Baskin. "Men with hawklike faces" aim their cameras at Howard in "Flowers for Marjorie." When the girl in "A Memory" finally identifies the terrible laugh she has been hearing unconsciously and focuses on "the motionless open pouched mouth of the woman," she could be looking at Edvard Munch's "The Shriek." The intense white and red make-up caked on Miss Baby Marie's face in "Livvie" and the faces of the bathers in "A Memory"—"metallic, with painted smiles in the sun"—recall the masked and menacing carnival figures in James Ensor's "The Intrigue." Mrs. Larkin's eyes are "puckered"; "her mouth was a sharp line"; Mr. Marblehall's "other wife" looks like "a woodcut of a Bavarian witch, forefinger pointing, with scratches in the air all around her"—these put-upon women are drawn with a striking clarity worthy of Callot or Goya; Miss Welty is compiling her own *Caprichos*. The affable fat guard in "The Purple Hat," who has "rather small, mournful lips . . . [a] vague smile," and a "look a little cosy and prosperous," might have been drawn by George Grosz: he "put his elbow on the counter, and rested his cheek on his hand, where he could see all the way down the bar. For a moment his eyes seemed dancing there, above one of those hands so short and so plump that you are always counting the fingers." The silent bartender's "mouth and eyes curved downward from the divide of his baby-pink nose, as if he had combed them down, like his hair." Miss Welty here anticipates the methods of contemporary artists such as Francis Bacon, who blur the edges of modeled forms in their still-wet canvases or thin their pigments with turpentine, allowing separate painted areas to run together in order to achieve visual forms that express corresponding psychic states. In "A Memory," the grotesque object of the narrator's revulsion is described in a manner that again anticipates important modern painters: the fat on the woman's arms is "like an arrested earthslide on a hill" and then her breasts themselves seem to turn to sand. The girl is experiencing something akin to the excremental vision of Jean Dubuffet, who paints his nudes with impasto pigments that are mixed with sand and pebbles, or of Willem de Kooning, whose monumental "Women" are painted in swirling and slashing brown, gray, and black strokes.[20]

Although it sometimes resembles caricature—the bartender's "enormous sad black eyebrows raised, like hoods on baby-carriages, and showed his round eyes"—Miss Welty's technique of the grotesque is essentially different from it. Caricature distorts and exaggerates the human physiognomy, but it leaves the form intact and never destroys it. But in the grotesque, as in a dream, a dimension of humanity may be displaced, missing, or replaced by an incongruous form; one detail may be stressed to the absolute exclusion of all others. In the Radio City melee of "Flowers for Marjorie," Howard stands close to a "large woman with feathery furs and a small brown wire over one tooth." Instead of a face we have the inanimate detail, in place of a body, the furs; the sense of lifeless anonymity defines Howard's crisis, his state of flux. In "The Purple Hat" our attention is continually drawn to the guard's plump little hands; they seem to have a life of their own. In a sense, he *is* his hands; they project his weakness and the absurdity of his being the Law.

The concentration on dissociated parts of the body is central to the grotesque vision: the body serves as the microcosm of a universal disorder—the lawless fragments threaten to disintegrate. In "A

Memory," "fat hung upon [the woman's] upper arms like an arrested earthslide on a hill. With the first motion she might make, I was afraid that she would slide down upon herself into a terrifying heap. . . . The younger girl . . . was curled tensely upon herself. She wore a bright green bathing suit like a bottle from which she might, I felt, burst in a rage of churning smoke" (153). The "confusion of vulgarity and hatred which twined among them all like a wreath of steam rising from the wet sand" (154) is almost as self-annihilating as the spontaneous combustion which consumes Krook and his Rag and Bottle Shop in Dickens' *Bleak House*. Existence is so oppressive to some of Miss Welty's characters that they literally seem to fall apart. When the Camp Fire Girl concludes her visit of charity by leaning over the old woman and asking for her age, the old face on the pillow "slowly gathered and collapsed." In her death throes, Miss Sabina all but comes apart at the seams, and, according to the fat man, when the woman with the purple hat was "murdered" with her hat pin, it "entered between the ribs and pierced the heart . . . [and] the old creature . . . simply folded all softly in on herself, like a circus tent being taken down after the show" (151).

Sometimes Miss Welty's technique of the grotesque involves the pathetic fallacy, the projection of human characteristics into the inanimate; the roses which Howard carries through the street—his "Flowers for Marjorie"—nod "like heads in his arms." Her basic technique, however, is to describe the human in nonhuman terms: animal, vegetable, or mineral. Because the young girl in "A Memory" perceives them as virtual avatars of chaos, the bathers embody all of these possibilities. The woman's "breasts hung heavy and widening like pears"—and later seem to turn into sand—"her legs lay prone one on the other like shadowed bulwarks, uneven and deserted," and her arms are a protoplasmic landslide. The man smiles "the way panting dogs seem to be smiling" and piles the sand higher and higher on her legs, "like the teasing threat of oblivion." The family rehearses a sequence of transformations that seem to transport them from a higher order to a lower order, and from a lower order into nothingness.

Miss Welty draws upon all the details of speech, dress, and setting to fashion grotesque analogies within the various orders; the animate and inanimate share each other's properties in startling and unsettling ways. The torpor of the traveling salesman in "The Hitch-Hikers" is reflected in the old dog that moves "stiffly, like a table walking." When the delirious and dying R. J. Bowman of "Death of a Traveling Salesman" remembers the congruent drabness of his sex life and his various living quarters, instead of an individual woman, he sees the "furniture of that room." As Mrs. Marblehall walks among the crowded "old things" in her house, she "looks like funny furniture—an unornamented stair post." And by the time the narrator projects the "other little boy's" view of his mother's incipient hysteria, she seems to have metamorphosed into furniture: "for a long time he supposed that his mother was totally solid, down to her thick separated ankles." Adversity creates automata: Mrs. Marblehall "rolls back into the house as if she had been on a little wheel all this time"; Mrs. Larkin works as tirelessly as a machine; and when Miss Eckhart, the piano teacher in "June Recital," stands over the grave of the man she loved from afar, she expresses her mute grief by rocking back and forth like the prized metronome which dominates most of her waking hours. In a rare moment, Miss Eckhart plays for herself, her body swaying ecstatically from side to side, "like a tree trunk." Clytie Farr's big straw hat sags down on each side with the rain, "until it looked even more absurd and done for, like an old bonnet on a horse." Caught out in the rain with the hens and chickens, she runs down the street with "her elbows out like hen wings." In death, Clytie's legs hang apart "like a pair of tongs." To the audience, Powerhouse looks like a monkey, has banana-like fingers, and eyes that are "horny like a lizard's"; the reader sees beyond the grotesque parts. In "A Visit of Charity," the first sound the girl hears is "like a sheep bleating." The old woman has "a bunchy white forehead and red eyes like a sheep," "claws," and a "square smile" that forces her old face "dangerously awry." She speaks in a "foggy" voice, for the damp and cold place is more like an ice box than an Old Ladies' Home. When her hand reaches over to the girl, "it felt like a petunia leaf, clinging and just a little sticky."

Plant imagery figures prominently in these virtual transformations. When the orphan Easter is pulled up from the muddy bottom of Moon Lake after almost drowning, "she was arm to arm and leg to leg in a long fold, wrong-colored and pressed together as unopen leaves are"; her wet hair "lay over her face in long fern shapes"; "her side fell slack as a dead rabbit's in the woods"; the whites of her eyes "showed under the lids pale and slick as watermelon seeds" (GA, 128). In "The Whistle," Jason Morton lies under his quilt "in a long shape like a bean," and when the frost threatens their crop, the Mortons undress and lay all their clothes over the *plants*. Because her overalls are stained green, Mrs. Larkin sometimes blends in with her garden. So complete is her victimization that when she swoons under the rain, her surrender to the absurd is orgasmic: "A wind of deep wet fragrance beat against her . . . as if it had swelled and broken over a daily levee, tenderness tore and spun through her." She sinks back into the plants, "with her hair beaten away from her forehead and her open eyes closing at once when the rain touched them. Slowly her lips began to part" (219). The widowed Mrs. Larkin submits to the falling rain as if to a man; it is the ultimate grotesque conversion. Because they have been treated like things, these characters seem to have been reduced to "thinghood," and the grotesque is a protest against their brutalization and abandonment. The grotesque configurations of each physiognomy reveal the price of consciousness.

The grotesque in Eudora Welty's fiction is not nihilistic, for it continually evokes our compassion and affirms the human worth of the individual. Mrs. Larkin's grotesque appearance—her man-sized overalls rolled up at the trousers and sleeves, and her wild, uncombed hair—underscores her suffering. The grotesque literally gives way to pathos when she lifts the hoe to strike Jamey: her clumsy sleeves both fall back, "exposing the thin, unsunburned whiteness of her arms, the shocking fact of their youth." Although Miss Welty's use of the grotesque sometimes precludes a sympathetic response, her intentions seem implicitly moral. Like Swift, Miss Welty might say that she hopes "to mend the world" through the grotesque satire of a story like "Petrified Man" or "A Memory." She exaggerates the ugliness of the bathers, isolating and "magnifying" it as a trauma, because she does not want her readers, like the bathers, to be "resigned to [human] ugliness"—to grossness and corruption and hatred.

4

FORM
AND
TECHNIQUE

THE MODERN SHORT STORY demands precision of style, and the distinction of Eudora Welty's art is due, in great measure, to her considerable technical resources; a decade ago the *Times Literary Supplement* pointed to her as "perhaps the best example of the polished craftsman" among the writers to gain prominence during and after the Second World War. Although Miss Welty began her own writing fresh from her discovery of Virginia Woolf, W. B. Yeats, Katherine Mansfield, and D. H. Lawrence, her style is based on the natural rhythms of American speech and, in this sense, she descends from Mark Twain, Stephen Crane, Sherwood Anderson, and Ernest Hemingway.

Yet the versatility of Miss Welty's style inhibits the inclination to categorize. Her wide range in points of view makes it almost seem as though each time Miss Welty has written a story she has felt the need to take a new angle out of a sheer joy in the uniqueness of the perspective. This does not mean that Miss Welty has indulged her virtuosity for its own sake, for, in her fiction, form and style are dictated by the special needs of the story; the oddest of angles turns out to be the right choice, the *only* choice for that particular story. It may seem arch to tell a story in the present tense, or coy to cast one in the second person, but the brilliance of "Powerhouse" would be diminished considerably if it were told in the past tense, and "Old Mr. Marblehall" would be bewildering if it were unfolded entirely in the third person, since that would make the narrator's observations blatantly omniscient and unreliable rather than a reflection of his own mind. Although not told in the first person, each of these stories possesses a slyly elusive narrative voice of it own. "Powerhouse" has a roving point of view that serves as a neutral observer in the long middle section. But in the opening and closing scenes it stations itself in the crowd and embodies a narrative voice which registers the collective attitude of those watching Powerhouse; "Nigger man?" it muses, slipping into the second person to create a sense of the hermetic intimacy of the crowd and Powerhouse's psychic distance from it. In "The Key" and "Old Mr. Marblehall," the voice is insinuating, personal, at certain moments the third-person narration imperceptibly shifting to direct address, involving the reader in the fictive process and in the fate of characters who might at first seem to be "special cases."

Miss Welty has been able to communicate the most tenuous aspects of reality through the precision, control, and concreteness of her language and, most specifically, through her use of what might be called verbal metaphors. These are verbs that in context seem unusual and unexpected, and are intended, in Joseph Conrad's familiar phrase, "above all, to make you see." They are used judiciously and afford the reader a succession of surprises that are a pleasure in themselves, as when Powerhouse plays the piano in a controlled fury, "kneading a dough of bass notes" (261). Through a richly suggestive verb we experience a place. In *Delta Wedding,* young Laura McRaven looks out upon the Delta from her train: "The land was perfectly flat and level but it shimmered like the wing of a lighted dragonfly. It seemed strummed, as though it were an instrument and someone had touched it" (4). The verbs "strummed" and "shimmered" are so imbued with the sense of place that the landscape, the heat, the very breath of all life there affronts the senses.

It is mainly through verbs that Miss Welty accomplishes the artful dislocations which render a character's acute state of apprehension, crisis, or reverie. The tensile atmosphere of the waiting room in "The Key" is reflected by the unnaturally motionless onlookers, who "sat in silence, their faces stung" and by the little girl who lies "as though sleep had struck her with a blow" (56). When the introspection of the girl in "A Memory" is interrupted by the gamboling bathers, the images of the large boy who "churned his overgrown body through the blue air onto a little bench," of the girl who ran "towards the bench as though she would destroy it" and then "dragged herself through the air and jumped over" it, and of the smaller boy "who flew out of the water to dig his fingers into her side" (155) become nightmarish because of the unexpected verbs, which suggest that the scene has been taken over by those phantasmagoric creatures of evil who fly over the landscape in a Bosch painting. This dreamlike retardation of action also projects the girl's state of mind in "A Piece of News"; through her window the stormy sky "hung full of lightning and thunder" (23) and "a whole tree of lightning stood in the sky" (27). In "Flowers for Marjorie," Howard is in shock when he runs through the city after killing his wife: trucks "contracted, as if on a bellows," and "people seemed to melt out of his way" (206). Mrs. Larkin's precarious hold on consciousness is felt throughout "A Curtain of Green," from the initial image of the sun which "seemed almost to spin in a tiny groove in the polished sky" (209) down to the tenderness which "spun through her sagging body" (218) as she fainted. When she thinks of her husband's death, memory "tightened about her" (213), so complete is its effect on her. She remembers the chinaberry tree, "suddenly tilting, dark and slow like a cloud, leaning down to her husband" (214). The slow-motion effects dramatize her refusal to accept the terrible fact of his death, the verbs keeping the tree in mid-air another instant, prolonging that moment when she tried to will him life. In the stillness that settles over the garden before she lifts the hoe to strike Jamey, "the sun seemed clamped to the side of the sky" (214). As she begins to sink down into the flowers, she looks "at the sky which had begun to move, to fold nearer in softening, dissolving clouds" (218). R. J. Bowman's distress is similarly rendered in "Death of a Traveling Salesman," when the feverish man

gazes up "where two chinaberry trees clutched at the air" (234).
All of these verbs enable Miss Welty to suggest an inside view of a
character without resorting to omniscient commentary.

When Miss Welty is not fashioning verbal metaphors, she is
using verbs as the fulcrums on which her metaphors and similes
turn. The sight of "the pale sobered winter dust where it chunked
out behind [R. J. Bowman's car] like big squashes down the road"
(239) suggests Bowman's stasis; for, to a normal eye, chunks of
dust do not keep their consistency long enough to look like big
vegetables; the verb—Miss Welty's invention—makes them seem
even larger and thicker. The distorting prism through which the
reader views this scene is Bowman's consciousness, as it is en-
veloped by delirium. In "The Winds," the heightened sensitivities of
the pubescent girl Josie are mirrored in the electric atmosphere of
the equinoctial storm, described in the curtains which "hung almost still, like poured cream, down the windows" (117) and by
the way in which "the house moved softly like a boat that has been
stepped into." (120). In the instant when everything stopped in
Mrs. Larkin's garden, when "the stillness had mesmerized the
stems of the plants and all the leaves went suddenly into thickness"
(214), the stasis of the scene and of Mrs. Larkin are one and the
same.

In Miss Welty's best imagery the reader not only sees the moment but often sees the entire fiction telescoped through that image.
But her imagery is not a matter of "fine writing," of studding the
prose surface with individual rococo constructs to be marveled
over. The substantial beauty of her imagery rests on the fact that
style and subject are nearly equivalent. In most of her stories (excepting some of her later work), diction, sentence structure,
rhythm, and figurative language derive from the setting and situation. The components of a metaphor may be drawn from the insect,
bird, animal, or plant life common to the place, from the weather,
or from the implements of daily life, and then expressed in a vocabulary possible to the ordinary people there, although Miss Welty
does not hesitate to reach out for effects beyond their range. The
benumbed farmers in "The Whistle" are "no more communicative
in their misery than a pair of window shutters beaten by a storm."
The wife's body is "as weightless as a strip of cane" (113). Just
before they burn their furniture, the "calm cold sink[s] into them

like the teeth of a trap" (118), summarizing their existence. When Lily Daw tells the three ladies about her "lover," they gasp, "the possible reality of a lover descend[ing] like a summer hail over their heads" (11). "The storm had rolled away to faintness like a wagon crossing a bridge" (31), at the end of "A Piece of News," and "the wavy heat of late afternoon came down from the watertank and fell over everything like shiny mosquito-netting" (64) in "The Wide Net."

In the opening paragraphs of "A Curtain of Green" are found two of the most resonant images created from the materials of a scene: "Every leaf reflected the sun from a hardness *like a mirror*. Nearly all the women sat in the windows of their houses, fanning and sighing," brushing their hair, looking down towards Mrs. Larkin's place in the garden. Two sentences later, "the intense light *like a tweezers* picked out her clumsy small figure" [italics mine] (209). Because the similes might have come off a dressing table belonging to one of those women they link together the social and cosmic indifference which formulate Mrs. Larkin's crisis and isolation. A more typical example of an organically developed image is provided by "The Key." The opening paragraph is devoted to the night sounds of insects, which are amplified to almost threatening dimensions by the awful stillness in the waiting room: "you could listen to the fat thudding of the light bugs and the hoarse rushing of their big wings against the wooden ceiling" (56). In the first sentence of the second paragraph one turns to the two rows of people, "their faces stung" into silence. At dusk in "Old Mr. Marblehall," the drone of insects sounds through Natchez. It is only natural that at night "when time is passing it's like a bug in his ear." In "Powerhouse," Scoot's rapid movements suggest a profusion of arms—"the drummer like a spider over his drums" (261).

Diction and metaphor are most likely to be homely and colloquial and folk expressions most frequent when the story is about a simple character. Miss Baby Marie, the amusingly vulgar cosmetics saleslady in "Livvie," asks the naïve girl, "Did you ever see so many cosmetics in your life?" " 'No'm,' Livvie tried to say, but the cat had her tongue . . . 'Try this!' she said. And in her hand was unclenched a golden lipstick which popped open like magic." Its fragrance reminds Livvie of chinaberry flowers and she visualizes a chinaberry tree from home, "dark and smooth and neatly leaved, neat as a guinea hen in the dooryard" (165). Sentence structure achieves similar effects. "Livvie" begins in this way: *"Solomon carried Livvie* twenty-one miles away from her home when he married her. *He carried her* away upon the Old Natchez Trace into the deep country to live in his house" [italics mine] (153). Although Livvie does not speak, the repetition of the subject-verb structure suggests her simplicity and the innocence of her voice. The smallest verbal elements can be meaningful. In the story's third sentence, Miss Welty writes, "She was sixteen—an only girl, then." The unexpected qualifier interrupts the rhythm of the sentence and stays in our mind because of its position. It implies that Livvie is no longer an only girl and that she looks back at the past with vague longing, suggesting her present loneliness.

The rhythm of style controls the tone throughout "Livvie," as it does in many of Miss Welty's stories. The humor of "Why I Live at the P.O." and "Lily Daw and the Three Ladies" is inherent in the glancing rhythms of the short sentences, and when a more "formal" device—such as word repetition—is used to introduce a homely analogy, the effect can be delightfully satiric: "Mrs. Carson was going on in her sad voice, sad as the soft noises in the hen house at twilight" ("Lily Daw," 7). Rhythm conveys the pathos in "Death of a Traveling Salesman." The sentences are loose, their rhythms slackened, sluggish, seeming to rise and fall with the fluctuations of Bowman's failing heart, slowing down even more as the story moves to its climax and Bowman's death. When the subject warrants, the style is sonorous. "A Still Moment" is set in the early nineteenth century and deals with three historic characters. The diction is formal ("ensconce," "prescience"), including at least one archaic word ("dumbrousness"), and the sentence structure is complex, abounding in subordinate clauses, parallel constructions, and word repetition. The gravity, measured pace and balance of the style is appropriate to the story's high seriousness.

The visual quality of Miss Welty's fiction reflects her background as a painter and photographer. Surely her ability to evoke light, color, and atmosphere, to render surface and texture, and to capture an elusive gesture suggest how much she has gained from her initial artistic interests. Some of Miss Welty's most virtuoso painterly effects are in "The Bride of the Innisfallen." The joyous girl

imagines, "I see Cork's streets take off from the waterside and rise
lifting their houses and towers like note above note on a page of
music, with arpeggios running over it of green and galleries and
belvederes, and the bright sun raining at the top" (82). The green
arpeggios are fauvist fantasy, and, when Miss Welty places "the
bright sun raining at the top," she seems to be setting a John Marin
watercolor to words. The description of Asphodel shows Miss
Welty's compositional eye at work, and how, with a few well-
placed "strokes," she can present an entire scene:

> It was a cloudless day. . . . It was noon, and without a shadow
> the line of columns rose in perfect erectness from the green vines. . . .
> It was a golden ruin: six Doric columns, with the entablature unbroken
> over the first two, full-facing the approach. The sky was pure, trans-
> parent, and round like a shell over this hill (WN, 95).

The ruins recall the disquieting effect achieved in surrealist paintings when the façade of a lone, empty building is silhouetted against
a blank sky.

Photography is brought to mind when the three old maids approach the ruins. It is as if the moment had been immobilized by
the click of a camera's shutter: " 'This is Asphodel,' they repeated,
looking modestly upward to the frieze of maidens that was satu-
rated with sunlight and seemed to fill with color, and before which
the branch of a leafy tree was trembling" (96). Miss Welty's eye
is extremely sensitive to the simple poetry of surfaces: "The old
circus posters on the store were nearly gone, only bits, the snow-
flakes of white horses, clinging to its side" (WN, 64); "the Confederate soldier on the shaft looked like a chewed-on candle, as
if old gnashing teeth had made him. On past him, pale as a rainbow, the ancient circus posters clung to their sheds, they no longer
the defacing but the defaced" (GA, 241); the tactile quality is
reminiscent of some of the photographs taken by Dorothea Lange
and Walker Evans for the Farm Security Administration. In re-
counting her experiences as a photographer, Miss Welty has defined the interrelationship of the arts as it affects her. She recalls
how, perhaps due to atavistic beliefs, people refused to pose for
her.

> . . . an eccentric old lady in Louisiana threatened to shoot me with
> her gun if I dared photograph a beautiful statue in her garden. It is
> clear that the fascination of a photograph of anything is that it im-

prisons a moment in time—and is that really different from stealing its spirit, its soul? Perhaps one does right to protest.

Yet this must be, in a sense, the purpose of nearly everything we do—certainly in the arts, painting and writing, we steal spirits and souls if we can, and in love and devotion, what do we do but pray: Keep this as it is, hold this moment safe? [1]

However thorough they may be, isolated remarks about a writer's style are by definition incomplete. To break a story into its component parts is to violate its form—to separate theme from technique. Perhaps only by the close analysis of two representative stories, "Death of a Traveling Salesman" and "The Hitch-Hikers," can one fully appreciate Eudora Welty's methods.

In these stories Miss Welty presents two salesmen who are representative Americans, rather than specifically Southerners, and who think of themselves as "adjusted" to the world about them, only to experience—through a brief relationship—a sudden discovery of their isolation. The setting of each story is in Mississippi, but the Southern place is very differently treated in each.

In "Death of a Traveling Salesman," R. J. Bowman is back on the road after a serious illness. The story is told in the third person and from his point of view, although the first scene contains some exposition dependent on an omniscience that quickly disappears by scene two. A brilliant study in autosuggestion, it is one of her stories in which the perspective slips from the objective to the subjective at precisely the right moment, achieving a deeply moving revelation of human need and desire—an effect she described metaphorically in *Place in Fiction*:

Some of us grew up with the china night-light, the little lamp whose lighting showed its secret. . . . The outside is painted with a scene, which is one thing; then, when the lamp is lighted, through the porcelain sides a new picture comes out through the old, and they are seen as one.

Miss Welty projects the story thematically throughout the first of its six scenes. In the opening paragraph, she writes:

R. J. Bowman, who for fourteen years had traveled for a shoe company through Mississippi, drove his Ford along a *rutted dirt path. It was a long day! The time did not seem to clear the noon hurdle* and settle into soft afternoon. The sun, keeping its strength here even in winter, stayed at the top of the sky, and every time Bowman stuck his head out of the dusty car to stare up the road, it seemed to *reach a long*

arm down and push against the top of his head, right through his hat
—like the practical joke of an old drummer, long on the road. It made
him feel all the more angry and helpless. He was feverish, and *he was
not quite sure of the way* [italics mine] (231).

Bowman's weariness is stated in a colloquial exclamation that
could be his own, and the images of the sun suggest several
meanings which are later confirmed. The sun's failure to "clear
the noon hurdle" defines the growth of his fever into delirium [2]
and, more abstractly, indicates that "time" has stopped for Bowman—the discovery he makes later in the story. The "long arm"
pushing "through his hat" is the first suggestion of Bowman's imminent death. Miss Welty skilfully completes the image with a
simile in keeping with Bowman's vocation—it's "like the practical
joke of an old drummer." The strength of the sun—"even in
winter"—is analogous to the mysterious strength later encountered
by Bowman in the cabin. As an extended metaphor, it is picked
up further on in fire imagery. Most important, the sun signals
Bowman's distance from the natural, organic world. Even after
fourteen years, Bowman remains unaccustomed to the Southern
sun because he is out of touch with the instinctual, life-giving
forces which it represents.

The sun is the archetypal symbol of life itself—fertility and
growth, power and passion. D. H. Lawrence, who made prominent symbolic use of the sun,[3] would have described Bowman as
having "lost the cosmos," and throughout the story the sun and
fire imagery symbolize this estrangement. When the sun bears
down upon Bowman's head, it is almost as if it regards him as a
personal affront, as if Bowman were a representative figure—a
symbol of the modern, materialistic temper, disconnected from all
organic life. While he drives, Bowman wonders how had he "ever
come to such a place?" Even though he has made this trip before,
he doesn't recognize certain hills and paths. His reactions to the
landscape project a feeling deeper than the mere loss of a sense
of direction. The mention of a "rutted dirt path" in the story's
first sentence can be read on the literal level. But in the last
scene, Bowman is overwhelmed by the discovery that his life has
followed a "rutted path," so to speak, and that—as Miss Welty
writes in the opening paragraph—he has *never* been "sure of the
way" and has always been "lost."

In the second scene, Bowman's car rolls over the bank of the backcountry road and he seeks help at a nearby cabin. His arrival there anticipates some kind of confrontation: "all of a sudden his heart began to behave strangely." Miss Welty now presents details as only Bowman sees them, and, entering his mind, she renders Bowman's thoughts within the descriptive passages. Much of the story's impact is dependent upon Bowman's limited point of view. The reader is aware of no more than what Bowman himself perceives. When Bowman looked at the woman in the cabin doorway, "he saw at once that she was old" and "set her age at fifty" (236). In the third scene, a man named Sonny enters the cabin: "There was the resemblance to his mother" (241). The "old woman" and her "son" allow Bowman to spend the night. In the fourth and fifth scenes, he fails to communicate with his hosts, and, in the domestic warmth of the physically and socially isolated backwoods cabin, Bowman begins to realize that *he* is the one who is isolated from mankind.

To Bowman, the world has always seemed askew or claustrophobic; the past can be summarized in a few phrases: "weren't [all hotels] eternally stuffy in summer and drafty in winter?" As for women, "he could only remember little rooms within little rooms, like a nest of Chinese paper boxes" (232). In contrast, the cabin represents the natural world: "the hearth and smoked chimney were of the stone he had seen ribbing the hills, mostly slate" (239); and "the whole cabin slanted a little under the heavy heaped-up vine that covered the roof, light and green, as though forgotten from summer" (235). This is no ordinary cabin in some random slice of Mississippi backcountry, but a symbolic landscape, blending myth and reality—a kind of pastoral scene, which, like the traditional landscape of pastoral, seems to occupy a middle ground between wild nature and urban society. It is the perfect metaphor to suggest the enduring contrast between the values and rhythms of a natural, organic existence and those of a commercial civilization:

And it was so still. The silence of the fields seemed to enter and move familiarly through the house. The wind used the open hall. He felt that he was in a mysterious, quiet, cool danger. It was necessary to do what? . . . To talk.

"I have a nice line of women's low-priced shoes . . ." he said (239).

The man and woman live in the spirit of their "place." Bowman is indeed a stranger here.

Until the middle of the sixth scene, Bowman—and the reader—have perceived the couple as mother and son. There have been no suggestions to the contrary, except for one detail: "her arms appeared pink and unexpectedly round" (237). But as Bowman sits at the supper table, Miss Welty manipulates her material in the manner of a movie cameraman who suddenly moves in for a close-up shot of his subject, revealing a startling, unexpected, intimate truth:

> Bowman had just happened to be looking at her. He set his cup back on the table in unbelieving protest. A pain pressed at his eyes. He saw that she was not an old woman. She was young, still young. He could think of no number of years for her. She was the same age as Sonny, and she belonged to him (250).

Thus, Bowman's complete inability to cope with reality is exposed by Miss Welty's handling of the point of view—Bowman was unable to see what was there all the time—and the reader experiences a shock along with the salesman when Miss Welty turns on her "china night-light." "She's goin' to have a baby," Sonny tells him. Bowman's realization of his estrangement is enormous: he is left speechless "with knowing what was really in this house. A marriage. . . . That simple thing. Anyone could have had that. . . . The only secret was the ancient communication between two people" (251). The incident reveals to Bowman his lifetime of isolation. In Franz Kafka's "The Metamorphosis," the absurdity of Gregor Samsa's life transforms that traveling salesman into a fantastic insect—a symbolic death-in-life. Although fact and fantasy have intermingled throughout her story, Miss Welty resolves the theme realistically. No "beast" appears. Bowman's shock of recognition comes with such violence that it stuns him—to death. He leaves the cabin and, as soon as he gets to the road—the "rutted path" that has been both his life and livelihood—he falls dead.

There is no sentimentality in this story. Although his visit to the cabin has shown Bowman the sterility and lovelessness of his world, he is unable to fill the vacuum; he can only summon up the conditioned responses of "a drummer, long on the road." Whenever reality seems about to overwhelm him, he reacts as a commercial man—offering to show a pair of shoes or to pay for staying overnight; thinking of a special January sale; and finally, on his way out, leaving money. Bowman is wedded to his way of life, just as the couple seem eternal in their marriage; the reader recalls the man's hotel rooms, "all, eternally, stuffy." One responds to his pathos; yet in the story he rouses suspicion. When Bowman asks if he can stay, Sonny searches him: "You ain't no revenner come sneakin' here, mister, ain't got no gun?" (247). Miss Welty's quiet irony destroys any trace of sentimentality without altering her deeply felt compassion, thus intensifying one's sense of Bowman as a figure of haunting futility.

There are critics who disparage women writers such as Miss Welty as "feminine"—meaning that these writers have overindulged their sensibilities and are guilty of "dressing-up" their stories by using poetic description as mere decoration. Most of Miss Welty's fiction stands in refutation of such charges, and "Death of a Traveling Salesman" is an excellent example of a story in which style tells all.

A startling quality of "Death of a Traveling Salesman" is the fact that—save for the title—the word *death* does not appear in the story. Instead, the story abounds in images and verbs calculated to express Bowman's delirium and to foreshadow his impending death. Several images that imply a "floating" sensation suggest his delirium. In the first scene,

All afternoon . . . and for no reason, he had thought of his grandmother. She had been a comfortable soul. Once more Bowman wished he could fall into the big feather bed that had been in her room (232).

When he watches a cloud, "it floated there to one side like the bolster on his grandmother's bed" (234). And in scene three, the design on the bed quilt in the cabin reminds him of "his grandmother's girlhood painting of Rome burning" (238). Miss Welty never says that "Bowman is going to die." Instead, Bowman's thoughts of his dead grandmother's soft, phantom-like "featherbed" project his imminent death and suggest his death-wish—he "wished he could fall into the big feather bed"—his subconscious desire for the comfort of senselessness. When his car goes off the road,

he saw that [it] had fallen into a tangle of immense grapevines as thick as his arm, which caught it and held it, *rocked it like a grotesque child in a dark cradle,* and then, as he *watched, concerned somehow*

that he was not inside it [italics mine], released it gently to the ground.
He sighed (235).

His death-wish is dramatized in this extraordinary accident scene.
The "floating" images become a leitmotif, appearing and reappearing at various intervals throughout the story. These passages are
rendered in the manner of a slow-motion picture, where everything is deliberately felt; the verbs carry much of the burden of
expression. After the accident, "all his anger seemed to have
drifted away from him" (235). In scene two, Bowman confusedly
stands before the cabin and drops his bags, "which seemed to
drift in slow bulks gracefully through the air and to cushion themselves on the gray prostrate grass near the doorstep" (236). In
the fourth scene, Bowman sees the man in the distance as he
moves toward the cabin: "His eyes searched the dusky air. The
white speck [the man] floated toward [him], like a leaf on a river,
growing whiter in the dark" (245).

The mythic aura about Bowman's visit to the cabin is symbolically underscored by his wish to reach his intended destination,
the town of Beulah, "by dark, to go to bed and sleep off his
fatigue" (233); one recalls the "Beulah Land" sung about in
Southern Baptist gospel hymns—the Beulah that in the *Pilgrim's
Progress* is associated with the peace to be found toward the end
of life's journey. Thus Bowman feels that the couple "withheld
some ancient promise of food and warmth and light." His arrival
at the cabin signals a return to the natural world and suggests a
movement backwards in time—into childhood and oblivion. As
he drives into the hill country, "it was as if he were going back,
far back" (232). His car—a kind of mechanical appendage to
the traveling man—is caught and held in an immense tangle of
vines "like a grotesque child" and Bowman is later "caught" inside the cabin which "slanted under the heavy heaped-up vine
that covered [it]." When Bowman sees the house, "he took a bag
in each hand and with almost *childlike willingness* went toward it"
[italics mine] (235). His month of sickness had been "an almost
inaudible life of heartbeats and dreams that came back" (240).
Bowman's most persistent dreams are of his grandmother. His
impulse is to see reality in terms of the past, to connect the living
with the dead. Like his car, he too is a "grotesque child"; he
longs to "embrace this woman who sat there *growing old and
shapeless before him*" [italics mine] (243). The adjectives key-

note Bowman's longing for death rather than life. When he first meets the woman he "looked at her carefully, and yet *in his distraction dreamily,* with his mouth open. . . . He saw her with the dark passage behind her" [italics mine] (236). He connects the cabin with his illness: "Inside, the darkness of the house touched him like a professional hand, the doctor's" (238). Bowman's immediate decision that the woman is old is an attempt to assign her to the "dark passage" of the past—the womb, perhaps? —and to subconsciously associate her with his dead grandmother; he seems to *force* her image to conform—she "grows old . . . before him." She has a quilt like his grandmother's, and in the moment following his recognition of her age, when his illusory sense of time and reality is shattered, "the pattern on the quilt moved." Bowman moves toward his "dark cradle." "He must get back to where he had been before," Miss Welty writes at the end of the story (252). He is on his way to Beulah.

Bowman's death is foreshadowed throughout the story by imagery that strikingly captures each fluctuation of his heart. Miss Welty develops and heightens this imagery until the climactic moment when the heart literally explodes. She constantly keeps the reader aware of Bowman's heart, beginning with scene two:

. . . all of a sudden his heart began to behave strangely. Like a rocket set off, it began to *leap* and *expand* into uneven patterns of beats which *showered* into his brain, and he could not think. But in *scattering* and *falling* it made no noise. It *shot* up with great power, almost elation, and *fell gently, like acrobats into nets.* It began to *pound* profoundly, then waited irresponsibly, *hitting* in some sort of inward mockery first his ribs, then against his eyes, then under his shoulder blades, and against the roof of his mouth when he tried to say, "Good afternoon, madam." But he could not hear his heart—*it was as quiet as ashes falling.* This was rather comforting; still, it was shocking to Bowman to feel his heart beating at all [italics mine] (235).

In this passage, the heart is congruent with the "floating" leitmotif, and the verbs are vividly metaphoric. "The pulse in his palm leapt like a trout in a brook" (240), and later, "Bowman's heart leaped again. It seemed to walk about inside him" (242). He hears his voice speaking over "the silent blows" of his heart and worries that the woman will hear them. The reader can almost feel the frenzied beat of the heart when Bowman's frustration is rendered in an interior monologue:

But he wanted to leap up, to say to her, I have been sick and I found out then, only then, how lonely I am. Is it too late? My heart puts up a struggle inside of me, and you may have heard it, protesting against emptiness. . . . *It should be full,* he would rush on to tell her, *thinking of his heart now as a deep lake,* it should be holding love like other hearts. It should be *flooded* with love. There would be a warm spring day. . . . Come and *stand in my heart, whoever you are, and a whole river would cover your feet and rise higher and take your knees in whirlpools, and draw you down to itself, your whole body, your heart too* [italics mine] (243).

The image of Bowman's heart as "a deep lake," along with the other water imagery, once again reiterates the "floating" leitmotif. As his delirium increases, the "water" metaphorically "rises higher."

Miss Welty does not manipulate her imagery or symbolism in a blatant or self-conscious fashion; as in the two long passages just quoted, it is immersed in the external reality of the story and tightly organized in the texture of the prose.[4] She does not fashion one central, overwhelming symbol, but lets the symbolic process work quietly. The imagery gradually gathers towards a concentration of effect. Spiritually, Bowman is the sum of his parts—sample cases, overcoat, old car. Only *once* is he described physically: "he was a man who always wore rather wide-brimmed black hats, and in the wavy hotel mirrors had looked something like a bullfighter, as he paused for that inevitable instant on the landing, walking downstairs to supper. . ." (233). The figure of Bowman as a "bullfighter" is a pathetic, absurd touch; the story's unfolding makes the irony apparent. In several of Miss Welty's stories, hats appear as phallic symbols (see "The Purple Hat," "Livvie," and "Music from Spain"). Bowman's black hat asserts his inadequacy and symbolizes his submerged, muffled sexuality. When he arrives at the cabin, he says,

"I am not strong yet. . . . May I come in?"
He stooped and laid his big black hat over the handle on his bag. It was a humble motion, almost a bow, that instantly struck him as absurd and betraying of all his weakness. He looked up at the woman, the wind blowing his hair (237–38).

And when Bowman first sees Sonny, the symbolism is most explicit: "On the back of his light hair he had a wide filthy black hat which seemed to insult Bowman's own" (241).

Sonny is indeed an "insult" to Bowman, for he is the antithesis of the salesman—strong, dignified, sexually vital, at peace with himself and his environment. He first appears, "plunging in at the door, with two hounds beside him." When he goes out to pull Bowman's car from the ravine, Sonny's powerful walk resounds on the hard earth. "Mischievously, at the suggestion of these sounds, Bowman's heart leapt again" (242). Bowman is rootless, but Sonny even manages to carry a sense of history about him: "He wore muddy blue pants and an old military coat stained and patched. World War? Bowman wondered. Great God, it was a Confederate coat" (241). Bowman finds the sun oppressive because he has lived in an emotional waste land; "if he thought of one woman he saw the worn loneliness that the furniture of that room seemed built of." A moment later, "he leaned out of the car again, and once more the sun pushed at his head" (233), as if infuriated by Bowman's remove from the organic world. Sonny, however, is symbolically identified with fire, the extension of the initial sun image; there is his name; his hair is blonde; his wife is pregnant; and he even has a "hot, red face." D. H. Lawrence would have admired him, for Sonny is similar to one of Lawrence's ideal "peasant" types; indeed, he is described in almost Lawrencian terms, and Bowman recalls the ineffectual husbands in Lawrence's "Sun" and "The Woman Who Rode Away." One verb communicates the way that Sonny's life is a judgment upon Bowman's: "Sonny's eyes lay upon him" (241).

Throughout the story, the woman is shown cleaning a lamp rather portentously. Before the recognition scene, the reader perceives Bowman's gnawing anxiety and sees much of his growing uneasiness through Bowman's reactions to the fire and lamp symbolism.[5] The symbolic correspondences are subconsciously made by Bowman himself and foreshadow the eventual impact of the couple's true relationship. His first view of the woman includes the lamp (236). The lamp immediately prompts him to make a symbolic association: "when she never said a word, and sustained her quiet pose of holding the lamp, he was convinced of the strength in her body" (237). Inside the cold cabin, the woman puts the lamp on a table in the center of the room and then crouches on the hearth. She makes no effort to light the fire. "Why is there no fire? he wondered" (239). The lamp fascinates, even obsesses Bowman: "He wondered over and over why the woman did not go ahead with cleaning the lamp" (240). While she waits, "her face was grave." In scene four she stands by the table. Again, "he wondered why she did not light the lamp. She stood there in the dark and did not light it" (245). His preoccupation with the lamp and Miss Welty's use of repetition invest the lamp with a kind of ceremonial importance. When the woman points to Sonny returning through the darkness, "it was as if she had shown him something secret, part of her life, but had offered no explanation. He looked away. He was moved almost to tears, feeling for no reason that she had made a silent declaration equivalent to his own. His hand waited upon his chest" (245–46).

The fire illuminates the oppressive "secret," both symbolically and actually. The woman opens scene five by announcing, "Sonny . . . you'll have to borry some fire" (247). Bowman desperately offers his help:

"But matches—I have matches—"
    "We don't have no need for 'em," she said *proudly*. "Sonny's goin' after *his own fire*."
    "I'm goin' to Redmond's," said Sonny with *an air of importance,* and he went out [italics mine] (247–48).

The fire-sun symbolism has been built-up with deft strokes, touch upon touch. Like a "guide," the woman had seated Bowman in a "chair with a yellow seat"; the room was enclosed in "yellow pine boards"; the quilt was red-yellow, like his grandmother's painting of Rome burning (238); and the man for whom he farms and who gives Sonny fire is named Redmond (red moon). Now, in anticipation of the recognition scene, the impotency-fertility contrast becomes more explicit; they don't want "matches," but real "fire," even though Sonny has to travel a mile. The flame he brings back has almost phallic overtones:

Sonny staggered in, holding a burning stick behind him in tongs, fire flowing in his wake, blazing light into the corners of the room.
    "We'll make a fire now," the woman said, taking the brand (248).

The room, once cold and dark, is brought to life by the flame:

. . . she lit the lamp. It showed its dark and light. The whole room turned golden-yellow like some sort of flower, and the walls smelled of it and seemed to *tremble* with the quiet *rushing* of the fire and the *waving* of the burning lampwick in its funnel of light [italics mine] (248).

Bowman has projected the couple's instinctual behavior into the male and female sexual correspondences of the fire and the lamp (and one is tempted to call the room a womb). He has symbolically imagined the truth about them by transforming his observations of some simple details into a kind of fertility ritual, in which the "lighting" of the "lamp" is perceived orgasmically—accompanied by "trembl[ing]," "rushing," and "waving." ("Livvie" ends in a similar way.) Bowman is left speechless and trembling. When he recognizes her true age, "the shifting yellow light [was] scattering over her head . . . trembling over her tall body. . . (250). Her teeth were shining and her eyes glowed" (251). She is revealed to him with all the power of the sun which pushed on his head in the first paragraph.

The story's symbolic action is enforced in a brief scene in which Sonny takes Bowman outside for some moonshine whiskey:

It was another excursion into the dark. . . . They came to a wilderness of thicket.
"Down on your knees," said Sonny.
"What?" Sweat broke out on his forehead.
He understood when Sonny began to crawl through a sort of tunnel that the bushes made over the ground. He followed, startled in spite of himself when a twig or a thorn touched him gently without making a sound, clinging to him and finally letting him go.
Sonny stopped crawling and, crouched on his knees, began to dig with both his hands into the dirt. Bowman shyly struck matches and made a light. In a few minutes Sonny pulled up a jug. . . . "You never know who's liable to knock at your door," he said, and laughed (249).

The "wilderness of thicket" is associated with the "immense grapevine" that had rocked his car "like a . . . child in a dark cradle" (235), and his movement through the "tunnel" furthers one's sense of the story's progression—Bowman literally seems to be *descending* into death. They have their drinks indoors: " 'This is good,' said Bowman. 'This is what I needed.' It was just as though he were drinking the fire off the hearth. 'He makes it,' said the woman with quiet pride" (250). The action and dialogue sustain the tightly packed yet unobtrusive symbolic level. Sonny's act of digging-up the jug symbolically places him at the source of his strength and fecundity, underlining his connection with organic and natural forces. Bowman's remark about the "drink" defines the exact nature of his failure. A few moments later, he recognizes the truth about the couple—and himself.

Later that night, he tries to sleep. Helpless, feeling "that he had been cheated," his life ebbs away:

> He lay stretched by the fire until it grew low and dying. He watched every tongue of blaze lick out and vanish. "There will be special reduced prices on all footwear during the month of January," he found himself repeating quietly, and then he lay with his lips tight shut (252).

During the night, at the sound of their breathing, "emotion swelled patiently within him, and he wished the child were his." "Swelled" is a well-chosen descriptive verb, at once reflecting the physical state of the woman and her pregnancy's impact on Bowman's consciousness. He gets up, and as he starts out he notices that "the woman had never got through with cleaning the lamp. On some impulse he put all the money from his billfold under its fluted glass base, almost ostentatiously" (253). Alienated from the possibilities symbolized by the lamp, he copes with the "lamp" in the only way he knows, commercially, substituting money for "fire"—his bankroll for his love and passion. Bowman's final, futile gesture signals, in Elizabeth Bowman's phrase, "the death of the heart." The symbolism is successful because it seems to have developed in Bowman's mind, rather than having been forced from without by the author.

In this last section, the story's main thematic threads coincide: "How many noises the night had: He heard the stream running, the fire dying, and he was sure now that he heard his heart beating, too, the sound it made under his ribs" (252). When Bowman leaves the cabin he is near death: his overcoat "felt too heavy on his shoulders." Outside, "the cold of the air seemed to lift him bodily" (253). Metaphorically, the "fire" is out and the "water" engulfs him; the heart and "floating" themes—death and delirium —merge in the culmination of Bowman's empty life:

> On the slope he began to run, he could not help it. Just as he reached the road, where his *car seemed to sit in the moonlight like a boat,* his heart began to give off tremendous explosions like a rifle, bang bang bang.
> He *sank* in fright onto the road, his bags falling about him. *He felt*

as if all this had happened before. He covered his heart with both hands to keep anyone from hearing the noise it made.

But nobody heard it [italics mine] (253).

Bowman dies as he had lived—alone. His inhibition reacts even at the moment of death, and he covers his heart to hide the noise. He feels "this had happened before" because it *had,* by installments, so to speak; he had been dying slowly throughout the story—physically, as made evident by the heart imagery, and psychologically, as shown by his attempt to identify reality with the dead past; the incident in the cabin provided the last stroke, presenting him with a sudden awareness of the deadness of the present and of his entire life.

The water, "floating," and drowning imagery which express Bowman's death recall T. S. Eliot's Prufrock: "We have lingered in the chambers of the sea/ . . . Till human voices wake us, and we drown." Some of Miss Welty's best effects, such as the water imagery in "Death of a Traveling Salesman," are realized in the manner of modern poetry. At the beginning of the story Bowman notices a cloud, and "thought shyly" about it. Later he hears and is disturbed by the "soft, continuous, insinuating" sound made by a nearby stream which, significantly, he cannot see because of "darkness." In the first passage about Bowman's heart, "the beats showered into his brain." His heart is first a "deep lake" and then, as his desperation rises, a "river," which, rising higher, creates "whirlpools." He thinks that his heart "should be flooded with love." Like Prufrock, he lingers "in the chambers of the sea." The "floating" imagery expresses Bowman's delirium, but when his delirium gives way to death—when "the human voices" in the cabin "wake" him—he symbolically "drowns" (Sonny first appears "like a leaf on the river"; metaphorically, he stays "afloat"). Bowman perceives his car—in itself a symbol of the traveling man's rootlessness—as if it "seemed to sit in the moonlight like a boat." When his heart exploded, he "sank" to the road. The tissue of water images has described his complete dissolution. Sun and water, the elements of growth and rebirth, spell death for Bowman—the intruder in the backcountry pastoral —who not only dies but seems actually to dissolve back into the region. The story is a triumph in technique.

The sun-flame imagery is symbolically effective because it is unfolded with the motion and progression of the story. Although the sun symbolism figures in several stories,[6] Miss Welty, unlike D. H. Lawrence, never uses it to preach. If she has never didactically "put" the sun into her work, it is because of her skill at rendering the entire natural world. One of the central characters in "A Still Moment" is Miss Welty's re-creation of Audubon, and she herself is often a kind of artist-naturalist in her stories. She knows the names of flowers and mosses and birds and can describe them precisely and evocatively, imprisoning the pulse of life in a phrase— the sight and sound of bluejays "whipping through their tunnels in the chinaberry trees," or of a hummingbird suspended over a flower, its whirring wings a haze "like the ring around the moon." Thus any images of the sun in her stories are first of all part of the natural world, which accounts for their success as symbols.

"The Hitch-Hikers" is also about the pervading mystery of relationship. Tom Harris, a thirty-year-old traveling salesman of office supplies, gives a ride to two hitchhiking tramps. One learns at the end of the story that the hitchhikers have been on the road together for two weeks. One of them carries a guitar, which he sometimes strums; the other, whose name is Sobby, is sullen and only speaks once. The three pause briefly at a roadside joint for hamburgers and beer. This is the extent of their fleeting relationship. Harris then drives on and stops the car at his usual local hotel; while he is inside, a boy enters and announces that the hitchhikers have tried to steal the car and that Sobby has attacked and almost killed the man with the guitar. That night, Harris goes to an especially dreary party. He returns to his cheap hotel room and recognizes his isolation. Later that night he has a pathetic encounter with a girl from the party, after which he learns that the man has died. In the morning he leaves town. He gives the dead man's guitar to a little Negro boy.

There's obviously more "plot" and "action" in "The Hitch-Hikers" than in "Death of a Traveling Salesman." Although the story is also told from the salesman's point of view, the unfolding is not as subjective as in "Death of a Traveling Salesman." The telling seems to be straightforward. But like all of Miss Welty's stories, it has its special perspective: the attempt to portray Harris' growing sense of isolation and his acceptance of it as conclusive and perhaps touching, yet essentially *non*dramatic—for the truth does not loom up before Harris, as it does for Bowman, whose whole life appears to him in that one instant of vision. Harris' self-knowledge is not so devastating; his life goes on, empty as it is. He is still young.

Miss Welty succeeds in rendering the flatness of his existence without writing flat prose. The form of the story is conceived with this in mind. It is composed of eight short scenes. There are no transitions between any of them; one seems to be juxtaposed upon the next in order to express the random, aimless quality of Harris' life. In the party scene, this technique is brought to bear upon all the mimetic components within the scene itself. The form is equivalent to the subject and it is a perfect framework in which to develop Harris' growing estrangement, which is echoed, secondly, in the landscape around him—or rather, *lack* of landscape, since it is almost nonexistent in "The Hitch-Hikers." Its absence becomes more apparent when one compares the story with Miss Welty's other stories or her remarks in *Place in Fiction* and in "Some Notes on River Country."

With the exception of a few other Southerners and Westerners such as Walter Van Tilburg Clark and Wallace Stegner, there are very few modern American fiction writers who share Miss Welty's almost reverent feelings about "the sense of place." In fact, except for these writers, the landscape—and "nature"—has all but disappeared in our prose literature, for most Americans seem unable to find in environment any confirmation of their identity. The insignificance of locality and community for many of our writers contrasts with Miss Welty's experience. "Like a good many other [regional] writers," she says, "I am myself touched off by place. The place where I am and the place I know, and other places that familiarity with and love for my own make strange and lovely and enlightening to look into, are what set me to writing my stories." To her, "place opens a door in the mind," and she speaks of "the blessing of being located—contained." Neither Bowman nor Harris are located or contained. In *Place in Fiction,* Miss Welty defines their plight, without mentioning either by name: "Being on the move is no substitute for feeling. Nothing is. And no love or insight can be at work in a shifting and never-defined position, where eye, mind, and heart have never willingly focused on a steadying point." In order to communicate Harris' state of flux, Miss Welty departs from her usual practice and abstracts any sense of "place" in "The Hitch-Hikers." Whereas Bowman's isolation was heightened by the fertile landscape (and couple), Harris' is paralleled by his sterile and empty environment. From Harris' point of view and by definition of his character the landscape is undefined and "unseen." He drives "somewhere in the middle of the Delta" (CG, 121); "there was a little town coming up; the lights showed for twenty miles in the flat land" (124); later, he "came to [a] bridge out in the middle of nowhere" (136); he recalls "the recurring sight of hitch-hikers waiting against the sky" (121). The atmosphere in the story is dependent upon what is *not* described. Only the hitchhikers are connected with "place." When Harris slows down to pick them up, one is standing by the side of the pavement, "with his foot stuck out like an old root," while the other is playing "a yellow guitar which caught the late sun as it came in a long straight bar across the fields" (121). The description frames them within the landscape, just as Harris remains figuratively apart from it.

Harris' isolation is formulated in the actions, characters, and details of each scene: the senselessness of the sudden murder; the roadside joint; the party scene; and the run-down, two-story Dulcie Hotel. Its proprietor, Mr. Gene, and his "ancient" collie dog mirror Harris' spiritual torpor: moving "stiffly, like a table walking," the dog shoves himself between the two men, putting his jaw in Harris' palm. " 'His spirit's gone. You see?' said Mr. Gene pleadingly" (129). Miss Welty's symbolism works quietly.

The violence in the car creates a good deal of excitement. Harris takes the injured man to the hospital. For perhaps the first time in years, Harris has been stirred out of his lethargy—and so has Mike, the dog: "It took it out of Mike, I'm tellin' you," Mr. Gene says, "first time he's barked since Bud Milton shot up that Chinese." The violence has bloodied Harris' car and clothes, but Miss Welty's irony and humor play back and forth, muting the crime's significance: while Harris puts on a clean shirt in his room, Mr. Gene lies on the bed with Mike across his chest. Talking in short breaths, Mr. Gene comments, "Ruined that Christmas tie you came in." After taking a swallow of whiskey, tears appear in the proprietor's warm brown eyes. "Suppose they'd done it on the porch" (131).

In place of a landscape, Miss Welty fashions apt juxtapositions, making judicious and expressive use of brand names, songs, and other images of commercial and human vulgarity, of cheap sex, lifelessness, dreariness, and dinginess: Ruth, the woman who gives the party, and her guests; that staple American drink, Coca-Cola; a pathetic "old Cadillac taxi"; "the ramshackle little hospital" (130); the dirty screendoor of the All-Nite diner (144); and the bare plaster walls and defective fan in Harris' room (140). When Harris stops for hamburgers, a girl car-hop in red pants leaps onto the running board and a man's voice calls out, "Come on in, boys, we got girls." The nickelodeon playing inside turns the window blue, red, and green. Before they leave, the car-hop says, "Hurry back," and after opening a heart-shaped pocket over her heart, she drops in her tip. " 'Aw river!' sang out the man with the guitar" (127).

The car-hop's gesture is a kind of charade, symbolizing the emotional impoverishment of the other characters. Everyone except the man with the guitar is either a lonely figure, like Harris, or a two-dimensional grotesque, like Ruth or Mr. Gene. The guitarist sings "Aw river!" at the sight of the girl's "open" heart because he alone stands out in contrast against this "waste land" atmosphere of tawdriness and isolation. There is a sense of the artist about him. "This Box? Just play it for myself," he tells Harris. He renders both moral and aesthetic judgments. When they stop to eat, "My," says the man with the guitar, "red sailor-boy britches." Harris expects a guitar note, but it does not come. "But not purty," says the hitchhiker. While they eat, a brassy swing record of "Love, Oh Love, Oh Careless Love" is playing.

"Same songs ever'where," said the man with the guitar slowly. "I come down from the hills. . . . We had us owls for chickens and fox for yard dogs but we sung true . . ." (125). "My ma, she was the one for ballats. Little in the waist as a dirt-dauber, but her voice carried. Had her a whole lot of tunes. Long ago dead an' gone. . . . Dead an' gone an' the house burned down." He gulped at his beer. His foot was patting (126).

Like the couple in "Death of a Traveling Salesman," the man and his guitar represent a deep-rooted source of natural, creative energy. The sun symbolism is evident again: it's a "yellow guitar," which catches "the late sun as it came in a long straight bar." At times the guitar serves as the man's voice: when Harris asks, " 'Anything to eat?' The man gave a pluck to a low string" (123); to a question about a place to sleep, he adds another pluck and yawns (124). The guitar is rendered as an almost natural extension of the man— a "note" repeated each time he is mentioned: "the man with the guitar was riding with it between his legs"; "once the man with the guitar started to sing. . . . Then in shyness he stopped" (122); and in the second scene, when Harris is called out to his car,

> It was the man with the guitar. The little ceiling light had been turned on. With blood streaming from his broken head, he was slumped down upon the guitar, his legs bowed around it, his arms at either side, his whole body limp in the posture of a bareback rider (129–30).

At the end of the story, his murderer whimpers, "He carried a gittar around."

The guitar is the central symbol in the story.

> Of course it was by the guitar that he had known at once that they were not mere hitch-hikers. They were tramps. They were full blown, abandoned to this. Both of them were. But when [Harris] touched [the guitar] he knew obscurely that it was the yellow guitar, that bold and gay burden in the tramp's arms, that had caused him to stop and pick them up (126).

As an emblem of a "bold," "full blown" though impoverished existence, the guitar does not "belong" to Harris. At the end of scene two, " 'I 'spec' he gonna die though,' said a colored child's voice mournfully. 'Wonder who goin' to git his box?' " (131) The boy returns for the seemingly forgotten guitar at the end of the story. Thus the last bit of action involves the guitar.

As a symbol, the guitar holds a deep attraction for Harris—and fills him with resentment for the man who carries it: "Just play it for myself," says the man, hitting the guitar with the palm of his hand. "Harris laughed delightedly, but somehow he had a desire to tease him, to make him swear to his freedom" (126). When Harris offered him a cigarette earlier, the man said, "Well . . . rarely," and Harris' cheek twitched "at the use of the unexpected word." The man seems to sense Harris' mixed feelings:

> "I bet you ain't got no idea where all I've slep'," the man said, turning around in his seat and speaking directly to Harris, with laughter in his face that in the light of a road sign appeared strangely teasing.
> "I could eat a hamburger," said Harris, swinging out of the road under the sign in some automatic gesture of evasion (124).

Harris' life has been a "gesture of evasion." His passivity is rendered with a "commercial" simile: his listening had become almost automatic, "like the way his hand went to his pocket for money" (125). Harris tries to provoke the man with the guitar:

> "You wouldn't stop and play somewhere like this? For them to dance? When you know all the songs?"
> Now the fellow laughed out loud. He turned and spoke completely as if the other man could not hear him. "Well, but right now I got *him.*"
> "Him?" Harris stared ahead.
> "He'd gripe. He don't like foolin' around. He wants to git on. You always git a partner got notions" (126–27).

Instead, the answers have a disquieting effect on Harris. The suggestion of some kind of mysterious code of the road—do tramps "always git a partner?"—aggravates his latent sense of isolation, which is later increased by the even greater mystery concerning the cause of the murder. Although they appear together in only one scene, the hitchhikers are the catalytic force in the story, as the title alone should indicate. The effect they are soon to have on Harris is sensed early in the story. As he slows down to pick them up, Harris thinks how "the recurring sight of hitch-hikers waiting against the sky gave him the flash of a sensation he had known as a child; standing still, with nothing to touch him, feeling tall and having the world come all at once into its round shape underfoot and rush and turn through space and make his stand very precarious and lonely. He opened the car door" (121–22). The guitarist gives Harris a vague feeling that *he,* and not the hitchhikers, is the real drifter, the *spiritual* tramp. (In the party scene, someone asks Ruth if Harris is her cousin; "no kin of mine, he's nothing but a vagabond," she says [134].)

The presence and then death of the man with the guitar help to separate Harris from his world of self-delusion. At first Harris resents him and tries to assert himself. As they pull out into the road again from the roadside joint, the man with the guitar calls out for Harris to drive back because Sobby had forgotten to return a bottle. " 'Too late,' said Harris rather firmly, speeding on into Dulcie, thinking, I was about to take directions from him" (127). After the attack, Harris listens to bystanders discussing the event:

> "The way I figure this thing out is," said a penetrating voice, as if a woman were explaining it all to her husband, "the men was left to

'emselves. So—that 'n' yonder [Sobby] wanted to make off with the car—he's the bad one. So the good one says, 'Naw, that ain't right' " (130).

But Harris instinctively balks at the idea of assigning the role of "the good one" in this little morality play to the guitarist: "Or was it the other way around? thought Harris dreamily" (130). " 'Who's got my car keys!' Harris kept shouting. He had, without realizing it, kicked away the prop, the guitar." But later his resentment turns to concern, and his apprehension is intensified by the events of the evening.

In scene three Miss Welty sets the mood which is developed in the subsequent scenes. Harris is surprised to learn that it has been raining for some time. "What time is it?" he asks. "Oh, it ain't *late,*" answers Mr. Gene. Significantly, he doesn't give Harris the time; Harris realizes later that "he himself had no time." The fact that he hasn't noticed the rain quietly alludes to his growing anxiety. The rain and mist later become evocative correspondences for Harris' feeling of isolation.

In the fourth scene, Harris phones Ruth, who invites him to a party she's giving; he'll be fixed-up with a young girl named Carol. The party scene is the longest in the story. Its importance is foreshadowed in the story's opening paragraph: "he was thinking he would like to do something that night." It is here that Harris first becomes aware of his condition.

Walking over to the party, so as not to use his car, making the only sounds in the dark wet street, and only partly aware of the indeterminate shapes of houses with their soft-shining fanlights marking them off, there with the rain falling mist-like through the trees, he almost forgot what town he was in and which house he was bound for (133–34).

The party aggravates his sense of lonely rootlessness: " 'So this is the famous "he" that everybody talks about all the time,' pouted a girl". . . . "I wish they'd call me 'you' when I've got here, he thought tiredly." Miss Welty's ear is perfect in catching the bits of dead conversation at a boring party—"What did you do?" "Same old thing" (135)—and in capturing the flatness of cliché speech— "More has gone on than a little bit" (134). They leave the party to pick up Harris' date. "She was a slight little thing, with her nightgown in some sort of a little bag"; the pathetic detail renders the meaninglessness of casual sex. On the way back to the party the two cars stop. When Harris had picked up the hitchhikers the reader was told that "on the road he did some things rather out of a dream" (121). At the scene of the violence, he "thought . . . dreamily," and now as the cars stop, the nascent dream-perspective prevails; the dialogue and action become disjointed, surrealistic:

> "Let's go holler off the bridge," said somebody in the car ahead.
> They drove over a little gravel road, miles through the misty fields, and came to the bridge out in the middle of nowhere.
> "Let's dance," said one of the boys. He grabbed Carol around the waist, and they began to tango over the boards.
> "Did you miss me?" asked Ruth. . . .
> "Woo-hoo!" they cried.
> "I wish I knew what makes it holler back," said one girl. "There's nothing anywhere. Some of my kinfolks can't even hear it. . . ."
> They drove around and waited to see if it would stop raining (136).

Instead of a landscape they seem literally to be in the "middle of nowhere"—the realization Harris soon makes about himself.

The atmosphere at the party is nerve-jangling, the "season of dreams" turning toward nightmare. Nearby actions aren't seen; they seem to happen in the distance: "Somewhere in the house the phone rang and rang" (135). Instead of Miss Welty's usual vivid imagery and sharp specification, the prose becomes static and the meaning it conveys oblique. "Back in the lighted rooms at Ruth's he saw Carol . . . give him a strange little glance" (136)—the glance is not explained. There are no chromatic colors in this scene; everything is in jarring blacks and whites: "Ruth, in a long black dress," a pouting girl in a white dress. The scene seems illuminated by a harsh, naked, overhead light—Miss Welty's china night-light stripped of its shade—recalling some of those sombre lithographs by Edvard Munch in which a group of dark, muffled figures stand and sit within a room, each strangely uncommunicative, each defining his own picture plane, all sharply outlined against the severe white background. And as in Munch, the party scene is two-dimensional, shadowless, and spectral. Miss Welty achieves this verbal analogue to Munch not only by shifting to a cold, static style but by not using the transitionary phrases which would logically link actions and movements and make them completely meaningful. The characters seem to come in and then out of focus, keeping the action firmly within "a season of dreams." Almost any passage in this scene is illustrative of Miss Welty's dream-rendering. Harris finds himself in the pantry with Ruth. Again a vague anxiety stirs in him: "Was she at all curious about him? he wondered," but "she stared off at nothing." Then, "as if under some illusion," he tells her about the hitchhikers. "What a stupid thing!" she says, her eyes flashing. The phone is ringing again, and Ruth glares at him, "as though he had made a previous engagement with the hitchhikers." When someone tells her the call was about the "murder in Tom's car," she cries out, "I know all about it! . . . He told me all about it. It practically ruined his car. Didn't it!" Without moving, Harris asks if he died. The rapid juxtaposing of sentences renders Harris' inner tension and creates a telling contrast between his unarticulated distress and Ruth's shrill vulgarity. The whole passage's oblique, slightly dislocated effect is achieved through the absence of transitional material and simple facts; one gradually realizes how much has been withheld. Who is at this party? We aren't told in very explicit terms: after Harris enters, "everybody was noisy again." There is no exposition. As in a dream, anonymous human forms appear and disappear. Neither Harris nor the reader ever sees the piano players ("at least two people" can be heard "playing a duet"). When he'd entered the party "he began shaking hands and set the bottle wrapped in the paper sack on the table" (134). The bottle looms more important than the people who are left unnamed and undescribed. Carol dances with "one of the boys." "Everybody was meeting them," writes Miss Welty; they are more like shadows than people. But the abstract, dreamlike atmosphere in the party scene is only effective because the other scenes are realistically presented; [7] the party stands in contrast to them because of the concreteness of Harris' experiences *earlier* in the story. The manner in which this scene is integrated into the story shows how Miss Welty maintains an effective equipoise between objective and subjective perspectives.

Harris phones the doctor; the guitar player is still alive. But the "murder" story has brought the party to "life," though one uses the word advisedly, because it is a liveliness by turns irrational and banal. "This is so exciting, tell us all," says a fat boy who "lived fifty miles up the river and had driven down under the impression that there would be a bridge game." Ruth says, "It's marvelous the way [Harris] always gets in with somebody and

then something happens"; and Carol agrees, "Oh, he's my hero."
Harris finally gets ready to leave the party, and says good-bye.

> "Let's all go to Greenville and get a Coke," said Ruth.
> "No," he said. "Good night."
> " 'Aw river,' " said the girl in the white dress. "Isn't that what the
> little man said?"
> "Yes," said Harris, the rain falling on him, and he refused to spend
> the night or to be taken in a car back to the hotel (139).

When the girl repeats what the guitarist sang out at the sight of
the car-hop's "heart," she completes the vulgarization of Harris'
experience. Ruth's insensitive suggestion to "get a Coke" at the
instant of Harris' weariest moment is typical of Miss Welty's expressive use of brand names. It creates the same kind of low-keyed,
emotional counterpoint one finds in many of Walker Evan's photographs of Southern scenes in *Let Us Now Praise Famous Men*. In
picture after picture of store fronts and one-room post offices the
only contrast on the bare, weather-worn wood-plank walls is afforded by the bright Coca-Cola sign—and its accompanying, almost man-size bottle effigy ("Ice Cold")—making the scene all
the more pathetic.

Back in the hotel, Mr. Gene tells Harris, "Poor Mike can't
sleep." Neither can Harris; the party scene has been equivalent
to Bowman's visit to the cabin. The full extent of his isolation
becomes apparent to Harris in the comalike silence of his room
(scene six). Miss Welty summarizes his life in the details of the
room, until his breath seems to merge with the room's "pulse."

> Harris lay down on the bed without undressing or turning out the
> light. . . . Half blinded by the unshaded bulb he stared at the bare
> plaster walls and the equally white surface of the mirror above the
> empty dresser. Presently he got up and turned on the ceiling fan, to
> create some motion and sound in the room. It was a defective fan
> which clicked with each revolution, on and on. He lay perfectly still
> beneath it, with his clothes on, unconsciously breathing in a rhythm
> related to the beat of the fan.
> He shut his eyes suddenly (140–41).

Harris thinks of the girls, but desire ebbs quickly. Miss Welty's
psychology is incisive and forbids sentimentality; self-protectively,
Harris tries to project his misery: "It was for relief, almost, that

his thoughts turned to pity, to wonder about the two tramps, their conflict, the sudden brutality." Harris thinks the evening is too like other evenings when there had been

fights, unheralded confessions, sudden love-making—none of any of this his, not his to keep, but belonging to the people of these towns he passed through, coming out of their rooted pasts and their mock-rambles, coming out of their time. He himself had no time. He was free; helpless (141).

The voice of Carol, the girl from the party, calls Harris to the window. He cannot see her and is so tired that he thinks of a girl from the wrong town. They go through the rain and mist to the All-Nite diner. Whereas the party scene was cold and abstract, the mood now changes to nostalgia. Miss Welty renders the rain motif like an impressionist painter (Turner rather than Renoir), adding small touches to achieve the atmospheric effect: "They walked past the tall wet church, and their steps echoed." Loneliness hovers above the scene like the mist as the young girl makes a nervous, awkward advance at Harris; she thinks they met at a summer hotel:

"You used to play the piano."
They passed under a street light, and she glanced up as if to look for the little tic in his cheek.
"Out on the big porch where they danced," she said, walking on. "Paper lanterns. . . ."
"I'd forgotten that, is one thing sure," he said. "Maybe you've got the wrong man. I've got cousins galore who all play the piano" (143–44).

In Miss Welty's best work a turn of phrase may communicate much of the intended mood. Following the girl's pathetic and even touching attempt to recall the past and to inject genuine feeling into an ambiguous relationship, Harris' disjointed syntax and the harshness of his response—"cousins galore"—have a jolting effect, revealing that he is indifferent and solipsistic, as well as helpless and unhappy. (Remembering the past, she says, "you talked about yourself.") The effect is to intensify the isolation of each.

They came to the little depot where a restless switch engine was hissing, and crossed the black street. The past and present joined like this, he thought, it never happened often to me, and it probably won't happen again. He took her arm and led her through the dirty screen door of the All-Nite (144).

When they finish their coffee, he puts her "into the old Cadillac taxi that always stood in front of the depot" (144). Again, the scene could be out of a photograph by Walker Evans. Miss Welty has used her photographer's selective eye to choose the few right details which suggest the whole scene and sustain its mood. And like Evans, she manages to squeeze a poetry of the commonplace out of materials of the bleakest sort.

Harris has, like Bowman, experienced a "death of the heart." He refuses Carol's overture and makes his own pathetic attempt at tenderness:

> Before he shut the taxi door he said, frowning, "I appreciate it. . . . You're sweet."
> Now she had torn her handkerchief. She held it up and began to cry. "What's sweet about me?" It was the look of bewilderment in her face that he would remember.
> "To come out, like this—in the rain—to be here. . . ." He shut the door, partly from weariness.
> She was holding her breath. "I hope your friend doesn't die," she said. "All I hope is your friend gets well" (144–45).

Harris' veiled distress has inspired this unlikely assumption. The irony of her closing remarks is apparent when one remembers Harris' initial resentment of the guitarist, who is declared dead at the end of this scene. His death is suggestively linked with Harris' own spiritual death: "He had been dying while Harris was sitting in the All-Nite."

In the morning, an unconcerned Sobby holds court; he almost smiles at all the men who have come to see him. But when he tells them about the dead man, he stands still, "as if he were trying to recall something particular and minute." He recalls it with an unexpected sense of urgency; looking up at their faces as though for support, he says, "He was uppity, though. He bragged. He carried a gittar around." Sobby whimpers. "It was his notion to run off with the car" (146). What had bothered Harris had also irritated Sobby—to the extent that it provoked him to kill. At the scene of the violence there was some ambiguity over whose idea it was to steal the car; the reader has probably taken it for granted, along with the bystanders, that it was Sobby ("the bad one"). But when Sobby claims "it was his notion," one may be tempted to criticize this revelation as a bit of heavy irony, or even worse, as an old-fashioned "surprise ending." In a story by a more conventional author this would be an O. Henry twist, but with Miss Welty this can only mean that the issue is still unresolved, the mystification deliberately maintained. Is Sobby telling the truth? He is probably not, but instead making a desperate attempt to assert himself against the memory of the man's independence and creative energy —and that final audacity: "He carried a gittar around."

Harris' kind of isolation is more typical than Bowman's: "fresh from the barbershop," his car polished, he is ready to get back on the road. He gives "the po' kilt man's gittar [which] even the policemens didn't want" to the small Negro boy. The little changing-of-the-guitar ceremony can be seen in the context of all of Miss Welty's work, for with few exceptions, it is the Negro characters who best endure their isolation, while the values symbolized by the yellow guitar are seldom found in Miss Welty's white characters. Earlier, the Negro boy had wondered, "Who goin' to git his box?"—and what it represents, one might add. Symbolically, the guitar belongs to the boy, and to the world of Miss Welty's Negro characters.

5

"THEY ENDURED": EUDORA WELTY'S NEGRO CHARACTERS

Phoenix went on. "We is the only two left in the world. He suffer and it don't seem to put him back at all. He got a sweet look. He going to last."

—EUDORA WELTY, "A Worn Path"

THE NEGRO CHARACTERS in Miss Welty's fiction have somehow avoided the overpowering forces of "reality" that engulf many of her white characters. As in William Faulkner's fiction, the prime role of the Negro in Miss Welty's stories is one of suffering and stoic endurance, pathos and a kind of heroism. Old Phoenix's remark about her sick grandson, "he suffer and it don't seem to put him back," is the history of the Negro in the South. Miss Welty, like Faulkner, seems to see the Negroes as a "chosen people." In "The Bear" (1942), Ike McCaslin says that the Negroes will endure because they are "stronger than we are," and Miss Welty writes that Phoenix has lasted "the whole enduring time." Her Negro characters withstand and even triumph over their isolation and adversity in a manner seldom approached by her white characters. But Miss Welty is not writing about race prejudice and the "Negro Problem" as such. The bitterly ironic recent sketch, "Where is the Voice Coming From?",[1] a monologue "spoken" by the murderer of an N.A.A.C.P.

leader obviously modeled on Medgar Evars, but written before any murder suspects were arrested, is a trenchant but uncharacteristically explicit statement for Miss Welty to have made, for her stories about Negroes are nearer to myth and legend than to social protest, extending their frames of reference and enriching their meaning.

The Negro characters in "The Burning," "Keela, the Outcast Indian Maiden," "Powerhouse," "A Worn Path," and "Livvie" exemplify the virtues that have all but disappeared from modern, polyglot life—the simple virtues necessary for survival—values which, to Miss Welty, seem to be most clearly defined in the resilient folk tradition of the Negro. If Miss Welty has recognized in Negro folk life the values in which she herself believes, then her experience resembles Ralph Ellison's discovery of this living folk tradition:

> For me . . . in the discontinuous, swiftly changing and diverse American culture, the stability of the Negro American folk tradition became precious as a result of an act of literary discovery. Taken as a whole, its spirituals along with its blues, jazz, and folk tales, it has . . . much to tell us of the faith, humor, and adaptability to reality necessary to live in a world which has taken on much of the insecurity and blues-like absurdity known to those who brought it into being. For those who are able to translate its meanings into wider, more precise vocabularies it has much to offer indeed.[2]

Since her childhood, Miss Welty has always loved folk tales and old legends and has liked to listen to the stories and songs of people whose culture is bequeathed orally. Her sympathetic response to the Negro folk tradition was almost inevitable. The Negroes are the South's greatest fantasy-makers, and the fabulous quality of two nonfiction sketches about Negroes, "Pageant of Birds" and "Ida M'Toy," shows how Miss Welty responds to their spirited acts of imagination. Rather than seeking a refuge in fantasy, her Negro characters renew themselves through their fantasy lives. In her five stories about Negroes, Miss Welty makes expressive use of the image of the trickster, the jazz musician, and elements from myth, the spirituals, and the blues—demonstrating that she is a writer who has been able to translate the meanings of the Negro folk tradition into a memorable vocabulary. In these stories, she uses folk materials in such a way that the characters' endurance assumes an archetypal significance.[3]

"The Burning" establishes the pattern of endurance manifest in the Negroes in "Keela, the Outcast Indian Maiden," "Powerhouse," "A Worn Path," and "Livvie." "The Burning" is Miss Welty's only story about the Civil War. It was published a decade *later* (1951) than the other stories under discussion, but should be considered first because it definitely establishes Miss Welty's attitude toward the Negro.[4] It is set in Jackson. Two Southern spinster ladies—Miss Theo and Miss Myra—made for nothing but antebellum life, witness with horror the arrival of soldiers from General Sherman's army. The ladies are sisters, and their father and brother are off to war. The rough Yankee soldiers are determined to burn their beauful home and desecrate their way of life; symbolically enough, a young drummer boy "caught both Miss Theo's peacocks and wrung their necks in the yard" (466). Their home is burned, along with all of Jackson, and the two sisters hang themselves grotesquely near a hammock on the side lawn. The only one left alive is their Negro slave, Florabel. She goes unharmed, but a child, Phinny, is burned to death in the house.

The sudden and terrifying sequence of events have left Florabel in a state of shock and her actions are characterized by an instinctual, deliberate, dreamlike quality. Florabel ignores the soldiers' command to help in the looting of the house. After the burning she hides amid the ashes and ruins of the gutted house until she senses that they have gone. Old Testament names pass through her delirious mind—King Solomon, and, three times, Jonah and the Whale. She exists in a timeless suspension—"even the command to loot was one more fading memory." An unexplained force moves Florabel; trancelike, she gets to her feet and rises from the ashes, "as if told to."

And so she saw what happened, the creation and the destruction. She waited on either one and served it, not expecting anything of it but what she got. . . . The world had not touched her—only possessed and hurt her, like a man. Her vision was clear. She saw what was there and had not sought it, did not seek it yet (475).

Florabel's endurance is not only stoic, but mystical, even saintly: "as a slave she was earth's most detatched visitor." The tone and the rhythm of the language is biblical, for Florabel is not just *any* Negro slave: "she saw what happened, the creation and the destruction"— much like Dilsey in Faulkner's *The Sound and the Fury* (1929), who says, "I seed de beginnin, en now I sees de endin" (the Faulknerian echoes are eliminated in the second version). Miss Welty seems to identify the suffering of Florabel and the slaves with the Jews of the Old Testament, an analogy that is expressed again and again in the Negro spirituals, in which the slaves reconstructed biblical episodes relevant to their own plight and hopes for freedom: "Go Down, Moses, tell ole Pharaoh to set my people free"; "Didn't my Lord deliver Daniel and why not every man?" The essence of the Negro spirituals is present in "The Burning." Miss Welty perhaps intends Florabel's preoccupation with Jonah as a symbolic comment upon the Civil War itself—that the Negro emerged from the depths of slavery as Jonah escaped from the Whale and that, through their suffering, the Negroes are to be "the chosen people" of the "new" South.

In spite of her shock, Florabel has one mission to perform before leaving the ruins: "She looked well in the ashes and found Phinny's bones all right. She ripped a square from her skirt and tied up the bones in it, and directly left that place." To follow the wheel tracks, the smell of fire and horses, and make her Exodus, "Florabel had to cross the river." In the Negro spirituals, the river is the central symbol of their hopes of physical freedom: "Deep river, my home is over Jordan, Deep River, Lord: I want to cross over into camp ground." Florabel goes toward the river as if by instinct. In Faulkner's *The Unvanquished* (1938), the thousands of slaves freed by General Sherman's army blindly follow the roads toward any river, singing and chanting, "Going to Cross Jordan." Writing about the same events, Miss Welty renders an individual Exodus while Faulkner's is panoramic. Although Miss Welty's attitude toward the Negro is not as complex as Faulkner's, their conceptions are very similar. Both of them are aware that the image of the river has deep, archetypal meanings in the Negro consciousness—see Langston Hughes' poem, "The Negro Speaks of Rivers"—and they join Mark Twain, T. S. Eliot ("The Dry Salvages"), and the unknown creators of the spirituals in a mythic representation of the river. In "The Burning," when Florabel wades into the water,

She went slowly, *gradually submerging herself to the waist and to the breast, stretching her throat like a stalk, holding her treasure over her head, not considering that she, Florabel, one life, might step too deep and the river smile and take her* [italics mine].

At that time it was only Friday, so it hadn't rained (476).

The story seems to end in the river. The power and legendary sweep of the Mississippi in Faulkner's "Old Man" (1939) is expressed in anthropomorphic terms: "de Ole Man" "whispers," "don't have to brag," and "debauchs." Miss Welty's image of the "smil[ing]" river also suggests, like the aforementioned writers, that the river is a power, a kind of deity with its own mind and will. Florabel has no fear of the "destroyer"; she never considers that she "might step too deep." In the words of the spiritual "Noah," she seems to believe that "God's gonna ride on the rain and the tide." Before Miss Theo and Miss Myra commit suicide, Florabel predicts the "deluge": "Won't rain till Saturday," she tells them (471). "At that time it was only Friday," Miss Welty writes at the end of the story, "so it hadn't rained." Florabel makes her Exodus before the Deluge. She is a personification of the deepened mysticism of the Negro spiritual. Instinctively, the river is for Florabel a symbol of freedom and a life-giving source: her act of "holding her treasure over her head"—the bones of the child—is a ritual reenactment of the spiritual "Dese bones gwine to rise again." Her name is significant. When Florabel responds to the water, thriving, even *growing* in it, "stretching her throat like a stalk," she experiences a symbolic rebirth. "My soul has grown deep like the rivers," runs the refrain of Langston Hughes' poem "The Negro Speaks of Rivers." The story does not *end* in the river, but, rather, it *begins* there. Florabel has the awareness of "thousands of years" of suffering. Her lack of fear and her relationship with the river epitomize Miss Welty's image of the Negro, and "The Burning" defines the two opposite extremes in human behavior: suicide and spiritual rebirth.

If Florabel's submerging in the river is a ritual of rebirth—or a kind of baptism—then she might be called spiritual parent to the contemporary Negroes who appear in "Keela, the Outcast Indian Maiden," "Powerhouse," "Livvie," and "A Worn Path." The Negroes in these stories are like Florabel and Sam Fathers in Faulkner's "The Bear": inheritors "of the long chronicle of a people who had . . . learned pride through the endurance which survived suffering."

Conversely, the suicides of Florabel's mistresses, Miss Theo and Miss Myra, are the most drastic embodiments of a tragic inability to cope with reality—the failure from which most of Miss Welty's well-born white characters seem to suffer. The world of Miss Welty's fiction is thus peopled with the spiritual descendants of at least two "family lines": the Negroes, descended from Florabel, inheritors of endurance and the powers of self-renewal; and the well-born Southern whites, willed a closet that contains several family skeletons, including the suicides of Miss Theo and Miss Myra. Metaphorically, the white characters in Miss Welty's stories who have descended from the Old Order are unable to function in the world and are victims of a kind of moral suicide (and in "Clytie" the suicide is actual). Along with the skeletons, their "family closet" may also hold memories of a tragic history.

"The Burning" may be read as a parable of the South's future, as a prophetic statement concerning the "new" or modern South and the Negro's role in it. Miss Welty writes that as Florabel left the wreckage of the house the "cinders were already springing weeds" (476). Miss Welty's work often seems to ask—if not demand—a symbolic reading. It is no ordinary weed that springs up through still-simmering ashes. Weeds are, of course, the only life that flourishes in a waste land or on the ruins of a dead culture. Their sudden emergence dramatically emphasizes the complete desolation of that land. "The Burning" represents not just the destruction of one house, but the spiritual "Fall" of an entire society. The various "weeds" that grew up "After the Fall" now "flourish" in the modern South that is seen in many of Miss Welty's stories: the rootless traveling salesmen of "The Hitch-Hikers" and "Death of a Traveling Salesman"; the family of "Why I Live at the P.O."; the inhabitants of Natchez who ignore "Old Mr. Marblehall" and his double life— "nobody cares," writes Miss Welty—and all the other characters who do not care, such as the neighbors of mad Mrs. Larkin in "A Curtain of Green," the Campfire Girl in "A Visit of Charity," the nurses in that story and in "A Worn Path," and the brutally vulgar women of "Petrified Man" and their virtually immobilized husbands; and, finally, the women in "The Purple Hat," "Clytie," "Lily Daw and the Three Ladies," and "Asphodel"—a group of ladies who appear to be direct spiritual descendants of Miss Myra and Miss Theo. But there are no "weeds" among Miss Welty's Negro characters; Faulkner's succinct summary of Dilsey's life applies to them: "they endured."

Perhaps the "springing weeds" in "The Burning" suggest a curse upon the land and people, a moral desolation having nothing to do with war destruction and the advent of a commercial economy or, as Faulkner has said, the curse of slavery. "Don't you see," cries Ike McCaslin in "The Bear," "Don't you see? This whole land, the whole South, is cursed." And "the black man . . . will be forever God's chosen own because He once cursed Him," says Joanna Burden in Faulkner's *Light in August*. Only Florabel has survived the holocaust of "The Burning" and has risen out of the ashes like the legendary Phoenix. All the principal Negro characters in Miss Welty's stories are Phoenix-like because, as a *group,* they are preserved by their living folk tradition "through the endurance which survives suffering." Significantly, the aged woman in "A Worn Path" is named Phoenix.

In the fiction of both Miss Welty and Faulkner the Negro not only is survivor of the curse of slavery but is also the reminder of the South's guilt. In Faulkner's story "Red Leaves," one of the Indians who is chasing the runaway Negro says, "Damn that Negro," and the other replies, "Yao. When have they ever been anything but a trial and a care to us?" And in *Light in August,* Joanna Burden tells Joe Christmas that she sees Negroes "not as a people, but as a thing" —a black shadow in the shape of a cross, under which all white people live and from which they struggle to escape. The black cross represents the weight of the white man's unexpiated guilt, the obsessive burden on the Southern conscience. The white man is thus often rendered helpless by the Negro. In the ironic relationship of Luster and Benjy in *The Sound and the Fury,* one sees the ultimate embodiment of the white man's helplessness before the Negro: a kind of symbolic reversal of paternalism. Benjy, the castrated idiot descended from a once-proud family, is completely dependent upon the Negro boy, Luster, "a man, aged 14."

This ironic triumph of the Negro at the expense of the white man is expressed in Miss Welty's "Keela, the Outcast Indian Maiden." Little Lee Roy, a crippled, retarded Negro man, had once appeared with a traveling carnival. Abducted and then dressed-up and made-over by the carnival owners, he had been exhibited in the freak show as the monster "Keela," eating live chickens. The show was eventually broken up by police. Little Lee Roy has lived a nightmare and, because of his mental deficiencies—he seems to suffer from some kind of anaesthesia—he exists in a permanent "season of dreams." But, interestingly enough, his grotesque experience was not imagined by Miss Welty. She has described the story's source:

> One day I was on an assignment at a fair and talked to a man who was building a booth at the fair grounds. He told me the story I used in "Keela"—about a little Negro man in a carnival who was made to eat live chickens. That's the only actual story I've used. I guess if you read it you must have known that it was true and not made up—it was too horrible to make up.[5]

But the story's main concern is not with the carnival horror.

The story takes place two years after Little Lee Roy's "retirement." Two white men visit him in his backyard in Cane Springs, Mississippi. Steve, the younger of the two, had been barker in the carnival and had actually believed Little Lee Roy to be "Keela." Confronted with the truth, Steve has, he says, "been feelin' bad ever since. Can't hold onto a job or stay in one place for nothin' in the world" (83) because "I was the one was the cause for it goin' on an' on an' not bein' found out—such an awful thing. It was me, what I said out front through the megaphone. . . . I think about it at night" (79). The "black shadow" has fallen full force upon him, and he struggles to escape from under it. He has vainly searched for "Keela" and, having found him, hopes to assuage his guilt. The story thus focuses on Steve who, like Coleridge's Ancient Mariner, has committed a crime and must try to reestablish his connection with humanity.

Miss Welty presents "Keela, the Outcast Indian Maiden" in the manner of a folk tale. Steve attempts to convince the other man, Max, an incredulous acquaintance, that the story about "Keela" and the carnival is true (if Steve suggests the "Mariner" then Max is the "Wedding Guest"). The two stand before Little Lee Roy—who sits on his porch, surrounded by barnyard fowl—and talk animatedly. The Negro, the topic of their discussion and therefore the subject of the story, is merely a listener:

> "Then it would pull the feathers out easy and neat-like, awful fast, an' growl the whole time, kind of moan, an' then it would commence to eat all the white meat. I'd go in an' look at it. I reckon I seen it a thousand times."
>
> "That was you, boy?" Max demanded of Little Lee Roy unexpectedly. But Little Lee Roy could only say, "Hee! Hee!"

The little man at the head of the steps where the chickens sat, one on each step, and the two men facing each other below made a pyramid [italics mine] (77–78).

In the presence of Little Lee Roy, Steve recalls every grotesque and haunting detail concerning the Negro's humiliation. He remembers that when the show was finally raided "Keela" " drug itself over to where the [sheriff] was standin' an' leaned down an' grabbed holt onto that white man's hand as tight as it could an' cried like a baby. It didn't want to hurt him!" (82). But Little Lee Roy only chortles with delight at each new revelation:

"They made it stay in jail to see if it could talk or not, and the first night it wouldn't say nothin'. Some time it cried. And they undressed it an' found it wasn't no outcast Indian woman a-tall. It was a little club-footed nigger man."
"Hee! Hee!" (83)

Miss Welty controls the form carefully. The story is revealed through Steve's dialogue. Descriptive phrases are at their barest minimum and the reader knows only what he is "told." "Keela" has many of the qualities of an oral story, although the narrative is not an uninterrupted monologue, a form which Miss Welty has mastered in "Why I Live at the P.O.," "Shower of Gold," and *The Ponder Heart.* The "listeners" are Max, Little Lee Roy, and the eavesdropping reader. The form of the story increases its power. The outpouring of Steve's "oral story" makes us believe in it and in his response to it more than if, say, Miss Welty had rendered it from a conventional third-person point of view.

Miss Welty depends upon description only in the dramatic and significant scene just prior to the story's end. Unable to release his guilt through "confession," Steve loses his temper, his mounting frustration triggered by the implacable former "Outcast Indian Maiden":

Little Lee Roy looked from one man to the other radiantly, his hands pressed over his grinning gums.
Then Steve sighed, and as if he did not know what else to do he reached out and without any warning hit Max in the jaw with his fist. Max fell off the steps.
Little Lee Roy suddenly *sat as still and dark as a statue, looking on.* . . .
"Say! Say!" cried Steve. He pulled shyly at Max where he lay on the ground. . . . Finally he got up.

"I can't figure out how I could of ever knocked down an athaletic guy like you. I had to do it," said Steve. *"But I guess you don't understand. I had to hit you"* [italics mine] (86).

Out of desperation, the men offer Little Lee Roy money—for which he has neither wish nor need. Steve leaves, unable to ease the pain of his guilt. The story ends on a brief, wonderful note of irony. The Negro's children return from the fields, and at the supper table he says: " 'Today while all you all was gone, and not a soul in de house . . . two white mens come heah to de house. Wouldn't come in. But talks to me about de ole times when I use to be wid de circus—' 'Hush up, pappy,' said the children" (88). Little Lee Roy has no comprehension of the wrong done him; his experience is more important than he and is beyond his powers of absorption. Thus the *real* unfortunate of the story is Steve. Little Lee Roy is in many ways an ironic version of the trickster, the major figure of the American Negro folk tale, who appears in two forms: as Brer (or "Buh") Rabbit, the innocent who can outwit wolf and fox, and as John, who appears to be an ignorant slave but can consistently outwit Ole Massa. Although he does it unwittingly, Little Lee Roy gets the best of the ex-circus barker, his former "Ole Massa." Unable to unburden his profound sense of guilt, Steve is the one who suffers—just as the South itself must bear the moral responsibility for its treatment of the Negro.

On another level the story may perhaps be read as a parable of the South's collective guilt concerning slavery. Little Lee Roy's tour in the carnival may be seen as a ritualistic reenactment of slavery in a contemporary setting. In his suffering, humiliation, dehumanization (he is called "it"), and endurance, albeit ironic, Lee Roy recalls the tragedy of slavery. The owners of the freak show had been " 'just travelin' along . . . and just seen this little deformed nigger man, sittin' on a fence, *and just took it. It couldn't help it'* [italics mine]. Little Lee Roy tossed his head back in a frenzy of amusement" (84). They "couldn't help it" is perhaps a history of the Negro. The extreme grotesqueness of "Keela's" freak show act keynotes this terse history, intensifying one's awareness of the suffering and denial of humanity undergone by both Little Lee Roy and the Negro race itself.

Steve may be said to represent the South that was burdened with the "curse" of slavery. Steve had been an unwitting participant in

"Keela's" act—"on an' on an' on" it had gone like slavery—but he is nevertheless morally responsible for his part in the show. The emancipated Negro—Little Lee Roy, freed from his "Keela" raiments—is no longer an "outcast," for he ironically turns the white man back upon himself, forcing a sense of guilt upon him. Thus the Negro turns white Southerners upon one another. When Steve cannot expiate his guilt, he strikes out unexpectedly at Max. "I had to hit you," he says, and somehow Max *does* understand him, for, rather than striking back, Max seems to assume and accept his own guilt, and looks up "at Little Lee Roy sitting cross-legged on the porch," a silent witness to the spectacle. Thus, in a story published in 1941, Miss Welty predicts a drama that, at least until recent times, when Negroes began to play a militant part in the race issue, has been paramount in the modern South: one white man pitted against another, while the Negro—the incarnation of the problem—watches and waits.

The Negro is at the apex of this triangle: "The little man at the head of the steps where the chickens sat, one on each step, and the two men facing each other below made a pyramid" (78). The symmetry of this symbolic arrangement suggests a kind of tribal altar. Flanked by his solemn chickens, Little Lee Roy seems to sit in mocking judgment above the two men, unmoved by Steve's outpouring of anguish. Not only do the chickens recall Little Lee Roy's ordeal, but their presence is grimly comic, since one would think that he had seen his last chicken. Little Lee Roy is an ironic folk hero. Although he resembles the trickster of the Negro folk tale, he is nearer to that figure's West African prototype: Legba the creator god's son in Dahomey, Spider on the Gold Coast, Rabbit or Tortoise elsewhere.[6] Little Lee Roy is presented much like the mocking figures who dance through West African mythology; his attitudes and expressions shift rapidly, as if a gallery of sculpted African fetish figures had been suddenly brought to life. He is at various moments "hunched," "huddled," "in a frenzy of amusement," "cross-legged," "a monkey," "radiant," misshapen, squealing, giggling, grinning; like the trickster hero of folklore, not quite animal, man, or god—"a dark statue" writes Miss Welty—a dwarfed, grotesque, and expressive effigy figure representing the American Negro, who stares down from his porch—or "tribal altar"—on the helpless and ineffectual representatives of an alien "tribe."

The spirit of rebirth introduced in "The Burning" is embodied in Little Lee Roy's children. In Miss Welty's fiction the Negro does not lose his life-giving powers, even if his body is twisted and crippled. The fact that Lee Roy has a family is purposely introduced at the end of the story: it is a final irony, highlighting Steve's isolation, for he—the "normal" man—is unattached and adrift.

Another kind of rebirth and endurance is expressed in "Powerhouse." It is Miss Welty's "Portrait of the Artist as a Jazz Musician" and presents a Negro who is a memorable folk hero. The story is a ritual of exorcism. The rebirth expressed in "Powerhouse" is one of self-determination: the renewal of the individual through the act of artistic creation. The education of the jazz musician can best be described as a kind of ritual. After learning the fundamentals of his instrument and the techniques and standard repertoire of jazz, the "apprentice" jazzman must attempt to find his own unique "voice" on his instrument, must, in essence, find his soul and be reborn as an artist, and must again and again "test" himself in the fiercely competitive arena of the jam session—an act of self-discovery and renewal that finds its parallel not in the pursuit of academic studies and degrees but in the archetypal cycle of the ordeal, initiation ceremony, and rebirth. As a folk tradition, jazz has produced a handful of Negro musicians who have risen above the vast field of competition by virtue of their improvisatory skills, and, like the "Fast Guns" of the American West, have been acclaimed as virtual folk heroes by their peers and public. The great improvising jazzman—such as Lester Young or Charlie Parker—has become a minor romantic figure in our time; he has even inspired a modest "jazz literature." He is essentially a soloist rather than just a bandleader, for most bandleaders tend to be "Organization Men." He is a folk hero because he is an improviser rather than a dance band musician—an instinctual, emotional, on-the-spot creator who tries never to play the same solo twice, functioning in a society that attempts to inhibit the individual, to make him conform and "play the same solo" continually. The Negro bandleader Powerhouse is a soloist of this rank. He is loosely modeled on the Negro jazz pianist, "Fats" Waller; by her own account, Miss Welty wrote the story after going to a dance where Waller and his band had played.

"Powerhouse" seems in answer to a statement by James Baldwin: "I have always wondered why there has never, or almost never, appeared in fiction any of the joy of Louis Armstrong or the really bottomless, ironic, and mocking sadness of Billie Holiday." Baldwin would no doubt find "Powerhouse" to his liking for, like the traditional blues line, "I'm laughing just to keep from crying," it is a dramatic juxtaposing of the extremes in human behavior. It is conceived very much in the spirit of the blues, for Miss Welty seems to have a sympathetic and sensitive understanding of this important body of Negro folklore. Her imagination has always responded to the welling, primitive poetry encountered in the best blues performances. Ralph Ellison defines the blues form as symbolic action: "The blues is an impulse to keep the painful details and episodes of a brutal experience alive in one's aching consciousness, to finger its jagged grain, and to transcend it, not by the consolation of philosophy, but by squeezing from it a near-tragic, near-comic lyricism." [7] Powerhouse is a jazzman who conquers the agony of life through a blues-oriented toughness of spirit. In essence, "Powerhouse" *is* a blues—an extended lament expressed in the short story form.

In "Powerhouse" a sense of deep alienation is experienced on several levels. Little "happens" in "Powerhouse" by way of external, dramatic action, and yet it is one of Miss Welty's most complex stories; although often anthologized, it is seldom commented upon. The scene is a Southern dance hall. The characters are Negro dance band musicians. Powerhouse is their leader and pianist—and, as his name implies, the dynamo of creative energy that drives the band. The story is told in the present tense—"Powerhouse is playing," Miss Welty writes in the first sentence. The principal level of action concerns only the playing of the musicians, a minor shift of scene when, during the intermission, they visit a cafe in Negro-town, and their return to the dance hall.

Miss Welty presents Powerhouse in mythical proportions: "There's no one in the world like him. You can't tell what he is. 'Nigger man?'—he looks more asiatic, monkey, Jewish, Babylonian, Peruvian, fanatic, devil. He has pale grey eyes when they're open. He has African feet of the greatest size . . ." (254). In his excesses he is a virtual Negro Paul Bunyan, or perhaps an image of John Henry as jazzman. He has a great head and stomach, "piston legs," a face like a "big hot iron stove" (268), a "vast oven mouth," and when they are at rest his "long yellow-sectioned strong big fingers [are] about the size of bananas" (255). In the cafe during intermission, Powerhouse opens his eyes "lazily as in a cave" and asks the waitress, "Where you going to find enough beer to put on this here table?" When they play the nickelodeon he says, "Here's a million nickels" (264). In this scene Powerhouse is seen as a Negro culture hero. When he leaves the dance hall, a hundred ragged, silent, and delighted Negroes come up from under the eaves of the hall and follow Powerhouse wherever he goes. When he enters the ironically titled World Cafe, "all the watching Negroes press in gently and bright-eyed through the door, as many as can get in." Powerhouse is held in awe. In the cafe, he is asked to meet the local hero:

> And out of the breathless ring somebody moves forward like a slave, leading a great logy Negro with bursting eyes, and says, "This here is Sugar-Stick Thompson, that dove down to the bottom of July Creek and pulled up all those drownded white people fall out of a boat. Last summer, pulled up fourteen."
> "Hello," says Powerhouse, turning and looking around at them all with his great daring face until they nearly suffocate.
> Sugar-Stick, their instrument, cannot speak; he can only look back at the others (269).

The local myth-maker had performed his feat by accident: "Can't even swim. Done it by holding his breath," someone explains. Powerhouse and the local hero do not communicate. This failure epitomizes Powerhouse's alienation from his own people (he looks at Sugar-Stick "seekingly"). Powerhouse, the urban Negro and the performing artist, is as isolated from the shy, ignorant country Negroes as from the white audiences for which he often performs.

While Powerhouse does not communicate with the Negroes in the cafe, his companions Scoot and Valentine do—after a fashion. Their dialogue demonstrates Miss Welty's subtle touch at rendering folk dialect as *dialogue,* her skill in placing just the right inflection without exaggerating the dialect:

> The waitress . . . comes up taut and apprehensive as a hen. "Says in the kitchen, back there putting their eyes to little holes peeping out, that you is Mr. Powerhouse. . . . They knows from a picture they seen."
> "They seeing right tonight, that is him," says Valentine.
> "You him?"
> "That is him in the flesh," says Scoot.

"Does you wish to touch him?" asks Valentine. "Because he don't
bite."
"You passing through?"
"You got everything right."
She waits like a drop. . . .
"Little-Bit, ain't you going to bring the beer?" (265–66).

In this passage Miss Welty renders the power and beat of Negro
music and Negro speech, a speech that is often so vivid because
it is private and forms the succinct means by which Negroes express complex relationships. The musicians' terse, sardonic replies
to the waitress are thus a kind of sleight-of-hand—an emotional
shorthand that captures the immense void existing between rural
Negroes and well-traveled urban Negroes.

As an improvising jazzman, Powerhouse is a folk hero. There
are several exuberant passages in which Miss Welty describes
Powerhouse's joyful explosions of improvisatory genius. But because of this genius, Powerhouse is even isolated from most of
the members of his own band: "He loves the way they all play,
too—all those next to him. The far section of the band is all studious, wearing glasses, every one—they don't count. Only those
playing around Powerhouse are the real ones" (257). The three
"real ones" are the clarinet player, the drummer, and the bassist—
the first a soloist, the latter two instinctive performers, and therefore acceptable to Powerhouse. He feels alienated from the studious
section men, wearing glasses, because they are the dance band's
necessary "long-hair" members, *reading* their music.

Moreover, Powerhouse is isolated from his audience. "Watch
them carefully," muse the onlookers, "especially what they say to
one another, in another language." The impersonal ambience of
the dance hall underlines Powerhouse's apartness. Utilizing her
keen, selective eye, sharpened by her experiences as a photographer,
Miss Welty needs only a few details to render the mood, and they
are seen with a cold clarity: it is a "shadowless steel-trussed hall"
and its sole decorations are "the rose-like posters of Nelson Eddy
and the testimonial for the mind-reading horse in handwriting magnified five hundred times" (255). The setting is alien enough, but
because "this is a white dance," Powerhouse's sense of alienation
is heightened. The white audience expects Powerhouse to perform
some kind of sexual ritual: when he opens his mouth, it is "vast

and obscene. And his mouth is going every minute . . . coming on
a light and childish melody—*smooch*—he loves it with his mouth"
(254); "he is in motion every moment—what could be more obscene?" Their attitude is a denial of his humanity. "You know
people on a stage—and people of a darker race—so likely to be
marvelous, frightening." Their reaction is in keeping with the popular stereotype that Negroes are all good dancers—a happy, childish, oversexed folk. To the white audience, Powerhouse is not a
human being, but a fixed image: "he's in a trance; he's a person of
joy, a fanatic" (255). Thus, the band stand is like an island unto
itself, isolated from "the white dance, [where] nobody dances, except a few straggling jitterbugs" (258), over which Powerhouse
rules, unleashing music "like a waterfall" with just a signal or a
word to the band, sometimes seeming lost—"down in the song,
yelling like somebody in a whirlpool"—but above all, exhorting
his musicians on.

The audience represents an alien world to Powerhouse, and,
when people hand him requests, "Powerhouse reads each one,
studying with *a secret face;* this is the face which looks like *a mask*
—anybody's" [italics mine] (256). Powerhouse hides his "secret
face" behind the several masks he presents to the audience: "On
the sweet pieces such a leer for everybody! He looks down so
benevolently upon all our faces and whispers the lyrics to us"
(257). Powerhouse is not unlike many of our most famous Negro
performing artists who hide their true emotions behind highly
stylized, carefully conceived masks—Ethel Waters, Duke Elling-
ton, and Louis Armstrong should come to mind. The persona is
often adapted in order to ease the psychic strain of simultaneously
being an artist, an entertainer, and a Negro. Ralph Ellison suggests
the possibility of interpreting the mask:

> Very often . . . the Negro's masking is motivated not so much by
> fear as by a profound rejection of the image created to usurp his iden-
> tity. Sometimes it is for sheer joy of the joke; sometimes to challenge
> those who presume, across the psychological distance created by race
> manners, to know his identity. . . . We wear the mask for purposes
> of aggression as well as for defense; when we are projecting the future
> and preserving the past. In short, the motives hidden behind the mask
> are as numerous as the ambiguities the mask conceals.[8]

When Powerhouse has a "leer for everybody" on the sweet pieces,
looking down "benevolently"—"whispering" the lyrics—he may

in fact be challenging those who presume to know his identity, rejecting the image invented to usurp his identity. In "Powerhouse" Miss Welty shows us the pain concealed by the "secret face." She probes beneath the mask. Powerhouse's "secret face" reveals the profile of the blues.

The blues is characterized by stoicism in the face of disaster and despair and by projections of fantasy and a humor of the absurd that help achieve the near-tragic, near-comic lyricism which enables one to transcend one's anguish. Ray West rightly notes that "Powerhouse," a story about musicians,

> . . . is constructed in much the same manner as a piece of music. Its development is thematic . . . [Miss Welty] has adopted the technique of the musician . . . [her] story attempts, by using the characters and events as symbols (motifs), to usurp the function of a musical piece, even to approximating the obscurity (inarticulateness) of the instruments.[9]

He goes on to suggest how the main characters function symphonically as motifs, and, although his approach is a valid one, he misses a basic, more obvious "musical" quality. Miss Welty is concerned with only four musicians: except for the clarinetist, they comprise the rhythm section, the band's propelling force. The prose rhythms of the story itself pulsate with a jazzlike beat. One can go a step further than West and suggest that if Miss Welty has "adopted the technique of the musician," the music which should be kept in mind is the blues, for the story's mood and depth of feeling are dependent upon Miss Welty's use of themes from the blues.

As a white writer, Miss Welty shows a rare, intuitive understanding of the blues form. She renders the blues lament with a sympathy one would expect to find in the fiction of a Negro writer, for the themes of the blues are found everywhere in Negro writing, especially the blues theme of leaving, travel, and journey: "Going to Chicago where de water drinks like cherry wine" and "how long, how long, has dat evenin' train been gone?" are typical refrains. A majority of blues lyrics involve some kind of movement from one place to another, and not surprisingly, for American Negro life has been characterized by an aimless horizontal mobility resulting from frustrated hopes for a vertical mobility: a Negro can change his job if he cannot rise in it; he can move to another place if he cannot live well enough in this place.[10] Then he may find himself with Bessie Smith's "Homeless Blues": "Homeless, yes, I'm homeless, might as well be dead [repeat], / Hungry an' disgusted, no place to lay my head." Thus Bigger Thomas' aimless running is the principal theme of Richard Wright's *Native Son* (1940). In Ralph Ellison's *Invisible Man* (1952) the movement is first out of the South to the Promised Land of the North. In New York City the narrator moves between Harlem and "downtown," finally achieving a surreal mobility: downward into a cellar. Powerhouse is conceived in terms of this aimless mobility.

Powerhouse, the traveling performer, belongs everywhere—and hence, *no where.* "They can't stay," Miss Welty writes of the musicians. "They'll be somewhere else tomorrow." Miss Welty renders the "Homeless Blues" in many ways. Powerhouse has "arched eyebrows that never stop traveling, like a Jew's—wandering-Jew eyebrows" (255). When the set is over, "he pulls a big Northern hotel towel out of the deep pocket of his vast pants" (262), and while they are playing, Powerhouse calls,

"What time is it? . . . What the hell place is this, Where is my watch and chain?"
"I hang it on you," whimpers Valentine. "It still there."
There it rides on Powerhouse's great stomach, down where he can never see it (261).

Powerhouse experiences the deepest kind of "Homeless Blues": he has lost track of time, physically and symbolically; "he can never see it."

In the cafe during intermission, the blues makes an in-person appearance:

"Nickelodeon, I request you please to play 'Empty Bed Blues' and let Bessie Smith sing."
Silence: they hold it like a measure (265).

Then they play "Sent For You Yesterday and Here You Come Today" on the nickelodeon. Although not included in the story, the lyrics of these blues are explicit comments upon Powerhouse's mute despair. "What you tell me the name of this place?" Powerhouse asks again. "White dance, week night, raining, Alligator, Mississippi, long ways from home," answers the other musician, defining their loneliness in the painfully blunt terms of blues-poetry.

In the blues, a compensatory grandiose fantasy often accompanies the despair or self-pity: "Say, I wisht I had me a heaven of my own [repeat], / I'd give all the poor girls a long lost happy home," sings Bessie Smith. This theme of grandiose fantasy runs throughout the blues, Negro writing, and "Powerhouse." Powerhouse has a fantasy of a "heaven of [his] own" that enables him to endure and transcend his despair. Late at night, when they are playing "the one waltz they will ever consent to play, 'Pagan Love Song,' " Powerhouse reveals a sense of alienation far deeper than his "Homeless Blues": groaning, he says, "You know what happened to me?" Valentine only hums a response. "I got a telegram my wife is dead," Powerhouse says. "Telegram say—here the words: Your wife is dead" (259). The rhythm and blunt finality of his words echo the Negro work song "Death Letter": "Got me a letter, / What you think it read: / 'Come home, come home, / Yo' mammy's dead.' " While he plays the piano he moans, "What the hell was she up to?" and shudders, "Tell me, tell me, tell me" (260). Finally something from within "tells" him, and Powerhouse weaves a complicated sequence of events, suggesting the details of the death of his wife Gypsy. A man named Uranus Knockwood, according to Powerhouse's legend, has been following Gypsy around and is somehow the cause of her death. The telegram is from Uranus Knockwood, Powerhouse says; "he take our wives when we gone." Powerhouse attributes all of his misfortunes to Uranus Knockwood, "that creeper that follow around after me, coming up like weeds behind me, following around after me everything I do and messing around on the trail I leave. Bets my numbers, sings my songs, gets close to my agent like a Betsy-bug; when I going out he just coming in. I got him now! I got my eye on him" (267). "That no-good pussyfooted crooning creeper" Knockwood is Miss Welty's version of the harbingers of bad luck who appear in many guises throughout the blues. "Black cat on my door-step, black cat on my window sill [repeat]," sings Ma Rainey in "Black Cat, Hoot Owl Blues," "If some black cat don't cross me, some other black cat will"—and the pun is triple, referring to animal, human being, and that creature of darkness, the devil.

Powerhouse credits Knockwood with finding Gypsy's body. As for Gypsy, the fact of her existence is ambiguous. When others mention her name, it is always questioningly. After Powerhouse announces his "telegram," Scoot, the drummer, says, "Not but four words?" Scoot is "a disbelieving maniac," and he asks Powerhouse, "Why you don't hear it straight from your agent? Why it ain't come from headquarters?" (261). The inconsistencies of Powerhouse's story suggest that he perhaps has no wife, and, if he *does*, she is certainly not dead; in the World Cafe he finally admits it "ain't the truth" (270). Powerhouse has developed Gypsy's story in much the same way as he plays the piano: it is improvised; while he announces the "telegram," his fingers "drag into the keys heavily," "walk up straight, unwillingly, three octaves," wander over the keys, and "put 4/4 over the 3/4" (259). While he is doing this, Valentine, significantly enough, is "dreaming at the bass." Both Valentine and Little Brother are in complete sympathy with Powerhouse's fantasy-making. Little Brother glares at Scoot when that skeptic presses Powerhouse about the telegram. And when Powerhouse reaches into his vast pocket and offers to show Knockwood's nonexistent telegram to the crowd, Valentine and Little Brother protectively implore him, "Now wait, now wait, boss," and again, as all eyes focus on Powerhouse, "Don't, boss, don't Powerhouse!" (270), for they do not want his story to be revealed as a hoax. The implication is that they have gone through this kind of experience before with Powerhouse and in behalf of fantastic improvisations brought off for similar reasons.

The actual story is not about the death of Powerhouse's wife, but about the inner turmoil which gives rise to his grandiose fantasy. Gypsy exists in Powerhouse's "heaven of [his] own"—his imagination. She is both a projection of Powerhouse's loneliness and a depiction of his love, including his jealousy and suspicion. The blues is a symbolic form, and, in this instance, Gypsy symbolizes all the painful and brutal experiences kept alive in Powerhouse's aching consciousness. Gypsy, the object of Powerhouse's love, is well named: for Powerhouse, love is a vagrant, transitory, elusive element—just as it is for almost every protagonist in the blues. Knockwood's name suggests Powerhouse's superstitious nature ("He come in when we goes out!"). And through Knockwood's "given" name Uranus, Powerhouse invokes the heavens. "Hell, that's . . . a star, boy, ain't it?" says Scoot (260). Through the blues fantasy, Powerhouse expresses his hope for Bessie Smith's "heaven of my own."

Miss Welty's use of blues fantasy enables the reader to see beneath Powerhouse's mask. The reader discovers that Powerhouse is anything but "benevolent" and hardly the "person of joy" that the white audience perceived. Miss Welty's merging of the blues and psychology is incisive and unique. Powerhouse's blues fantasy provides him with a home and wife on "white dance, week night, raining, Alligator, Mississippi, long ways from home." When he first announces "I got a telegram my wife is dead," he has apparently forgotten the previous night. Scoot, the skeptic, immediately says, "Gypsy dead? Why how come her to die, didn't you just phone her up in the night last night long distance? (259). (The last phrase is an example of the prose-poetry that Miss Welty can create out of Negro speech.) Powerhouse's fears and his unrealized emotional and physical needs—or "Empty Bed Blues"—are so great that the phone call was not enough—if, in fact, it was *actually* made and is not the enactment of another fantasy, a charade of the blues as sung by Jimmy Rushing: "Thought I would write her, but I b'lieve I'll telephone [repeat], / If I don't do no better, Baby, look for your daddy home." Powerhouse needs more than just a wife at home. Before playing the nickelodeon, he "makes [a nickel] vanish like a magician" (264) and now, "looking into the ketchup bottle" like a medium and "slowly spreading his performer's hands over the cloth with the red squares" (266), he imagines and re-creates Gypsy's "death." He will settle for nothing less than a woman who kills herself out of love for *him*:

"Listen how it is. My wife gets missing me. Gypsy. She goes to the window. She looks out and sees you know what. Street. . . . People walking. . . . What she do? Jump out and bust her brains all over the world" (266).

The death-wish is manifest in many blues. Powerhouse's despair approaches this total gloom. Gypsy's "suicide" is perhaps an enactment of Powerhouse's own death-wish, projected and released through the activated fantasy. In clinical terms, his fantasy becomes a kind of psycho-drama. He "improvises" Gypsy into existence and imagines the details of her loneliness for him, projecting his *own* anxieties into the fantasy. When the absence of love and his sense of isolation become most oppressive to him, Powerhouse turns on his fantasy in frustration. He "kills" Gypsy, the embodiment of his unrealized love, to exorcise his own death-wish. At the moment

Powerhouse announces Gypsy's death the band is appropriately playing "Pagan Love Song." He "kills" her with a vengeance, like a voodoo medicine man stabbing a pin into an effigy. His reaction to her death is not sorrowful; rather, it shows his release of a deep feeling of aggression: she "bust her brains all over the world," Powerhouse exclaims; *"Sssst! Plooey!* See, there she is in her little old nightgown, and her insides and brains all scattered round" (268). "Me and the devil was walking side by side [repeat] / I'm going to beat my woman until I get satisfied," sings Robert Johnson in his "Me and the Devil Blues."

Powerhouse's creation of "that creeper" Knockwood may be a folk image of the devil, on whom Powerhouse and the other Negroes in the cafe blame any despair and bad luck. "Old Uranus Knockwood . . . look down and say Jesus!" says Powerhouse (268). The scene has the rhythm, excitement, and tone of a gospel meeting. Early in the story Powerhouse is described as "look[ing] like a preacher when his mouth is shut" (254), and now he assumes the stance of a preacher leading his cafe "congregation." "Brains and insides everywhere, Lord, Lord," he cries (267). The rapid-fire dialogue seems intended to chase the devil or at least "chase the blues away":

". . . look down and say Jesus. He say, Look here what I'm walking round in!"
They all burst into halloos of laughter. . . .
"Why he picks her up and carries her off!" he says.
"Ya! Ha!"
"Carries her *back* around the corner!"
"Oh, Powerhouse!"
"You know him."
"Uranus Knockwood!"
"Yeahhh!"
"He take our wives when we gone!"
"He come in when we goes out!"
"Yeahhh!"
"He standing behind the door!"
"Old Uranus Knockwood!"
"Middle-sized man."
"Wears a hat."
"That's him."
Everybody in the room moans with pleasure (268–69).

With this moan one feels that a certain collective catharsis has occurred, just as Powerhouse may have experienced a catharsis through his fantasy-projection.

In the memorable blues performance there seems always to be a transcendence and a catharsis that is achieved through a kind of humor of the absurd—a bitter mocking of sadness. Disaster may be met with this kind of mocking: "If your house catch on fire, Lord, and there ain't no water around [repeat], / Throw your trunk out the window and let the shack burn down." The lament may be turned to ironical self-ridicule:

> Gwine lay my head right on de railroad track [repeat],
> Cause my baby, she won't take me back.
>
> Gwine lay my head right on de railroad track [repeat],
> If de train come 'long, gwine snatch it back.

Powerhouse knows this bitter mocking. At the end of the intermission, before leaving the World Cafe, Powerhouse admits, about his story of Gypsy and Knockwood, "No it ain't the truth." He says,

"Truth is something worse, I ain't said what, yet, it's something hasn't come to me, but I ain't saying it won't. And when it does, then want me to tell you?" He sniffs all at once, his eyes come open and turn up, almost too far. He is dreamily smiling (270).

For Powerhouse, the "truth" will be that moment when he ceases to endure his loneliness, when his despair will give way to personal disaster. He "ain't saying it won't happen" to him—Knockwood may yet be the ultimate winner and the real "powerhouse"—but Powerhouse knows there is only one way to avoid it when it "come to me": by "laughing just to keep from crying," in the words of the blues. Thus Powerhouse is "dreamily smiling," and, when he and his sidekicks leave the cafe, he invokes his fantasy again, not because it's the "truth," but to mock it—"If de train come 'long, gwine snatch it back"—and to mock what it represents.

"Take a telegram!" Powerhouse shouts suddenly up into the rain over the street. "Take a answer. Now what was that name?" [Powerhouse has already forgotten the name of his "enemy"!]
They get a little tired.
"Uranus Knockwood."

"You ought to know."

"Yas? Spell it to me."

They spell it all the ways it could be spelled. It puts them in a wonderful humor.

"Here's the answer. I got it right here. 'What in the hell you talking about, Don't make any difference: I gotcha.' Name signed: Powerhouse."

"That going to reach him, Powerhouse?"

"Yas, yas."

All hushing, following him up the dark street at a distance . . . the Negroes are afraid they will die laughing. . . (271).

The blues laughter rips and tears one with pain, but it achieves the necessary near-tragic, near-comic lyricism. Powerhouse and his colleagues achieve a catharsis through this laughter; Powerhouse holds up his arm.

"Reach him and come out the other side."

"That's it, Powerhouse, that's it. You got him now."

Powerhouse lets out a long sigh (272).

Gypsy's alleged death "don't make any difference" now, because Powerhouse is past his crisis. "I gotcha," he dictates aloud: in other words, *I gotcha Knockwood, I caught hold of my blues.*

Powerhouse's primitive myth-making is filled with a comic extravagance that has long been a major element in American humor. Characteristically, the story is virtually oral, and it oscillates between extremes in the manner which Constance Rourke ascribed to the native humor: Powerhouse's fantasy is by turns violent and wildly comic, sad and meditative; his delivery is soliloquizing and covert, yet also boastful and almost megalomaniacal. Although the emotions which activate Gypsy's story are no hoax, the musicians enjoy it as another of Powerhouse's improvisatory tall tales, and, like a long line of native straight men and gulls, they take a great, peculiarly American delight in being hoaxed. When the ever-skeptical Scoot would seem to have devastated the veracity of Powerhouse's telegram and story—"What you been doing, getting telegrams in the *corridor,* signed nobody" (261)—they all simply laugh, perhaps at poor Scoot for being so literal-minded. Each facet of Powerhouse's hyperbolic humor is much in the American grain: when the musicians step out into the rain, Powerhouse warns, "Watch out Little Brother don't shrink. . . . You just the right size now, clarinet don't suck you in" (263). Powerhouse's joke is reminiscent of the grotesque, hallucinatory American frontier humor which involves a sudden upset in the laws of nature—of gravity, mass, or form—such as the story in the *Crockett Awl-Man-Axe* for 1839 which tells of "a certain gentleman who being subject to the occasional absence of mind, one evening lit a candle, and instead of going to bed walked down his own throat."

The mood of despair in "Powerhouse" is heightened by Miss Welty's use of an image that occurs with expressive force throughout the blues: rain. In the blues, rain is a frequent metaphor for sadness. The theme of rain has connotations of tragedy as well as ennui, for rain in the neighborhood of the Mississippi River could mean disaster. In "Powerhouse," the waitress in the World Cafe announces, "Mississippi River's here" (266). The rain is a blue-note sounded throughout the story. It is the leitmotif associated with Powerhouse, a reminder of the lingering despair that haunts him:

> "Come on!" roars Powerhouse. He is already at the back door, he has pulled it wide open, and with a wild, gathered-up face is smelling the terrible night.
> They step out into the drenching rain.
> "Well, they emptying buckets," says Powerhouse. . . . On the street he holds his hands out and turns up the blanched palms like sieves (262).

The weather helps set the mood for Gypsy's "suicide," for it is a "terrible night" in every way. When they enter the World Cafe—its "screen door warped like a sea shell, bitter in the wet"—they are "stained darker with the rain" (263). In the cafe, "the wall and the rain and the other Negroes watching them enclose them" (266). The rain becomes a sustained chord as they walk back to the dance hall. "Powerhouse shouts up into the rain" (271); he "throws back his vast head into the steaming rain, and a look of hopeful desire seems to blow somehow like a vapor from his own dilated nostrils over his face and brings a mist to his eyes" (272); the others follow him "like old rained-on black ghosts" (271); and the scene ends as "they go on up the street, shaking the rain off and on them like birds" (272). Miss Welty's use of the rain image communicates the feeling of Joe Turner's "World of Trouble": "You walk the streets all night long, feet soakin' wet" because "you in a world of trouble, whole world got its back on you." And when Powerhouse walks the rain-soaked streets, like Joe Turner, he "ain't seen nobody look like [his] baby yet." But he has achieved a catharsis, and, in the rain—the metaphor of sadness—he comes to grips with himself. The other Negros are perceived as "black ghosts" in the rain, but Powerhouse responds to the downpour, "and a look of hopeful desire seems to blow somehow like a vapor" from his nostrils. He throws back his head into the rain and then "holds up his arm in the rain" (272). Powerhouse completes his ritual of exorcism by experiencing a kind of emotional rebirth in the rain, analogous to the ritual enacted by Florabel in "The Burning" when she waded into the river, "stretching her throat like a stalk."

Powerhouse's endurance is made striking by Miss Welty's use of the themes of the blues. As in a classic blues, "Powerhouse" expresses both the agony of being and the possibility of conquering and transcending this agony by virtue of a resilient toughness of spirit. The psychology of Powerhouses's fantasy-making is consistent with the folk context and his endurance is heroic because one perceives his suffering and witnesses that, in the end, he must depend only upon self; he renews himself through his creative acts. The blues is the ideal idiom for "Powerhouse," for the story is a comment upon the Negro race itself: their suffering and endurance, their stratagems for self-protection and survival in the white world, and their combination of skepticism and belief, of reality and imagination. Powerhouse adheres to the archetypal pattern of endurance followed by the other Negroes in Miss Welty's stories. But Powerhouse is not only a Negro; he is also a performing artist.

The isolation of Powerhouse the artist is a realization of the hopes expressed by Constance Rourke in *American Humor,* for Miss Welty has achieved an instinctive alliance between native and old world traditions.[11] She invests the story with an oral quality and a rich abundance of improvisatory humor that are characteristically American and uses the nomadic strain in the blues to express the artist's situation as it is represented in so much post-Romantic art and literature. The alienation of the "private" creator—the painter or writer—is projected in an image of the "public" artist—the street musician, cabaret dancer, or circus performer—who, as in the work of Lautrec, Roualt, Degas, Picasso, the Goncourt brothers, Kafka, and Rilke, is seen as a tragic or comitragic figure performing his public role before a callous audience which is unwilling to become involved. "When somebody, no matter who, gives everything, it makes people feel ashamed for him" (259). Yet they are greedy for distraction:

> When . . . any performers come to town, don't people always come out and hover near, leaning inward about them, to learn what it is? What is it? Listen. Remember how it was with the acrobats? Watch them . . . don't let them escape you; it's the only time for hallucination, the last time (256).

This passage may bring to mind the evocation of acrobats in the opening lines of Rainer Maria Rilke's fifth *Duino Elegy*. Miss Welty had not yet read the *Duino Elegies* when she wrote "Powerhouse," but Picasso's great painting "The Family of Saltimbanques" inspired Rilke to write that elegy—and the sense of isolation experienced by the performers in Picasso's painting seems to express Powerhouse's situation. Although the six "Saltimbanques" are a family, each of them, as an artist, experiences an apartness from the world around him. The figures are grouped together, but they avert one another's gaze. As traveling performers, they too are "homeless." And most important, the "Saltimbanques" and the Negro musicians are isolated from their audiences. When the conceptual similarity between the story and the acrobats in the painting was pointed out to Miss Welty, she remembered an unpublished story of hers, "Acrobats in the Park," about the appearance in Jackson of some traveling performers, written shortly before "Powerhouse" (ca. 1940). Recalling that in her description of the acrobats she had had Picasso's performers in mind, she suddenly realized that she had unconsciously written part of that forgotten story—and, by implication, Picasso, too—into "Powerhouse": explicitly in that one line, "remember how it was with the acrobats" and implicitly in the whole conception of Powerhouse himself. The acrobats and jazz musicians symbolize their creators' own apartness. By creating Powerhouse, who in turn creates his own fiction, Miss Welty succeeds in presenting the artist's timeless search for an identity and his attempt to sustain it and survive.

Although Powerhouse is at the height of his powers at the end of the story, his improvisational genius is wasted on the unsympathetic audience. To them, Powerhouse is no different from the inarticulate Sugar-Stick, whose heroic deed was a chance happening, since he could not swim; to the audience, Powerhouse's creative acts are just as accidental—"they are just inspired remarks that roll out of his mouth like smoke" (272). *Just* is indeed the most frightening condescension an artist can receive. When Sugar-Stick had been pushed through the crowd of Negroes, he was seen as "their instrument." Similarly, Powerhouse is the white crowd's "instrument": they "play" him, seeing in him what they want to see—"a person of joy," a mechanical man—a comic grotesque. The story ends as Powerhouse addresses his song to the dancers in an attempt to express his deepest drives, exactly as his unconscious improvised the fantasy of Gypsy's death:

> They've requested "Somebody Loves Me," and he's already done twelve or fourteen choruses, piling them up nobody knows how, and it will be a wonder if he ever gets through. Now and then he calls and shouts, " 'Somebody loves me! Somebody loves me! I wonder who!' " His mouth gets to be nothing but a volcano. "I wonder who!"
> "Maybe. . . ." He uses all his right hand on a trill.
> "Maybe. . . ." He pulls back his spread fingers, and looks out upon the place where he is. A vast, impersonal and yet furious grimace transfigures his wet face.
> "Maybe it's You!" (273–74)

Miss Welty captures the moment of masking. When he looks out, he knows how alone he is, and the mask appears. He fights his oppressive sense of isolation in the only way he, or any artist, knows: "Powerhouse is playing." And through his playing he is renewed, for he has achieved that crucial identification between his instrument and his deepest needs which enables him to transform these needs into art. Powerhouse reaches the reader, if not the audience, with his song, for one recognizes that whatever his race and whatever his special idiom, Powerhouse's attempt to communicate is a paradigm of *all* human isolation and all attempts to transcend it. As an all-encompassing symbol of the artist, Powerhouse embodies and formulates the doubts and fears of all races: he is proclaimed "Sheik! Sheik!" when he wraps a towel around his head; he looks "Asiatic, monkey, Jewish, Babylonian, Peruvian . . . African," and his band is named the Tasmanians. The story is memorable because it starts with Powerhouse's specific lament and ends with his blues metaphoric for a universal condition.

Transcending acts of imagination seem to Miss Welty to be the special province of the Negro. In the sketch, "Pageant of Birds," [12]

her courage and single-minded devotion, her buoyancy, serenity, and strength, she experiences something akin to God: "We is the only two left in the world," she says of her grandson; "he suffers and it don't seem to put him back at all. He got a sweet look. He going to last" (288). Phoenix is as indomitable as the Natchez Trace, one of the last regions to preserve its identity. The Negroes are part of their tragic history and living folk tradition just as the Trace stretches into the past. They *both* represent values that have been obscured in the confusion of modern life. In "Some Notes on River Country," Miss Welty writes: "Whatever is significant and whatever is tragic in a place live as long as the place does. . . . Though they are unseen . . . the new life will be built upon those things, regardless of commerce and the way of rivers and roads and other vagrancies." [14]

Created in the spirit of the "place," ageless Phoenix seems to span the years that extend from the death of the white heron ("A Still Moment") to the emergence of the modern town ("Petrified Man"). She transcends her region's geographical boundaries, for her celebration of life and her endurance—and that of the Negroes in the other stories and sketches—are presented by Eudora Welty as human qualities that man, whether Southerner or Northerner, Negro or white, must possess if, as Phoenix says of her grandson, "He going to last."

6

THE
"SEASON OF DREAMS"
AND THE
NATCHEZ TRACE

THE LINES BETWEEN fact and fantasy, dream and reality are often blurred in Eudora Welty's fiction, but, in *The Robber Bridegroom* and *The Wide Net,* dream and fantasy become the dominant mode. Her predilection for fantasy was evident in *A Curtain of Green.* Even in a "realistic" story such as "The Hitch-Hikers," events are perceived as uncertain and ambiguous. Some of the characters in her first volume, like the salesmen in "The Hitch-Hikers" and "Death of a Traveling Salesman," have managed to keep contact with the outer, everyday world through self-deception, but, when they discover the aimlessness of their lives, reality assumes dream-like dimensions. For others, like the narrator of "Why I Live at the P.O.," the inner world is that reality, whereas the world which the rest of us regard as actual is for them irrational. But though Miss Welty has an astute understanding of how the imagination creates a private world in order to enrich or endure the public one, the "season of dreams" is not simply an escape mechanism; witness

Mrs. Larkin's paralysis of will. The child in "A Memory" indulges in a dream world, but this is the only story in which the issue is left in suspension. Wherever Miss Welty presents characters whose lives are circumscribed by fantasy, reality inevitably impinges upon the privately constructed world—and this clash between dream and reality takes place in the *actual* world. The results are as varied as the range in techniques. Clytie Farr's attempt to narrow the gulf between the two worlds in "Clytie" ends in her suicide. In "A Piece of News" and "The Whistle," only the dream manages to sustain the isolated characters. When characters transcend their isolation through creative acts—like the jazz musicians in "Powerhouse"— or through love—like Phoenix in "A Worn Path"—fantasy plays a part in their triumphs. Phoenix has her little dreams, sees herself as an embodiment of the landscape ("I walking in their sleep"), and Powerhouse manages both to create and kill a "wife." Fantasy-making is in itself the subject of "Old Mr. Marblehall"; the process is the story. Fantasy has its freest play in *The Robber Bridegroom,* and the dream world emerges most fully in *The Wide Net,* particularly in "The Purple Hat," which *is* a fantasy.

"Whatever happened, it happened in extraordinary times, in a season of dreams" (WN, 3)—thus the opening sentence in *The Wide Net* warns the reader that he is about to enter a special world in which illusion, fantasy, and dream are paramount. There is a dreamlike portent and retardation in much of the action. Even where the events and their ordering are most "realistic," the stories themselves belong to the "season of dreams" by virtue of their mood, their special perspective. The subject matter of *A Curtain of Green* is more varied, but Miss Welty makes some of her most delicate explorations of the inner life in *The Wide Net.*

In addition to its ambiguities and elusive mysteries, the "season of dreams" is realized on a literal level. In most of the stories in *The Wide Net,* the characters are seen responding to the actual season, experiencing dream states that are appropriate to the weather and atmosphere of that particular time. In "First Love," it is winter; in "Livvie" and "At the Landing," spring; in "Asphodel," the hot summer day stimulates the old maids' "season of dreams"; in "The Wide Net," the summer is just turning to autumn, and Hazel's pregnancy has inspired in her the secret "elation that comes of great hopes and changes, sometimes simply of the harvest time" (56);

and in "The Winds," the dreams of a young girl approaching adolescence are punctuated by a terrible equinoctial storm. But setting plays as important a part as season in these stories.

The Robber Bridegroom and all the stories in *The Wide Net* (except "The Purple Hat") take place on or near the legendary Natchez Trace, the prehistoric buffalo path that became the route of the Chickasaw and Choctaw Indians. In its violent heyday, the Natchez Trace was called "The Devil's Backbone." As the main road of colonization for Louisiana and the lands west of the Mississippi River, it was traveled by fabled and brutal highwaymen, merchants, mail riders, and by American soldiers on their way to fight in New Orleans or Mexico. Figures such as Henry Clay, Sieur de Bienville, Aaron Burr, Lorenzo Dow, John James Audubon, and Rachel and Andrew Jackson rode along it. Because of its clay composition, original sections of the Natchez Trace exist even today. The preservation of much of the Trace's identity increased its imaginative appeal for a writer growing up in its vicinity. In a 1942 interview, Miss Welty said, "When I decided just to go ahead and write stories I no longer could meet as many people [as on her W.P.A. job], but that doesn't seem to matter much. Why, just to write about what might happen along some little road like the Natchez Trace—which reaches so far into the past and has been the trail for so many kinds of people—is enough to keep you busy for life." [1]

Its dramatic history makes the Natchez Trace the ideal backdrop against which to unfold various "seasons of dreams." Along the Trace passed men haunted and driven by their dreams and ambitions. But no one will ever know what drove the fanatical evangelist Lorenzo Dow on his quest for a Kingdom of Souls, or the number of murders committed by John Murrell, or the motivations behind his alleged plans for a great slave insurrection, or his reasons for naming his organization of outlaws the Mystic Confederacy. Many of the famous events which occurred on the Trace, such as Meriwether Lewis' death and the Aaron Burr conspiracy, are still a mystery to historians. But "whatever happened, it happened in extraordinary times," writes Miss Welty, and the mysteries have been projected in her fiction. *The Robber Bridegroom,* "A Still Moment," and "First Love" are set in the "extraordinary times" of the Trace's frontier past and present storied characters from its history—Burr, Audubon, Dow, Murrell, the Harpe brothers, and, from its folklore, Mike Fink.

The Natchez Trace may be available to tourists, but Miss Welty seems to feel that its essence is now dormant; her sense of loss is felt keenly, and, like Faulkner's, it includes the period before antebellum days.

> The Old Natchez Trace has sunk out of use, it is deep in leaves. The river has gone away and left the landing. Much beauty has gone, many little things of life. . . . To light up the nights there are no mansions, no celebrations, just as, when there were mansions and celebrations, there were no more festivals of an Indian tribe there; before music, there were drums. . . .[2]

The Natchez Trace is for her very much like T. S. Eliot's river in "The Dry Salvages"—"the strong brown god" which is "almost forgotten/ By the dwellers in cities," but is a "reminder of/ What men choose to forget."

In combining the Trace and the "season of dreams," Miss Welty creates a fictive world that is elegiac, unearthly, timeless— a setting appropriate for characters who are striving to discover the most tenuous, fundamental mysteries about themselves. Her re-creation of the Natchez Trace is another version of the retreat from civilization that has been a continuous theme in American literature—in Cooper, Melville, Thoreau, Twain, Cather, Hemingway, and Faulkner. This impulse to create what Bruno Snell, describing Virgil's Arcadia, calls a "half-way land [where the] currents of myth and empirical reality flow into one another"[3] might be called pastoral;[4] it describes Miss Welty's Natchez Trace and the plantation of *Delta Wedding*. The backcountry in "A Worn Path" has an otherwordly quality, and Miss Welty had already given suggestions of pastoral in "Death of a Traveling Salesman." The image of the cabin—"the whole cabin slanted a little under the heavy heaped-up vine that covered the roof, light and green, as though forgotten from summer" (CG, 235)—echoes descriptions of the Bower of Bliss in *The Faerie Queene* and *Paradise Lost* (IV, 690–97). This pastoral quality is sustained throughout *The Wide Net*. In "A Still Moment," the artist-naturalist Audubon comes upon the Trace. He walks quietly by the silver roots of the high cedars, which trail down "like veins of deepness in this place. . . . All life used this Trace, and he

liked to see the animals move along it in direct, oblivious jour-
neys, for they had begun it and made it, the buffalo and deer and
the small running creatures before man ever knew where he
wanted to go, and birds flew a great mirrored course above" (82).
"A Still Moment" may seem to describe the world as it appeared
"Before the Fall." Yet, however archetypal and primal this landscape may be, one must mention "The Fall" advisedly, for a
consciousness of evil is very much present in this "Eden." The
Natchez Trace in *The Wide Net* does not represent an escape
from the complexities of being. Unlike many of the American
writers who have retreated to the territory that lies safely behind
us, Miss Welty's preoccupation with the past is not an exercise in
piety or nostalgia.

Whether they take place in the historic past or in the present,
the stories set on the Trace have a legendary quality. Except for
"Asphodel," the title story, and a brief interlude in "Livvie," there
is no humor in *The Wide Net;* the stories are told gravely, as
befits their subjects. The deliberate quality of the action often
seems to approach allegory, but meanings are finally rendered by
a tissue of symbols rather than by an allegorical system. The
stories in *The Wide Net* are written in a style which is in keeping
with their mood of acute apprehension. Rich in metaphor, the
prose is the most poetic she has ever written. The critics who
found the style too fancy—"falsely poetic," "insincere," and "out-
weigh[ing] the uses to which it is put" [5]—who criticized the language and syntax for having "the improbable inexactitude of a
verbal dream," [6] and who accused Miss Welty of "forc[ing] a
compensatory poetry upon her prose" because of a "fear [that]
she may have lost the heart of her experience" [7] had themselves
failed to grasp the total experience and design of the book. And
they failed also to see that with the exception of two stories
("Asphodel" and "The Purple Hat"), *The Wide Net* presents
variants of a basic theme, unfolded in a language appropriate to
the elegiac world which it describes. Miss Welty's critics overlooked the strong sense of pastoral in her Natchez Trace: it is
certainly not urban, nor is it real wilderness either; she re-creates
it as a symbolic terrain in which to enlarge upon the theme introduced in "A Memory"—a story that presented the polar contrasts
of innocence and experience, yet left them unresolved. But in *The*

Wide Net the individual makes the vital effort to reconcile these extremes; the dream is carried to and submitted to the world.[8] Miss Welty seems to feel that this effort must be made, however doomed to failure it may be, for through such efforts, the human manifests itself as human. The stories to be considered next intensify this basic theme in her work: all are somehow concerned with an individual's awakening or "initiation" into the mysteries of life or into a realization of his essential nature. This moment of discovery is presented in triplicate in "A Still Moment."

This is Miss Welty's most probingly metaphysical story. Three historical characters meet on the Natchez Trace at sunset, each possessed by a consuming desire: "what each of them had wanted was simply *all*"—Lorenzo Dow, "to save all souls"; John Murrell, "to destroy all men"; and Audubon, "to record all life that filled this world—all, all" (WN, 88).

Lorenzo Dow is a madman of God with an impossible mission. As he rides down the Trace, "all the souls that he had saved and all those he had not took dusky shapes in the mist that hung between the high banks, and seemed by their great number and density to block his way . . . so that he feared his passage was to be difficult forever. The poor souls that were not saved were darker and more plentiful" (73). His desire to "have more souls" is kept at manic intensity by his sense of unworthiness as both a Man of God and a sexual man; he fears that he is more susceptible to natural than to divine beauty and that he may be of the devil's party. When he calls out to the souls that were not saved, "Light up, in God's name," a swarm of fireflies instantly flickers around him—proof "that his eyes were more able to see the fireflies of the Lord than His blessed souls." He cries out to Him, "Do not let my eyes remain in this failing proportion to my loving heart always" (74). But his loving heart is also unfulfilled. As he rides faster, he sent "thoughts of love . . . to his wife Peggy in Massachusetts. He found it effortless to love at a distance." And the first words he had spoken to her were, "Would she accept of such an object as him?" In his frequent encounters with savage Indians or bears, an inner voice always gives him "lightning-quick" directions that arouse sudden strength and cunning in him, and, "turning half-beast and half-divine, dividing himself like a heathen Centaur," he escapes his death once more. But "each time when he acted so it was at the command of an instinct that he took at once as the word of an angel, until too late, when he knew it was the word of the devil," for "God would have protected him in His own way, less hurried, more divine." "I know you now!" he cries at a serpent crossing the floor of the Trace. Thus he races through the forests, peering ahead and shouting into the treetops as he carries his message from one camp meeting to another: "Inhabitants of Time! The wilderness is your souls on earth! . . . These wild places and these trails of awesome loneliness lie nowhere, nowhere, but in your heart" (78).

Whereas Dow is consumed by divine love, Murrell believes that he is being used by Evil; when he was young he would sometimes stop a traveler by shouting, "Stop! I'm the Devil!" Murrell's passion is to "destroy the present! . . . the living moment and the man that lives in it must die before you can go on" (79). Murrell chooses Dow as his next victim, and, drawing alongside him, he begins to talk as they ride. His murders are carried out like "a kind of ceremony." While they ride, he tells the victim long tales, always about a murder that Murrell committed "yesterday," and in this place. Never looking at his victim until the moment of confrontation, Murrell murders in order to peer into the eyes of "a man fixed and stayed at the point of death . . . hands spreading to reach as if for the first time for life," for "in laying hold of a man [he] meant to solve his mystery of being. It was as if other men, all but himself, would lighten their hold on the secret, upon assault, and let it fly free at death. In his violence he was only treating of enigma" (81). The evangelist and the murderer come to a low marshland and dismount; each involved in a furious quest, they stand next to one another "like brother[s] seeking light" (82). But Audubon's appearance "cheats" Murrell of his opportunity.

Audubon approaches, walking quietly, "disturbing nothing in his lightness." He doesn't answer Dow's greeting because he has gone for days without speaking; his thoughts of the birds and animals are not susceptible to words. Although the young student is a "sure man, very sure and tender," he too is consumed by an obsession—his insatiable need to remember and "record all life." But when Audubon looks into the dark, flinty eyes of Murrell, he feels his concept of beauty challenged, his secret of life withdrawn:

. . . is it true . . . that man is a cave man, and that the openness I see, the ways through forests, the rivers brimming light, the wide arches where the birds fly, are dreams of freedom? If my origin is withheld from me, is my end to be unknown too? Is the radiance I see closed into an interval between two darks, or can it not illuminate them both and discover at last, though it cannot be spoken, what was thought hidden and lost? (85–86)

Audubon's eyes have persisted in "looking outward" in the hopes that they will open to "look inward." His search for identity is interpreted too literally and too superficially by the people along the Trace. Rather than just trying to find out whether or not he is the Lost Dauphin, Audubon walks on and on in the wilderness as if looking for some legendary beast or bird that would, if found, release the secret of all life.

The three men stand silently in the twilight. A snowy white heron then slowly alights on the marsh before them and begins to feed serenely: "a single frail yearning seemed to go out of the three of them for a moment and to stretch toward this one snowy, shy bird in the marshes. It was as if three whirlwinds had drawn together at some center" (88). Overwhelmed by its beauty, the three men are unburdened of their obsessions for "a still moment." Dow triumphantly proclaims, "Praise God, His love has come visible." Before he shades his eyes, Murrell "saw only whiteness ensconced in darkness," an image that at first ignites his visions of satanic glory: he sees himself as the leader of the Mystic Rebellion, unfurling the Devil's banner before all the slaves, criminals, and outcasts of the Natchez country. But he is overtaken by a sudden desire for confession: "was this the end—the sight of a bird feeding at dusk?" His crimes now "thick in his heart," he flings himself to the ground and wearily imagines the day when the Trace will be levelled and all his stone-loaded victims will be pulled up. His eyes ask for pity, and he looks back at the bird as though it had a divine power capable of both accusing and forgiving him. Audubon watches the heron wondrously, "steadily, in his care noting the exact inevitable things." But because "it was not from memory that he could paint," he shoots it. As he fires he sees in Dow's eyes a look of such horror "that he recognized it for the first time. He had never seen horror in its purity and clarity until now" (91). Audubon then puts the heron in his bag and the three men disperse.

The incident is revelatory; it is as if each of their destinies had been confirmed. The heron's quick death assures Murrell that it was an innocent creature rather than the harbinger of his doom: he hides and awaits his next victim, dark dreams rolling about his head; "his faith was in innocence and his knowledge was of ruin. . . . Now what could possibly be outside his grasp?" (91).

As Lorenzo Dow rides slowly away, his body shakes with cold, for it suddenly seems to him that "God Himself, just now, thought of the Idea of Separateness." He has a terrifying realization that God had "given Love first and then Separateness, as though it did not matter to Him which came first," and that there is no divine order in the world because God is outside Time and will "let the whole world come to grief in a scattering moment" (93). The death of the heron horrifies Dow because it is a microcosmic vision of God's indifference toward men: He created the bird, allowed Dow to see and love it, and then let it be destroyed, just as God has created human yearning—Love—and then left man to fend for himself in an orderless world of Separateness, the condition of life constant throughout Miss Welty's fiction. Dow stares back at the marsh, "as if nothing could really take away what had happened to him, the beautiful little vision of the feeding bird. . . . The sweat of rapture poured down from his forehead." His fears and doubts are confirmed. He is overwhelmed by the knowledge that he is more susceptible to natural than divine beauty and is unable to make his religious definition of reality accommodate the "natural" emotion which overcomes him. Dow shouts into the darkening marshes, "Tempter!"—a cry that seems to admit the pointlessness of his divine mission to save all souls. But his desperate faith drives him on to that night's camp meeting to "deliver his address on the subject of 'In that day when all hearts shall be disclosed' " (94). Dow looks forward to the end of Time when Love and Separateness will be one.

Unlike Murrell and Dow, Audubon can find no solace in dreams of a glorious future. Audubon loves nature, but his desire to paint the heron involves him in a paradox: to paint it he must "know" it, feather by feather, and to do so, he must kill it. In accepting the paradox he discovers his identity.

The gaze that looks outward must be trained without rest . . . and then, Audubon dreamed, with his mind going to his pointed brush, it must see like this, and he tightened his hand on the trigger of the gun and pulled it, and his eyes went closed. In memory the heron was all its solitude, its total beauty. All its whiteness could be seen from all sides at once (90)

In the past, as an "innocent" student, "what he would draw and what he had seen, became for a moment one to him then," but, having killed the bird and seen the horror deep in Dow's eyes, he knows that even the sight "had not been all his belonging" and that "the best he could make would be, after it was apart from his hand, a dead thing and not a live thing . . . only a sum of parts; and that it would always meet with a stranger's sight." Audubon had hoped to communicate with others through his commemoration of the heron's beauty. But now, "as he had seen the bird most purely at its moment of death, in some fatal way, in his care for looking outward, he saw his long labor most revealingly at the point where it had met its limit" (92). Audubon knows that the painting can only be anticlimactic to his vision of the heron—a moment of beauty which can never be recaptured or communicated, can "never be one with the beauty in any other man's head in the world" (92). Images from the visible world can be rendered, but nature itself remains mysterious, inviolable.

Like "Powerhouse," the story is an exploration into the problems of the artist. Miss Welty may have found its antecedents in Hawthorne's "The Artist of the Beautiful." As a symbol, the white heron resembles the butterfly created by Owen Warland in Hawthorne's story. The two symbols of ideal beauty "test" the sensibilities of those who come in contact with them and serve to highlight the artist's position in the world. Rather than bringing Audubon and Owen Warland closer to other men, the bird and the butterfly define the "limits" of their "long labor," establishing their isolation from others.

Through her characterization of Audubon, Miss Welty resolves the issue left in suspension in "A Memory." The potential artist in that story could only present her dream as "simultaneous" with the image of the grotesque bathers. But Audubon's "initiation" from innocence to experience suggests that just to exercise a sensibility and sustain a dream—like the girl in "A Memory"—is not enough; the dream must be submitted to the world, whatever the consequences. Thus Audubon learns that there is a pathos inherent in the artist's task: the artist must not only endure his isolation but suffer in the realization that the product of his labor is the sum, "never the essence," of his dream, the realization that moved Owen Warland to leave "half his conception on the canvas to sadden us with its imperfect beauty." [9] By killing the heron, Audubon discovers and fully accepts the meaning of his life. He walks "on into the deeper woods, noting all sights, all sounds, and was gentler than they as he went" (92).

The question of identity is also central to the meaning of *The Robber Bridegroom,* a fantasy that lightheartedly combines elements of American frontier humor with situations and character types drawn from Grimms's *Fairy Tales.* Rosamond, Clement Musgrove's beautiful daughter, is abducted by the bandit of the forest, whose face is always disguised by berry-juice stains and with whom she chooses to remain. Jamie Lockhart, the dull young gentleman who saved Clement from being murdered by Mike Fink and who has met Rosamond at her family's dinner table, comes in search of the robber bridegroom at her father's request.

Rosamond's life with the bandit leader is idyllic. She lives with him freely, visiting her family whenever she pleases; only one thing is denied her: as in the Cupid-Psyche myth, she is prohibited from ever seeing her bridegroom's face. "She contented herself with loving all that was visible and present of him" (86) until her stepmother, playing the Tempter in Rosamond's Eden, gives her the recipe for making a berry-stain remover. Rosamond can wait no longer for his "true" identity; while he sleeps, she wipes away the stains, awakening him: "You are Jamie Lockhart!" she says. "And you are Clement Musgrove's silly daughter!" he answers, rising out of his bed and leaving her (135). They are equally disappointed in one another. But identity is not simply a matter of appearance. As Clement Musgrove observes of Jamie,

"If being a bandit were his breadth and scope, I should find him and kill him for sure," said he. "But since in addition he loves my daughter, he must be not the one man, but two, and I should be afraid of killing the second. *For all things are double, and this should keep us from taking liberties with the outside world, and acting too quickly to finish things off* [italics mine] (126).

Rosamond complains that "too much of this secrecy goes on in the world for my happiness" (174), but, as in "The Key," Miss Welty is suggesting that every individual has a right to keep his secret private and that its inviolability is a psychic necessity. Just as the narrator creates "Mr. Marblehall's" second, equally "real" family, so too must respectable young men be permitted to fancy themselves robber bridegrooms and rich men's sheltered daughters be granted their adventuresome fantasy lives as kidnapped brides. *The Robber Bridegroom*'s unique mode suspends disbelief, allowing these "fantasies" to become actual and, in the special terms of the book, "realistic." Although most of the book's commentators have been satisfied with admiring the purity and simplicity of its prose style and the verve with which Miss Welty created her own genre, it has a far more substantial appeal.

The three characters in "A Still Moment" want to know "all" about themselves and the universe, but in *The Robber Bridegroom* Miss Welty is saying that to press too hard for definitions about another human may "finish things off" and lead to disenchantment; *not* to ask all is also a way of coming to terms with reality. At the end of *The Robber Bridegroom,* Rosamond and Jamie Lockhart have settled in New Orleans. "All his wild ways had been shed like a skin" (183) in exchange for the conventional life of a rich merchant who is the father of twins, owner of a handsome marble house and one hundred slaves, and who even goes "boating with other merchants and their wives, the ladies reclining under a blue silk canopy" (184). But "the outward transfer from bandit to merchant had been almost too easy to count it a change at all, and he was enjoying all the same success he had ever had. But now, in his heart Jamie knew that he was a hero and had always been one, only with the power to look both ways and to see a thing from all sides" (185). Ideally, then, the actual world and the dream world should be hospitable to one another, in the way that Jamie accepts his dual nature, integrating the two "worlds" beautifully. Dreams must have their play, even if an adjustment such as Jamie's is perhaps possible only in a work of art, in the dream-country of the tale.

The "season of dreams" is inherent in *The Robber Bridegroom*'s unusual mode, but in "First Love" the actual weather sets the special perspective. The story takes place in "the bitterest winter of them all": "The north wind struck one January night in 1807 with an insistent penetration. . . . Afterwards there was the strange drugged fall of snow. . . . The Mississippi shuddered and lifted from its bed, reaching like a somnambulist driven to go in new places." Boats float downstream through the ice, but the spectral sight of their huddled, motionless passengers inspire bets on shore "as to whether they were alive or dead." Travelers go "through the glassy tunnels of the Trace" like insects, "for all proportion went away"; "in the fastness of Natchez it began to seem then that the whole world, like itself, must be in a transfiguration" (4). As announced in the story's first sentence, "whatever happened, it happened in extraordinary times, in a season of dreams," and the muted, frozen landscape and dreamlike atmosphere are appropriate to the experiences of Joel Mayes, a twelve-year-old deaf-mute orphan, and the man with whom he has a brief but intense relationship, Aaron Burr, whose mysterious conspiracy and legendary trial take place in the penumbra of the story, as it were.

Joel had come to Natchez from Virginia, "through great worlds of leaves, and the whole journey . . . had been to him a kind of childhood wandering in oblivion," for he had been separated from his parents in a terrifying encounter with Indians and had since remained to himself, even in his job as boot-boy at the Inn. Walking through frozen Natchez, his eyes fill with wonder at the sight of breath coming out of people's mouths; he marvels at the infinite designs of speech made visible in formations on the air, and his awe turns to tenderness whenever he sees people meet and exchange words. There is no dialogue in the story; trying to express his "secret desire" as he walks through the silence, Joel pushes his own breath into the air and watches with pleasure as the "words" take shape. Joel has his own little room at the Inn, on the ground floor behind the saloon. Late each night he gathers up all the boots and brings them here. The job has dignity to him, for it is dangerous in Natchez to walk about among sleeping men. As the flames move gently on the floor stones, he contentedly cleans the boots; his life now seems "safely alighted, in the sleep of everyone else, like a bird on a bough." At night, when his carefully polished candlestick is lighted, "all the messages of love carved into it with a knife in Spanish words . . . came out in black relief, for anyone to read who came knowing the language" (9). It is in his room that Joel tries to communicate his own "message of love." Its recipient is Aaron Burr.

Joel awakens very late one night to find two tall, mysterious men talking together at his table. As he sits bolt upright in bed, one of the men makes a gesture which transfixes Joel. He "lifted his right arm—a tense, yet gentle and easy motion—and made the dark wet cloak fall back. To Joel it was like the first movement he had ever seen, as if the world had been up to that night inanimate. It was like the signal to open some heavy gate or paddock" (11). Burr's single gesture awakens in Joel his "first love" and a sense that this love is to remain forever unspoken. He somehow knows that the men are Burr and Harman Blennerhassett and is "seized and possessed by mystery." Every night Joel sits in the shadows and adoringly watches Burr transform the room with the "flame" that seems to spring from him. "Everything in the room was conquest, all was a dream of delights and powers beyond its walls." They accept his presence but ignore him ("his defect seemed to him a kind of hospitality"). All his love goes out to the talkers, but the only way he can express it is to bring them food saved out of his own suppers and to suffer in silence with his premonitions of disaster. It is Joel himself who pastes the notice on the saloon mirror which announces that the treason trial of Aaron Burr would be held at Jefferson College.

One night, after Blennerhassett and his wife have left the room, Burr astonishes Joel by stretching out and falling asleep on the table; the boy knows that Burr's departure is imminent. "Why would the heart break so at absence? Joel knew that it was because nothing had been told. The heart is secret even when the moment it dreamed of has come" (27). As he gazes at the sleeping face, Joel senses that, even if he *could* speak, he would not find the words to express his love—its history of sorrow and the dreams it has contemplated. The best he can do is to stop Burr's nightmare cries from being heard by eavesdroppers: "Whatever words they were, they were being taken by some force out of his dream." Joel puts out his hand in horror and Burr's fingers clasp it fiercely. At last the words stop, and his burning hand relaxes. The sequence dramatizes Burr's own sorrow, while at the same time denying, in a modest way, the efficacy of history. It is Burr's tragedy that "whatever words" they *were,* they went unrecorded, for the legend of his unspoken dream of power has obscured his earlier eminence, relegating him to a shadowy corner of American history.

The next night a disguised Burr makes his escape, using Joel's boot rag to darken his face. The boy follows on foot in the direction of Burr's route of departure. Knowing that Burr will never return, he feels a strange mourning: he "would never know now the true course, or the true outcome of any dream: this was all he felt. But he walked on, in the frozen path of the wilderness, on and on. He did not see how he could ever go back and still be the boot-boy at the Inn." The final image of "First Love" reasserts that his love is always to remain inarticulate: "He saw that the bodies of the frozen birds had fallen out of the trees, and he fell down and wept for his father and mother, to whom he had not said good-bye" (33). The mysteries of the heart may be more elusive to a deaf-mute child, but to Miss Welty, Joel's is perhaps everyman's fate, magnified by affliction.

"The Winds" is another intuitive exploration into the sensibilities of a child, set in more recent times. Young Josie is awakened one night by what she mistakes to be the cries of "big girls" out on a hay-ride: "At once she could see in her mind the source of it, the Old Natchez Trace, which was at the edge of her town, an old dark place where the young people went, and it was called both things, the Old Natchez Trace and Lover's Lane" (114). But in reality it is her father, lifting her out of bed as he moves the family into the living room to await the full impact of an equinoctial storm. The electric quality of the atmosphere, rendered in several fine images, is a fitting correlative for the body metabolism of a girl entering puberty. "Summer is over," sighs Josie's mother; autumn—and adolescence—await Josie.

Awaiting the storm, Josie dreamily recapitulates all the joys of childhood—the friends, games, songs, and superstitions. She is stimulated by the sudden atmospheric changes, the strange shifting lights and noises of the approaching storm. In a series of flashbacks, she sensitively re-creates the sights and sounds, the idle diversions available to a girl growing up in a small Southern town during the First World War. Foremost in her mind is a "big girl," Cornella.

"I see Cornella. She's on the outside, Mama, outside in the storm, and she's in the equinox."

But her mother would not answer.

"Josie, don't you understand—I want to keep us close together," said her father. She looked back at him. "Once in an equinoctial storm," he said cautiously over the sleeping Will, "a man's little girl was blown away from him into a haystack out in a field."

"The wind will come after Cornella," said Josie (118).

Cornella lives with her cousins "only by the frailest indulgence" in a motley, menacingly fenced-in place known as the "double-house." Never daring to speak to Cornella, Josie watches her constantly, adoringly—as Cornella darts out of the house to escape "the nagging odor of cabbage cooking" and the shrill taunts of her aunt; as she brushes and dries her silky golden hair in the sun; or as she walks in her high heels, swaying from side to side "in some kind of secrecy." One conviction grips Josie: "No matter how old I get, I will never catch up with Cornella." As the storm arrives, taking their house to its "very breast," Josie suddenly lies "as still as an animal" and in panic thinks of the future. For the first time in her life she thinks, "might the same wonders never come again?" (134). She realizes that to become a "big girl" like Cornella she will have to leave behind the joys of her childhood; growth involves a loss. The breaking sound of the first thunder is heard. "It's over," says her father. Josie's expanding perceptions have been delicately tuned to the storm's course. The calm and steady falling of rain begins. Returning to her bed,

She listened for a time to a tapping that came at her window, like a plea from outside. . . . There, outside, was all that was wild and beloved and estranged, and all that would beckon and leave her, and all that was beautiful. She wanted to follow, and by some metamorphosis she would take them in—all—every one. . . (139).

The next morning she finds on her porch the wet fragment of a letter which she reads. Cornella's name is on it, and it says "O my darling I have waited so long when are you coming for me? Never a day or night goes by that I do not ask When? When?" (140). Lost in the equinoctial storm that symbolizes her passage from adolescence to womanhood, Cornella's life is indeed "stormy" because she is "on the outside": without a father or mother, her home life is devoid of the kind of structure and warmth which Josie enjoys and which will give stability to her own efforts to emerge from childhood into adolescence, the change heralded by "The Winds."

The "initiation" theme is explored in a more complicated fashion in "The Wide Net," which also takes place "in the changing-time" and in "Livvie" and "At the Landing," the story of Jenny Lockhart. Living alone with her grandfather and a servant, Jenny, like Clytie Farr, is trapped in the house of tradition, pride, and death. As in "Livvie," it is spring, and her house is filled with symbolic details: the cord and tassel of her grandfather's brocade robe "seemed to weigh upon his fragile walking like a chain" (179); in her room is a "great box-like canopied bed" and "the great wardrobe in which she had sometimes longed to hide"; Jenny and her grandfather are served dinner in a pavillion which is surrounded by "an ancient circling thorny rose" (182), a detail subtly echoed by her late mother's painting "The Massacre at Fort Rosalie," which hangs in the parlor (180). These images of containment all symbolize her predicament. Because she is forbidden to talk to the "inferior" townspeople, Jenny Lockhart's house *is* a fort: she never performs any act for herself. "It might seem that nothing began in her own heart" (183). The story chronicles the opening of Jenny's locked heart, her painful rebirth from the womblike confines of her house.

As in "The Wide Net," the river symbolizes the life forces and the world of experience from which Jenny is isolated. At the beginning of the story, her grandfather has a dream of "high water" which symbolically projects the action of the story:

> The river has come back. That Floyd came to tell me. The sun was shining full on the face of the church, and that Floyd came around it with his wrist hung with a great long catfish. "It's coming," he said. "It's the river." . . . That Floyd's catfish has gone loose and free. . . . And all of a sudden, my dear—my dears, it took its river life back, and shining so brightly swam through the belfry of the church and downstream (178–79).

Billy Floyd, who fishes on the river, is a beautiful, wild, sun-burned creature whose origins are mysterious. The catfish in the old man's dream symbolizes Floyd's freedom, his easily and naturally expressed sexuality, and his divinity; for like William Wallace in "The Wide Net," who dances with a big catfish on his belt, Floyd is a river god, and, when he rides the Lockhart's rusty-red horse through a pasture of butterflies, he is also a field god.[10] To Jenny, "Floyd was in the world." The town is still called The Landing, even though the river is gone, three miles away, and comes back only in flood. When it reappears, both literally and in the person of Floyd, Jenny is brought into the world, just as the catfish in her grandfather's dream "took its river life back."

Billy Floyd represents the beauty of Eros; a network of sexual symbols proclaims his role in the story. "It was said by the old ladies that he slept all morning for he fished all night" (185); "they always [said that] he caught enormous fish wherever he fished in the river, and always had a long wet thing slung over his wrist when he went by, ugh!" (207); "in the long shadows . . . they could see his figure with the gleaming fish he carried move clear as a candle over the road. . . . And if in each day a moment of hope must come, in Jenny's day the moment was when the rude wild Floyd walked through The Landing carrying the big fish he had caught" (184). Jenny is thus drawn to him because she knows that he lives "apart in delight." Floyd's sexual violation of Jenny is foreshadowed in their first meetings in a ravine and a pasture which, significantly, adjoin the Lockhart cemetery. She watches him leap into the ravine as though "into something dangerous." In the pasture, "the sun and the grazing horse were on his side, the graves on hers, and they each looked across at the other's." Their initial encounters are tender and tentative, and the symbolism is rendered lyrically:

The whole world seemed filled with butterflies. At each step they took, two black butterflies over the flowers were whirring just alike, suspended in the air, one circling the other rhythmically, or both moving from side to side in a gentle wave-like way, one above the other. . . . Jenny and Floyd stopped and looked for a little while at all the butterflies and they never touched each other. When Jenny did touch Floyd, touch his sleeve, he started (187).

The action is most explicitly symbolic when Jenny catches "the horse he had excited. Then he was jumping on its bare back and riding into a gallop . . . [Jenny] threw herself down into the grass. Never had she known that the Lockhart horse could run like that" (188). As Floyd rides, she lies in the grass, thinking that "he might even have jumped across her," transforming his "riding" into anticipatory thoughts of the male and female sexual postures—"the vaunting and the prostration of love" (189). At the end of the story, the sexual symbolism takes a violent turn, as does the action.

In the first part of "At the Landing," Jenny is waiting "for the calling back that was in the world" (192). She learns about the mysteries of love and separateness just by watching Billy Floyd, by responding to his untamed beauty. When Floyd drinks deeply from a spring without once lifting his face and then falls into a sleep of satiety, she watches him and "felt it come to her dimly that her innocence had left her, since she could watch his" (186). He rides off into the woods. She knows what she would find if she followed him. "As she was living and inviolate, so of course was he, and when that gave him delight, how could she bring a question to him?" (188). Although they have not spoken, she has intuitively learned how love "would have a different story in the world if it could lose the moral knowledge of a mystery that is in the other heart." Her discovery is similar to those made by William Wallace in "The Wide Net" and Rosamond in *The Robber Bride-groom*—the discovery that Howard ("Flowers for Marjorie") and Ellie Morgan ("The Key") refuse to accept. Because Jenny senses the "fragile mystery" in Floyd, the knowledge comes to her that this mystery "was in everyone and in herself" and that, however well one may know that another's mysteries must be respected, the inevitable human impulse nevertheless is to press for such knowledge: "whatever she did, she would be bound to ride over and hurt" because "the secrecy of life was the terror." Yet in her dreamy anticipation of the sexual act, she perceives that sexual experience will not reveal the essence of identity nor by itself bring two people closer together; "the vaunting and prostration of love told her nothing—nothing at all" (189).

Part two of "At the Landing" records Jenny's arrival "in the world." She goes down the hill into The Landing to announce her grandfather's death. Entering the dim and dingy village store, she sees Billy Floyd. Trapped in a confined place, he is a different man; there is now something "used and worldly about him," like the "odor of the old playing cards that the old men of The Landing shuffled every day." Jenny senses that here she can corner him and discover his identity. The old ladies in the town think he is "really the bastard" of one of the old players. But to Jenny his wild beauty insists upon a more mysterious origin. Perhaps, as one of the old women suggests, "Floyd had the blood of a Natchez Indian, though the Natchez might be supposed to be all gone, massacred. The Natchez, she said . . . were the people from the lost Atlantis . . . and took their pride in the escape from that flood, when the island went under" (208). But whatever his identity, Jenny fears that any definition made in the store would include the odor of those playing cards, and, not wanting to shame the Floyd of the woods and river, she walks out and lets him "escape." He returns with the flood.

The arrival of the flood is suggestive of childbirth: "Each day the storm clouds were opening like great purple flowers and pouring out their dark thunder. Each nightfall, the storm was laid down on their houses like a burden the day had carried" (198); "when at last the river came, it did come like a hand and arm"; "the clouds lowered and broke . . . . Boat whistles began crying as faint as baby cries in that rainy dark" (199); and, when Jenny returns to her house after the flood, it seems "crouched like a child going backwards to the womb" (204). Floyd, whose shining eyes "held the whole flood," brings Jenny in his boat to a hill above the submerged graves of her family and there takes her, bringing her into the world. They celebrate her "birth," and ceremoniously partake of his field and river "divinity" by eating fresh wild meat and fish: "She knew from him . . . that what people ate in the world was earth, river, wildness, and litheness" (201). But when she finally speaks to him, "I wish you and I could be far away, I wish for a little house," he does not answer her. And when the flood recedes he too leaves, for he is more like a natural force than a man; it is as if it were enough that he has brought her out of her "dream of love" and has started her on her journey through life. "She herself did not know what might lie ahead, she had never seen herself. She looked outward with the sense of rightful space and time within her, which must be traversed before she could be known at all" (206).

Jenny's first love was born in the spring. With the coming of summer the little town seems to stretch and swoon in the stupor and languor of the heat. The enveloping fecundity of "the dream of July" sends her in search of Floyd, for she is "lost in wonder again. If she could find him now, or even find the place where he had last passed through, she would gain the next wisdom" (211). Jenny leaves The Landing, and her quest leads her into deep, paradisal woods which are like underwater depths (212), recalling William Wallace's plunge to the bottom of the Pearl River in search of the causes of his wife's "old trouble."

Emerging into what is for her yet another new world—the camp of the primitive river people—she asks for Floyd. "They said he was out on them now, but would come back"—like the tide. The men that had been throwing knives at the tree when she entered the camp now put her inside a grounded houseboat and, one by one, the men come in to her. "About them all and closer to them than their own breath was the smell of trees that had bled to the knives they wore."

A rude laugh covered her cry, and somehow both the harsh human sounds could easily have been heard as rejoicing, going out over the river in the dark night. By the fire, little boys were slapped crossly by their mothers—as if they knew that the original smile now crossed Jenny's face, and hung there no matter what was done to her. . . (214).

In the protective, stifling fold of her family, Jenny had been denied knowledge of both good *and* evil, love *and* hate. Floyd introduced her to love; "but if innocence had left," she thinks while he sleeps, "she still did not know what was to come" (186), and later she imagines herself like a house in which each "room" (or compartment of unrealized knowledge) had to be "lighted" (or experienced) "before going to the next" (206). Evil is "next," for loss of innocence is not necessarily followed by a knowledge of evil, and, to move completely from the house of death, the world—including evil—must be re-created for her, the history of the race relived (she has "the sense of rightful space and time within her"). This is achieved through the destructive violence enacted in a place where "all things, river, sky, fire, and air, seemed the same color . . . the color of day when vision and despair are the same thing" (212); hence, the "original smile" on Jenny's lips. The old woman who looks into the houseboat and asks, "Is she asleep? Is she in a spell? Or is she dead?" understands this. When she is told, "she's waiting for Billy Floyd," she nods, "and nodded out to the flowing river, the firelight following her face and showing its dignity." To gain full knowledge of the world—the flowing river—one must know and endure both the good and evil possibilities of experience or, in the terms of the story's sexual symbolism, the delights of fishing and the painful assaults of knives. The story ends as "the younger boys separated and took their turns throwing knives with a dull *pit* at the tree" (214); their day will arrive. Beauty and horror, innocence and experience, good *and* evil are for Jenny "in the world": she is "at the landing," the point of debarkation, waiting for Billy Floyd and the next stage in her journey.

In "Livvie" another young woman returns to life from a house of death. When Livvie was sixteen she was married to Solomon, a dignified old colored man who owned his own land. Solomon had brought Livvie back to his isolated house in the deep country of the Natchez Trace. Nine years go by, with Solomon getting so old that he becomes a bedridden comatose. When he dies, Livvie is reborn through her sexual surrender to Cash McCord, one of Solomon's tenant field hands; "Livvie is Back" was the story's original title. Although her return is more joyous than Jenny Lockhart's, Livvie's new life is achieved at the expense of certain positive values from the old life; the story is thematically more complicated than its simple, straightforward narration of events might suggest.

Solomon is a moral, pious man whose Bible is always by his side. The iron bed in which he sleeps all day has "polished knobs like a throne" (154) and above the bed "there was a picture of him when he was young. Then he had a fan of hair over his forehead like a king's crown" (160), for Solomon is well named: he exemplifies wisdom, order, control, and, at the end of the story, forgiveness. When Miss Welty carefully describes the inside and outside of his tidy, well-furnished house (154–56), she is not simply cataloging, but brilliantly projecting the quality of Solomon's life—its dignity, discipline, and order. The three pages of tightly written description could well serve as a textbook example for writers to illustrate how the naturalistic details of a scene can work symbolically without ever announcing themselves as Symbols. Everything is patterned and balanced: there are three rooms in his "nice house"; in the living room all the furniture is grouped around a three-legged table "on which was set a lamp with three gold feet"; there are three objects on the kitchen table; and outside, rose bushes grow in threes on either side of the steps. In the kitchen there are four baited mousetraps, one in each corner. The porch is also symmetrically arranged. Each detail is relevant. Solomon sleeps soundly under "a big featherstitched piece-quilt in the pattern 'Trip Around the World,' which had twenty-one different colors, four hundred and forty pieces, and a thousand yards of thread, and that was what Solomon's mother made in her life and old age" (155). His mother's laborious task symbolically describes how all Solomon's "life he had built, little scrap by little scrap, respect" (173). Multiple meanings are suggested by the colored bottles which Solomon has placed on the ending of each branch of the bare crape myrtles along the path coming up from the deep cut of the Natchez Trace below. Solomon doesn't say what they are for, but Livvie knows how bottle trees keep "evil spirits from coming into the house—by luring them inside the colored bottles, where they cannot get out again. Solomon had made the bottle trees with his own hands over the nine years, in labor amounting to about a tree a year, and without a sign that he had any uneasiness in his heart" (156). While the "precautions" are inspired by folk superstition and characterize the safety and security which Livvie enjoys, they also attest to Solomon's mute anxieties over having a young wife. She is forbidden to see anybody, especially the field hands. The "spirits" which Solomon is guarding his house (and wife) against are implicitly sexual, and the bottle trees set up the symbolism which is later developed. The life-giving radiance of the sun makes the bottles "look prettier than the [sexually barren] house"; similarly when Livvie gives herself to Cash at the end of the story, "the sun [is] in all the bottles on the prisoned trees" (177)—the sexual force of a young man making Livvie look prettier than she ever did in Solomon's lifetime, when the bottles, metaphorically, were "unfilled."

Livvie's temperament is serene, and she serves Solomon with a sweet and singular dedication. But she longs for companionship. Her isolation in Solomon's house of respectability and in Time is symbolized by his ever-present silver watch: he sleeps with it in his palm, and she thinks he dreams "what time it was," for he awakens "knowing where the hands were." One day she steals away down the still, deep Trace, beneath trees enclosed by great caterpillar nets. The landscape symbolizes her entrapment: "she felt as if she waded a river when she went, for the dead leaves on the ground reached as high as her knees, and when she was all scratched and bleeding she said it was not like a road that went anywhere" (157). She longs for a release—"Oh for a stirring of the leaves and a breaking of the nets!"

The "nets" are "broken" on the first day of spring. The shouts of men and girls plowing in the fields come to her through the air "and rouse her as if . . . they were telling her, 'Jump up!' " (161). Her release is hastened by a white woman named Miss Baby Marie, a traveling cosmetics saleslady who, like the bathers in "A Memory," impinges upon the poetic innocence of Livvie's dreamlike world. Miss Baby Marie is a humorous figure, but her arrival suggests that the encroachments of commercialism are unstoppable; her "little car [is] steaming like a kettle out in the field-track—it had come without a road" (164). Miss Baby Marie is country cousin to the beauty-parlor women of "Petrified Man." The story's grave tone gives way to her breezy vulgarity.

The saleslady is the "tempter" in Livvie's prison-paradise. Livvie has never used cosmetics before, and Miss Baby Marie offers her a purple lipstick—an emblem of sin and of the knowledge of life. "A fragrance came out of [the lipstick] like incense, and Livvie cried out suddenly, 'Chinaberry Flowers.' " "Oh, no, not chinaberry flowers—secret ingredients," replies Miss Baby Marie. When Livvie looks in the mirror and applies the lipstick, "her face dance[s] before her like a flame." She has tasted the original apple. Miss Baby Marie "took a look at what she had done, and said, 'That's it' " (166). Because Livvie cannot pay for it, Miss Baby Marie takes the lipstick with her. But the "tempter's" visit has been successful; the lipstick—or "apple"—has made Livvie explicitly aware of her needs. "It seemed as if her heart beat and her whole face flamed from the pulsing color of her lips" (168). Realizing that Solomon's death is imminent, she leaves the house.

Livvie comes upon Cash McCord on the Old Natchez Trace, "looking like a vision" in his gaudy new Easter clothes; he has a "guinea pig in his pocket" and "all of him was young." His Dionysian vitality recalls Mr. Don McInnis ("Asphodel"), King MacLain (*The Golden Apples*), and William Wallace ("The Wide Net"). But he is unlike the other Negroes in Miss Welty's stories. When he sees Livvie, he begins to look himself over, starting at the bottom with his pointed shoes. After he lifts his peg-top pants higher to see his bright socks, his gaze moves across his long, wide, leaf-green coat, high-up tawny pants, and luminous baby-pink satin shirt. At the end, he reaches up and with one finger gently touches the emerald green feather in his wide, platter-shaped round hat, which is the color of a plum. Cash may be a black buck and a field god, as Robert Penn Warren says,[11] but he is a field god in a zoot suit, a "transformed field hand" (170) whose name is significant, for his flamboyant city clothes have been bought with cash stolen from Solomon, and his hat is the same color as Miss Baby Marie's lipstick. Livvie tries to "see hope in [his] insolence," but when he moves along kicking the flowers he looks as if he could "destroy anything in the world," and a chill runs through her when Cash "laughs just to see Solomon's house sitting there." Cash is no Noble Savage. When Livvie kisses him, she feels Solomon's death is at hand and runs for the house. Laughingly, Cash picks up a stone and throws it into the bottle trees. "She put her hands over her head, and sounds clattered through the bottle trees like cries of outrage. Cash stamped and plunged zigzag up the front steps and in at the door" (172). The "cries" and the violence of Cash's virtual assault upon the house suggest to Livvie that any new freedom found with Cash will only be won at the expense of the dignity, balance, security, and moral order of her life with Solomon. Thus Miss Welty's attitude should not be confused with romantic primitivism, the faulty impression which this story may make upon a quick or superficial reading.

Livvie runs to Solomon's bedside, where he lies wrapped in his quilt, asleep. The only sounds in the house are the ticking of his watch and Cash's foot steps ("a noise like a hoof pawing the floor"). While Solomon sleeps his face tells them "like a mythical story" how he had built "respect":

When Solomon was young . . . he could see no end to the respect he would contrive and keep in a house. He had built a lonely house, the way he would make a cage, but it grew to be the same with him as a great monumental pyramid and sometimes in his absorption of getting it erected he was like the builder-slaves of Egypt who forgot or never knew the origin and meaning of the thing to which they gave all the strength of their bodies and used up all their days. . . . in his dreams he might have been an ant, a beetle, a bird, an Egyptian, assembling and carrying on his back and building with his hands, or he might have been an old man of India or a swaddled baby, about to smile and brush all away (173–74).

Through its antitheses, the passage manages simultaneously to suggest both admiration and criticism of Solomon's life-labor. Respectability is the dream which has withered. Yet his simple dignity is nevertheless undeniable.

Solomon suddenly awakens, and Cash raises his arm to strike down. But it stays in mid-air, as if held; a "tiny illumination" flickers in the ancient face, causing a "crisis, a mystery in the room that would not permit a blow to fall." The relentless inner strength of the frail, helpless old man cows the straining, powerful field hand, who steps "back behind Livvie, like a round-eyed school boy on whose unsuspecting head the dunce cap has been set. 'Young ones can't wait,' said Solomon." The great dignity, grace, and magnanimity with which he releases his hold on life suggest that Solomon himself, rather than his obsessively neat and "respectable" house, is his own greatest achievement. (Livvie earlier thinks he "look[s] like somebody kin to himself" [160].) Without bitterness or rancor he accepts the fact of his inevitable failure ("so here come the young man Livvie wait for. Was no prevention" [175]) and the irony that "it come to be somebody I know all the time, and been knowing since he were born in a cotton patch, and watched grow up year to year, Cash McCord, growed to size, growed up to come in my house in the end." With his lips moving like a chanter's, and Livvie's sobs following his words "like a soft melody repeating each thing as he stated it," he confesses and asks forgiveness "for sins great and small. God forgive Solomon for carrying away too young girl for wife and keeping her away from her people and from all the young people would clamor for her back" (176). As his last gesture he offers her his silver watch, the symbol of his life and of her isolation. "He dangled it before her eyes, and she hushed crying. . . . For a moment the watch could be heard ticking as it always did, precisely in his proud hand. She lifted it away. Then he took hold of the quilt [the symbol of his quest]; then he was dead" (177). By symbolically forgiving and releasing Livvie to Cash, Solomon gravely inaugurates the "rites" which herald her joyful rebirth.

Unlike the standard "black bucks" in Southern romance fiction (in *Porgy,* for example), Cash does not ravage Livvie; Miss Welty avoids making the Natchez Trace into Catfish Row. Instead, the brief final scene has the quality of a rite rather than an overt act; the initial moments of their union are enacted in a strange, deliberate, and ceremonial manner that can best be explained by examining the thread of "time" symbolism that runs through the action. In the description of the house, mention is made of a plow-wheel, "just a pretty iron *circle nailed up* on one wall" [italics here, and in the following quoted passages are mine]. This combines the image of "unplowed" Livvie with the image of the wheel, suggesting an immobilized wheel of life (155). Shortly before Miss Baby Marie's arrival, Livvie is described in the kitchen, watching and hearing the fertile motion and noise of the field plowing going on all around her: "High above everything, the *wheel* of fields, house, and cabins, and *the deep road surrounding like a moat to keep them in,* was the *turning* sky . . . serene and still as high flames. And sound asleep while all this went on around him that was his, Solomon was like a little *still spot in the middle*" (161–62). This is the traditional image of the absolutely still spot at the very center of the wheel that T. S. Eliot uses in the *Four Quartets* and *Murder in the Cathedral.* Cash, who is described as having a "round head, a round face, [and a] round hat" (170), brings Livvie out of the still center and back into the motion of the wheel of life: outside of Solomon's house "she went closer to him and his *swinging* arm drew her in at once" (171)—a symbolic movement which is completed after Solomon's death.

As they reached the front room, he seized her deftly as a long black cat and dragged her *hanging by the waist round and round him, while he turned in a circle,* his face bent down to hers. . . . They moved *around and around* the room and into the brightness of the open door (177).

But Livvie is not immediately submissive: "the first moment, she kept one arm and its hand stiff and still, the one that held Solomon's watch"—as if she were reluctant to finally part with the values it symbolizes. "Then the fingers softly let go, all of her was limp, and the watch fell somewhere on the floor," signaling her return to Time and the rotating wheel of life ("outside the redbirds were flying and crisscrossing"). The watch "ticked away in the still room, and all at once there began outside the full song of a bird. . . . She rested in silence in his trembling arms, unprotesting as a bird on a nest . . . the sun was in all the bottles on the prisoned trees, and the young peach was shining in the middle of them with the bursting light of spring" (177).

The story's joyful ending represents the culmination of a tissue of sexual symbols. While Livvie's isolation is projected in nature imagery (she is enclosed by "nets," knee-deep in "leaves"), her sexual predicament is rendered by various symbols of covered phalli. Surely Solomon's meticulous placing of bottles on the ends of the branches suggests this line of interpretation, which is later underscored by Cash's assault upon the bottle trees, a gesture that foreshadows the story's conclusion, when "the sun was in all the bottles." Two traditional phallic symbols are invoked in the references to Solomon's black hat—"the blackest thing in the world" (171)—hanging always over the doorknob "with a pearl in the end" (156). Unlike Solomon's hat, Cash's is the color of a plum (fecundity), and Livvie unconsciously seems to compare their "hats" (170), much to the advantage of Cash's, with its impressive green feather which "shone like a light" at the end of the story. The first unobstructed phallic symbols significantly occur *after* Livvie has applied the lipstick, which reminds her of a chinaberry tree by her family's home. She remembers her mother on one side of the tree "holding up her heavy apron [which] was loaded with ripe figs, and on the other side was her papa holding a fish-pole over the pond" (165), a symbolic coupling echoed in the story's last sentence when, to express Livvie's unfettered orgasmic joy, Miss Welty draws her sexual correspondences from nature: Livvie responds to Cash as the "young peach" among the bottles (female and male organs) responds to the "sun"; their passion reaches its climax, "shining with the bursting light of spring."

Although "Livvie is back," she knows that her return has been built upon the death of Solomon and his values. Like many of the characters in *The Wide Net,* she has submitted her dream to the world and will live with the consequences.

Delta Wedding belongs with the Natchez Trace stories, for it represents an enlargement upon the pastoral theme of the two preceding books. The novel is set in 1923 at Shellmound, the large Delta cotton plantation of the Fairchild family, where preparations are underway for the marriage of Dabney Fairchild and

Troy Flavin, the overseer. Troy is from the hill country of northern Mississippi, and theirs is considered a "bad match." As a
family, writes Shelley Fairchild in her diary, "together we have
a wall, we are self-sufficient against people that come up knocking,
we are solid to the outside." The town is named after the family,
for countless generations of Fairchilds have lived at Shellmound
and drawn their living from the land. Confusion, violence, and
death are overlooked, if not denied by them. Within the family
shell the past is kept alive. The portraits of Fairchild ancestors
are hung everywhere through Shellmound, their books and diaries
are about; under the aegis of the elderly Fairchild aunts, the family
continually rehearses the past in an effort to order the present.
Nine-year-old Laura McRaven, a Fairchild cousin who has arrived
from Jackson for the wedding, recalls how from her earliest memory the Fairchilds "never seemed to change at all." Their world
is a self-styled pastoral idyl. Just before the train pulls into Fairchilds, Laura "felt what an arriver in a land feels" (5).

The conventional paradox of pastoral is invoked. Laura thinks,
"Jackson was a big town, with twenty-five thousand people, and
Fairchilds was just a store and a gin and a bridge and one big
house, yet she was the one who felt like a little country cousin
when she arrived" (54). At intervals throughout the novel, the
sound of a piano can be heard from another room. It is played by
Mary Lamar Mackey, a cousin from Lookback Plantation [!], and,
in a moment of silence during a minor family crisis, she can be
heard "playing a nocturne—like the dropping of rain or the calling
of a bird the notes came from another room, effortless and endless,
isolated from them, yet near, and sweet like the guessed existence
of mystery. It made the house like a nameless forest, wherein
many little lives lived privately, each to its lyric pursuit and shy
protection" (156). Thus the family myth of beauty, honor, and
grace points to the perfection of the pastoral vision.

Everything must conform to their vision, and almost everything
does. One afternoon when the Fairchilds are crossing the railroad
trestle, retarded cousin Maureen gets her foot caught in the track.
As the Yazoo Delta train moves toward her, its engineer asleep,
everyone scatters, except George Fairchild, the living embodiment
of Fairchild man, who stays behind to try to free her. While
George wrestles with her foot, Maureen spreads out her arms to

halt the train, which comes to an obedient stop just when it is upon them. It is not in the Fairchild destiny to be killed by a train.

There *is* death in this world—a lovely, mysterious girl from the woods is killed on these same tracks—but the Fairchilds prefer to ignore it. Dabney remembers an incident from her childhood in which she had come upon George in the woods and had seen him bloodied when he stepped in and stopped a knife fight between two little Negroes. "All the Fairchild in her had screamed at his interfering—at his taking part—*caring* about anything in the world but them" (36). Maureen's father Denis had been killed not long before in the First World War, but he is already a legend, safely ensconced in the pantheon of fallen Fairchilds, already part of the daily ritual which preserves the family's identity and stays the forces of time and change. The novel's title describes this process: the book is concerned with the wedding, the ritual, not the marriage, and, although they have prepared for it over the course of a week (the novel's duration), the marriage ceremony is described in only one sentence. "Mr. Rondo married Dabney and Troy" (214). Their ritualization of life is examined from the inside as well as from the outside. By filtering the action through the separate consciousnesses of several characters, Miss Welty takes us behind the façade of what John Crowe Ransom calls their "comedy of love," where self-sufficiency may be seen as loneliness, where the Fairchild ethos may be scrutinized and even criticized by Fairchilds themselves.

The wedding preparations are disturbed by the absence of Robbie Reid, the "common" little store clerk from town whom George Fairchild married. Because of the incident on the trestle two weeks earlier, Robbie has run away; "George Fairchild, you didn't do this for *me!*" she had said. The Fairchild family cannot understand why Robbie would question George's heroic near-sacrifice; when she does return to Shellmound for the wedding, the old aunts excoriate her. The trestle incident nevertheless preys on the thoughts of several characters and forces them to examine the complex interaction of familial and conjugal love as it affects them. It also serves as the novel's main unifying device. But the wedding goes according to plan, and at the end of the novel life seems to be as tranquil as ever. Ellen Fairchild is pregnant again; her husband Battle has accepted the marriage of Dabney and

Troy; and the newlyweds have happily returned from a short honeymoon. The Fairchild clan goes on an evening picnic on the bank of the Yazoo River, where they talk and sing and watch a falling star.

There are ominous undertones in this final scene, however. Troy, the outsider, is now taking over the empty plantation house, Marmion. George, who lives in Memphis, says that he is thinking of coming home and ousting his two spinster sisters from the other family place, the Grove. He heretically plans on planting fruit trees instead of cotton and perhaps bringing in some livestock. Troy thinks it's a good idea. "What would the Delta think!" Aunt Tempe demands. Her voice shaking a little, Aunt Primrose says, "I forgot to tell you until now—there are rats at the Grove" (245). She is not simply trying to discourage George, for the rats have been mentioned earlier. They symbolize the nascent disorder of the Fairchild world; the pattern of life is soon to be broken. This is felt in the climactic scene following Robbie's return to Shell-mound, when Ellen Fairchild is overwhelmed by her sense of all the predicaments that have been averted. "The Yellow Dog had not run down George and Maureen; Robbie had not stayed away too long; Battle had not driven Troy out of the Delta; no one realized Aunt Shannon was out of her mind; even Laura had not cried yet for her mother. For a little while it was a charmed life . . ." (166).

For a little while. *Delta Wedding* recaptures the past at the moment it is about to become the present. The novel may have evolved out of a long passage in *The Robber Bridegroom* in which Clement Musgrove interrupts the fantasy to expound on the muta-bility of all things (141–44): the woods are becoming fields, the heroes are being replaced by murderers, "the time of cunning has come" (142). "So while Clement was talking so long to himself on the lateness of the age, the Indians came closer and found him. A red hand dragged him to his feet. He looked into large, worldly eyes" (144). Because he is Miss Welty's version of the American Adam, Clement always extricates himself from the hands of evil forces. Yet this element of the fable is not successfully integrated with the identity question that is central to the book. The beautiful digression on time's passing remains just that, a digression. "The settlement has come, and the reckoning is here," says Clement's wife, Salome. "Punishments and rewards are in order!" (144) But *The Robber Bridegroom's* light tone and special mode limit the possibility of a fully meaningful "reckoning"; the theme thus receives a full orchestration in *Delta Wedding*, although the same Northern critics who misunderstood *The Wide Net* could not see the "punishments" for the "rewards."

Isaac Rosenfeld and Diana Trilling both complained that Miss Welty did not show the relationship between the Fairchild's mode of life and the rest of Southern society and that she was not critical of the Fairchilds.[12] These critics failed to perceive that "the South" is not the subject of *Delta Wedding;* it is about the family and their exclusion of "the world," and, in presenting the Fairchilds' story, Miss Welty does exercise moral discrimination. The pastoral vision is *their* view of themselves, and Miss Welty submits it to her subtle irony. The novel's pervading irony lies in the way several individual Fairchilds belie that vision, examine it, and find it wanting. The irony is felt from the first sentence. "The nickname of the train was the Yellow Dog. Its real name was the Yazoo-Delta." Everything is personalized, made familiar; they often call "their" train simply the "Dog." The bridesmaids all bear shepherdess crooks that have been sent from Memphis by train. When George announces his plans for the Grove, Aunt Tempe says, "Well, Denis wouldn't . . . Selfish, selfish! Spoiling the picnic" (245). But Denis is dead, and their idyl is doomed.

George's wife Robbie sees the family with the eyes of an outsider. "It meant coming to touch the real, undeceiving world within the fairy Shellmound world to love George," but to get through the Fairchilds to George was "like parting a shiny curtain" (149). Plain little Robbie understands that the "spectacle" of Fairchild love is a kind of collective narcissism. Even Dabney comes to a critique of them. She thinks that her family never "looked deeper than the flat surface of any tremendous thing." Reflecting on the story of how her grandfather was killed in a duel over land, Dabney thinks, "Honor, honor, honor, the aunts drummed it into their ears. . . . To give up your life because you thought that much of your *cotton*—where was the love, even, in that? *Other* people's cotton! Fine glory! Dabney would not have done it" (120). As a declaration of her independence from the otiose Fairchild traditions, she breaks the little night-light heirloom that her aunts have given her as a wedding present.

Ellen Fairchild's new perspective is informed by her sense of George's detachment. At the wedding dance she realizes that "their legend was *happiness*. 'The Fairchilds are the happiest people!' They themselves repeated it to each other." But George risks more than their "legend" allows. As she dances with him, Ellen intuitively knows that her solicitude for him had been gratuitous because George is "ready for anything all the time." He alone, of all the Fairchilds, confronts experience unflinchingly, "stretching the opposite ways the self stretches" (222). George is the one person "who relieved the heart's overflow" for her: he epitomizes the need for both love and separateness, the polar extremes that are most nearly reconciled in Eudora Welty's next book, *The Golden Apples.*

7

THE
WANDERERS
AND THE
GOLDEN APPLES

Though I am old with wandering
Through hollow lands and hilly lands,
I will find out where she has gone,
And kiss her lips and take her hands;
And walk among long dappled grass,
And pluck till time and times are done
The silver apples of the moon,
The golden apples of the sun.

—W. B. YEATS [1]

ALTHOUGH EACH WAS first published separately, the seven inter-related stories in *The Golden Apples* can best be read as a novel. The sections are numbered like chapters, and each informs the other, gaining in resonance as the narrative unfolds. With the exception of one story, all the action takes place in the same small town over a period of forty years, and the book opens with a full-page listing of its dramatis personae: "Main Families in Morgana, Mississippi." The book's cohesive action is thematically and symbolically telescoped in its title, which is taken from Yeats's poem "Song of the Wandering Aengus." The source is not supposition: lines from this poem cross the mind of Cassie Morrison several times in the book's longest section, "June Recital," which first appeared in *Harper's Bazaar* (September, 1947) under the title "Golden Apples." This version ended with a quotation of the last two lines of Yeats's poem (see above), but they were omitted in the book.

Yeats's poem is about the Celtic hero-god Aengus—"The Master of Love"—who represents a restless and passionate seeker (perhaps a persona for the poet himself). The "fire" in Aengus' head drives him to go fishing at dawn in a "hazel wood," where with his "hazel wand" he catches "a little silver trout" which changes into "a glimmering girl/ With apple blossoms in her hair/ Who called me by my name and ran/ And faded through the brightening air." He grows old searching for this beautiful visionary creature—his one glimpse at perfection—but he still hopes to find and kiss her and to finally pluck the now blossoming golden apples which will enable him to enjoy complete emotional and sexual fulfillment.

Yeats's golden apples provide Miss Welty with the book's controlling symbol. She has said that "in any group of stories we might name as they occur to us, the plot is search. It is the ancient Odyssey and the thing that was ancient when first the Odyssey was sung." [2] All the major characters in *The Golden Apples* are conducting the search that is symbolically described in Yeats's poem; like Aengus, they too are wanderers engaged in an endless quest that is at once personal and universal.

The first wanderer to appear in *The Golden Apples* is the amorous and irrepressible King MacLain, whose carreer as seducer and cuckolder is comically narrated by Katie Rainey in "Shower of Gold." By opening *The Golden Apples* with Mrs. Rainey's monologue and closing it with her funeral, at which King MacLain is a most conspicuous guest, Miss Welty invests the book with a cyclical, novelistic unity. The events which Mrs. Rainey describe happened around 1910, and her funeral in "The Wanderers" occurs some forty years later. Her narration is strategically placed, for her shrewd and humorous observations, delivered while she churns butter at her roadside selling post, give one an immediate sense of life in Morgana, and the vacillations in her attitude toward King— ranging from outrage to adoration—project the town's varying reactions to his gay, willful, pagan ways.

King stands in open defiance of all social and moral order. Over the years he creates his own legend by appearing and disappearing unexpectedly and mysteriously, selling his spices and tea in distant places, and by mocking all conventions as if he were ready, in Yeats's words, to "pluck [the golden apples] till time and times are done." He puts men to shame not only because of his sexual prowess but because of his generosity—he is always bringing people surprise gifts—and his spontaneity—"Fate Rainey ain't got a surprise in him, and proud of it," Mrs. Rainey says of her husband (6)—and above all, his gift at making every woman feel unique, like a queen, an achievement that as an old man still fills him with pride. At Mrs. Rainey's funeral, he remembers how he gave her a swivel chair to use at her roadside stand. "Oh, then, she could see where Fate Rainey had fallen down, and a lovely man too; never got her the thing she wanted. I set her on a throne!" (224) King is well named. Yet his carefree ways are not altogether admirable: his gentle and faithful wife Snowdie has quietly suffered through the years while King has pursued the golden apples, leaving behind him "children known and unknown, scattered-like" (4)—"And don't nobody know how many chirren he has," says one fearful husband (92).

The title "Shower of Gold" points to its appropriate mythic source: the wayward King is a small-town Zeus and his wife represents Danaë, who, in the Greek myth, is impregnated by Zeus when he visits her in the form of a "shower of gold." As an albino, Snowdie is especially sensitive to sunlight, and when she informs Mrs. Rainey that she is pregnant, "It was like a shower of something had struck her, like she'd been caught out in something bright" (6). And after King has Mattie Will Sojourner in the woods ("Sir Rabbit"), he leaves her in light "like golden smoke" (95); when she approaches Morgana, it is "all in rays like a giant sunflower in the dust of Saturday" (97). King always wears a "luminous" golden panama hat, signaling his fecundity, and his "known" children, the twins Randall and Eugene, have golden hair, as does Easter, the rebellious orphan who may be one of his "unknown" offspring, and Fan, his grandchild, whose hair is like a "band of sunlight" (184) or "a gold rain hat" (168).

King MacLain's Jovian "glow" is visible throughout *The Golden Apples,* for his "known and unknown" children figure prominently in five of its seven sections, strengthening the book's structural, thematic, and mythic unity. If gold is the MacLain family color, it is not because the quest to find and taste the golden apples—to achieve self-fulfillment—is theirs alone, but because they conduct their search with such relentless passion.

In the last story "The Wanderers," King has returned home

permanently. Snowdie now reveals that "I spent all Mama and Papa had tracing after him." Although over sixty, the voluntarily retired wanderer remains unsatisfied, driven, defiant. While Mrs. Rainey's funeral is in progress he has a snack—loudly breaking chicken bones with his teeth, wagging his tongue in the air after tasting hot coffee, and then making a hideous face at Mrs. Rainey's daughter Virgie that is to her like "a silent yell at death" (227). All his life, King "had butted like a goat against the wall he wouldn't agree to himself or recognize" (233). He remains uncowed by any of the tragic implications of life. Even though "they all knew he was next—even he," King still asserts his joyous wish to live. After the funeral, Miss Snowdie leads her husband down a path, saying to him, "but mainly, Mr. MacLain, you should remember to keep off rich foods." Even as he is led away, King continues to eat (229).

"Sir Rabbit" humorously reinforces King's identification with Zeus or some satyr-god. King encounters Mattie Will Sojourner and her stupid husband Junior Holifield out on a hunting foray in the woods. A volley of buckshot aimed just over Junior's head sends him sprawling in a faint and looking "like the preternatural month of June" (94), King is suddenly upon Mattie Will—who plays woodland nymph to his Zeus, or, more specifically, Leda to his swan, for the passage describing their sexual union paraphrases and echoes Yeats's poem "Leda and the Swan." "When she laid eyes on Mr. MacLain close, she staggered, he had such grandeur." Wanting to become part of King's legend, she happily submits to him: "she was caught by the hair and brought down as suddenly to earth as if whacked by an unseen shillelagh" (Aengus' shillelagh? or Leda's great beating wings?). As she looks into King's eyes above hers, "keenly bright and unwavering and apart from her life," there is the suggestion that for some dark, inexplicable reason, King will always remain unsatisfied:

> But he put on her, with the affront of his body, the affront of his sense too. No pleasure in that! She had to put on what he knew with what he did—maybe because he was so grand it was a thorn to him. Like submitting to another way to talk, she could answer to his burden now, his whole blithe, smiling, superior, frantic existence (95).

But this is the only hint at complexity in the characterization of King. He leaves her, and she now feels that "she was Mr. Mac-

Lain's Doom, or Mr. MacLain's Weakness, like the rest, and neither Mrs. Junior Holifield nor Mattie Will Sojourner; now she was [part of] something she had always heard of"—the legend of King MacLain. She does not stir.

King's sexual prowess may be Olympian, but he is nevertheless treated as a comical as well as heroic figure. In "Shower of Gold," his twins' Hallowe'en prank frightens him into leaving town, and, when Mattie Will later finds King snoring against a tree, his body "looking no more driven than her man's now," she can only think of a silly little rhyme:

> *In the night time,*
> *At the right time,*
> *So I've understood,*
> *'Tis the habit of Sir Rabbit*
> *To dance in the wood*—(97)

Although King MacLain is the most fulfilled of the wanderers, he is also the least complicated. Like Uncle Daniel in *The Ponder Heart,* he possesses no moral or rational intelligence; he gets older, but he does not develop or change. By turns comical and mythical, his exploits are achieved outside of the moral world; significantly, even his *wife* comes to him in the woods in "Shower of Gold." He thus exists as an *emblem* of freedom and joyousness, rather than as an example of tenable behavior, and it is only as a pagan emblem that he is to be taken seriously by either the other characters or the reader; he is "Sir Rabbit," a nimble and inspirational embodiment of Eros.

King's appetite for life sets him apart from most of Morgana. When the "unmysterious" Snowdie leads King away from the funeral, Virgie Rainey watches the old man's "mysterious, vulnerable back" (229). The distinction goes a long way in describing the prevailing nature of Morgana's citizens. Almost all are "unmysterious," taking part in all the stabilizing community rituals from afternoon card parties to funerals, living their lives quietly, working, marrying, procreating, dying but somehow trying to remain unaffected by this cycle and to conceal from one another any sense of individual pain and loneliness by ignoring the inexorable movement of time—and forty years of it flows by them in *The Golden Apples.* "Time goes like a dream no matter how hard you run," says Mrs. Rainey, Morgana's chorus, "and all the time we heard things from out in the world that we listened to but that still didn't mean we believed them" (9). Thus they maintain their tidy little world, suppressing any passions or ambitions which might disturb the course of daily life, admitting neither tragedy nor heroism, and attempting to contain the "mysterious" few—King MacLain, Virgie Rainey, Miss Eckhart, Loch Morrison—who fight the confinements of small-town life and refuse to accept their imprisonment in Time: "What fortress indeed would ever come down, except before hard little horns, a rush and a stampede of the pure wish to live?" (233) King and Loch know that self-fulfillment is only to be had "out in the world"; Virgie and Miss Eckhart demonstrate that the community thwarts and even destroys those talented members whose transcendent acts would unforgivably remind the "unmysterious" inhabitants of the vast range of human potential and, by implication, remind them too of all human limitations before the unyielding passing of time.

"June Recital," the book's second story, takes place in 1920 and is mainly concerned with Miss Eckhart, the piano teacher, and Virgie Rainey, her "star" pupil, then sixteen years old—two wanderers at very different stages of their life's journey. It is the longest and perhaps most boldly experimental of Miss Welty's stories. Divided into four sections, the point of view is alternately shared by young Loch Morrison and his older sister Cassie. The restless, curious boy is confined to his room with malaria, but his boredom keeps him at the window, peering out through his father's telescope at the strange activities which take place next door in the large, almost abandoned MacLain house. Loch's comprehension of the mysterious events is limited and distorted by his youth, fever, and imagination, which interprets experience in the melodramatic terms of the movie serials at the Bijou theater. In the room next to Loch's, Cassie is busy dyeing a scarf and practicing on her ukelele for a hayride that is to take place that night. She too goes to the window, but the afternoon sunlight obscures her view into the MacLain house. Instead, Cassie recalls the past, and, as her recapitulations unfold, the reader discovers himself relating them to the events which are directly seen by Loch. By balancing and combining the two limited points of view and by following the story's "camera eye" as it sweeps up and down and in and around the two houses and the street below, the reader enjoys a unique perspective. And when to get a better view Loch climbs from his window into a tree and then hangs upside down from a branch like "a folded bat," Miss Welty is also out on a proverbial limb with her narrative technique as she records the action seen by the dizzy young boy as he sways back and forth.

From his two vantage points Loch looks into the MacLain house. As on every afternoon, old Booney Holifield, a night watchman, is asleep in a downstairs room. Loch sees a sailor and a girl go in the back door and then "play" (make love) on a bare mattress upstairs. They gaily chase each other around the mattress "like the policeman and Charlie Chaplin." More interesting to Loch is the appearance downstairs of an old woman whom he mistakenly assumes to be the sailor's mother. She busily hangs ribbons of newspaper all over the room—"she was putting up decorations," he thinks (27). Festooning the piano until it "rayed out" like a Maypole, she then ceremoniously places a ticking metronome on it (he thinks it a bomb). When she closes all the windows and begins stuffing the cracks with paper, Loch realizes that she is planning to set fire to the room. Before doing so she plays a few bars on the piano, three times.

"Für Elise"—thus opens the second section, told through Cassie's consciousness (30). *Für Elise* is the name of the piece which Virgie Rainey always played when she was Miss Eckhart's pupil, and it is the opening bars of this piece which the old woman now plays. *"Für Elise*. It came again, but in a labored, foolish way. Was it a man, using one finger?" (52) When Loch hears it, "it came like a signal, a greeting. . . . It took him back to when his sister was so sweet, to a long time ago" (24). Like the little phrase from Vinteuil's sonata in Proust's *Remembrance of Things Past,* the *Für Elise* theme is a reflexive link to the past. Each time it sounds, Cassie's memory is stirred. When she first hears it, "Cassie looked up from what she was doing and said in response, 'Virgie Rainey, *danke schoen*'" (30), which had been Miss Eckhart's grateful response after every performance by her only talented pupil. In Cassie's two sections the reader discovers that the girl romping upstairs with the sailor is Virgie, that the old woman below is really Miss Eckhart, who once gave lessons in the very room that she is now "decorating," and that this grotesque, destructive ritual is aimed at Virgie Rainey.

Miss Eckhart is the most thwarted and least fulfilled of all the wanderers, and she has traveled the greatest distance only to find continual frustration and disaster. The repeated musical phrases twice bring to Cassie's mind appropriate lines from an unidentified poem (Yeats's "Song of the Wandering Aengus")—*"Though I am old with wandering/ Through hollow lands . . ."* (33)—for Miss Eckhart's wandering is almost over. No one knows where Miss Eckhart came from—probably Germany—or why she chose little Morgana to settle in. Arriving with her crippled old mother, she rents a room in Snowdie MacLain's house and turns it into a "studio." Her whole life seems centered solely on giving lessons and taking care of her wheelchair-ridden mother. The little girls of Morgana, including Cassie and Virgie, dutifully but fearfully attend the "studio," for Miss Eckhart, a large, "heavy brunette woman whose age was not known," is a severe task-master. The untalented students are subject to the twin discipline of Miss Eckhart's tyrannical, ever-ticking metronome and her frequently used fly swatter. "The studio was in some ways like the witch's house in *Hansel and Gretel*," says Cassie's mother, "including the witch" (34). But the stern, forbidding Miss Eckhart becomes an increasingly sympathetic character as the story unfolds. At times pathetic—"a small, mint-white bust of Beethoven, all softened around the edges with the nose smoothed down, as if a cow had licked it," stands on the corner of the piano, an emblem of her disappointment—at others grotesque—she locks the worshipped metronome in a safe each night, symbolizing immobilized Time and all her thwarted hopes and ambitions—she is finally revealed as a touching, even tragic figure.

Virgie Rainey is Miss Eckhart's only gifted student. Not only is Virgie musically talented, but her independence and spirited abandon suggest that King MacLain might well be her unacknowledged father. In "The Wanderers," King is described as having all his life butted against the "walls" he wouldn't agree to recognize, and Cassie recalls how one rainy day in school "when recess was held in the basement [Virgie] said she was going to butt her brains out against the wall, and the teacher . . . had said, 'Beat them out, then,' and she had really tried" (38). Virgie plays the piano with such passion that when she finishes her number at one annual "June Recital," her clothes are wet and stained with perspiration.

She is the piano teacher's last hope—the only consolation and artistic justification for her boring and frustrating existence. But in her fearlessness Virgie only intensifies Miss Eckhart's private agonies, for Miss Eckhart has a "timid spot in her soul," a little vulnerable place, and Virgie finds it and shows it to others. Virgie refuses to use the metronome, throws sheet music on the floor, and insists on playing pieces her own way; having made an exception of Virgie, Miss Eckhart now falls "humble before her impudence." All the little girls can tell that Virgie is turning Miss Eckhart from a teacher "into something lesser. And if she was not a teacher, what was Miss Eckhart?" (41)

Miss Eckhart's vulnerability was vividly revealed to Cassie and Virgie one afternoon during a thunderstorm when for the first and only time Miss Eckhart played in their presence—a sonata by Beethoven, performed with passion and fury, "her solid body sway[ing] from side to side like a tree trunk." But "coming from Miss Eckhart the music made [them] . . . alarmed; something had burst out, unwanted, exciting, from the wrong person's life. This was some brilliant thing too splendid for Miss Eckhart" (50). To them she is more accurately defined by episodes such as her mute and thwarted love for Mr. Hal Sissum, a shoe clerk who also played cello in the Bijou. Mr. Sissum is attracted to Miss Eckhart because of her surprisingly pretty ankles, but he is drowned in the Big Black River. When Miss Eckhart appears at the cemetery, her repressed anguish is in keeping with their relationship and the essential quality of her life. As if she had been metamorphosed into her metronome, she vigorously and silently nods back and forth above the grave. Her way of "crying" moves several ladies to stop their little girls from learning any more music.

Miss Eckhart has a predilection for disaster. If King MacLain is a natural-born conqueror, then Miss Eckhart is the victim incarnate. In "Sir Rabbit," Mattie Will remembers that "disappointments are not to be borne by Mr. MacLain, or he'll go away" (95). On the street, King and Miss Eckhart "always passed without touching, like two stars, perhaps they had some kind of eclipse-effect on each other" (44)—as though two natural forces—personifications of Eros and Thanatos perhaps—were side-stepping one another. Soon after she arrived in Morgana her fate as Victim was established, accounting in part for the town's surprising hostility to her. One night she had been attacked and beaten by a crazed Negro. People had hoped and expected that after her recovery she would move away—"then they wouldn't always have to remember that a terrible thing once happened to her"; "perhaps more than anything it was the nigger in the hedge, the terrible fate that came on her, that people could not forgive Miss Eckhart" (51). But she "stayed, as though she considered one thing not so much more terrifying than another. (After all, nobody knew why she came!)" She is an uncomfortable reminder to Morgana that the worst tortures are not physical, that human loss and separateness sends individuals roaming "like lost beasts," and that there are hopes and ambitions "in the world"—such as Miss Eckhart's for Virgie—which transcend the provincial, narrow-minded aspirations of a small town. The time marked by Miss Eckhart's metronome points elsewhere, beyond Morgana, and Cassie is correct in perceiving that "perhaps nobody wanted Virgie Rainey to be anything in Morgana any more than they had wanted Miss Eckhart to be" (56). To the ladies of Morgana, music is part of the local social life; to Miss Eckhart and to Virgie, it is the very substance of life, although Virgie does not realize this until years later.

Miss Eckhart wants Virgie "to be heard from, in the world." Again and again she says that Virgie has a gift and must leave Morgana and study and practice her music for the rest of her life. In repeating this, Miss Eckhart suffers, because she senses that Virgie's irrepressible nature will betray her hopes. Thus at fourteen, when Virgie finishes school, she goes straight from classical music to playing the piano in the Bijou; *Für Elise* is replaced by "You've Got to See Mama Every Night," and she matures suddenly, bypassing adolescence. But when she stops her lessons with Miss Eckhart, "Virgie's hand lost its touch—that was what they said."

Cassie thinks "it might have been Virgie's stopping that took away Miss Eckhart's luck for good." Snowdie sells her house and moves home to MacLain, seven miles away, displacing Miss Eckhart, who soon loses all her pupils. After her mother dies, the broken, bitter, and lonely woman goes "down out of sight," most likely as a charity case on the County Farm. And now, perhaps somehow having found out what Virgie is using the house for, she has returned to destroy everything once dear to her—the studio, piano, metronome, Virgie, and even herself. The second section ends with Cassie's fond, out of sequence recollection of a typical "June Recital." Miss Welty achieves an expressive contrast by placing this long and detailed evocation of Miss Eckhart's proudest, most glorious day *after* Cassie has ostensibly completed the piano teacher's history, for it is immediately followed by Loch's blunt, "eye-witness" report of Miss Eckhart's ineffectual attempts to burn that very room in which the annual gala was held, and the incendiary strips of newspaper are now seen as a monstrous burlesque of the decorations for a "June Recital." This juxtaposing of the past and present communicates a deep pathos.

Even Miss Eckhart's attempts at destruction are fated to fail. In the third section Loch watches two comical characters, Mr. Fatty Bowles and Old Man Moody, the marshal, arrive to awaken the sleeping night watchman. They are followed in by a man Loch mistakes for a former boarder, Mr. Voight. His puckered lips and golden panama hat suggest he may be King MacLain, unexpectedly returned from a trip, and, after the three put out the fire, Miss Eckhart recognizes King and mumbles his name.

The fourth section is Cassie's. Miss Eckhart's hair has been burned off, and looking out the window, Cassie sees the men carry out an old woman with "some nameless kitchen rag" wrapped around her head, "wearing a gray housedress prophetic of an institution." Loch has jumped down from the tree, and Cassie runs out into the street in her petticoat, crying, "You can't take her! Miss Eckhart!"—which is the first time that the old woman has been identified by name (78). Naked from the waist up, the sailor runs from the smoky house and dashes toward the river. But Virgie emerges, unconcerned. Wearing a bright apricot voile dress, swinging her mesh pocketbook on a chain, and clicking her heels "as if nothing had happened in the past or behind her, as if she were free, whatever else she might be," she passes the hushed and curious group of ladies who have just come from a "Rook party," and walks toward the Bijou.

Instead of showing surprise or concern for Miss Eckhart, the ladies only speculate about the sailor—"Why, Kewpie Moffit!" they cry, who is he staying with, "what ever became of his mother? I'd forgotten all about him!" Cassie thinks,

People saw things like this as they saw Mr. MacLain come and go. They only hoped to place them, in their hour or their street or the name of their mothers' people. Then Morgana could hold them, and at last they were this and they were that (79).

To "place" people is to deny their humanity, to avoid all that is enigmatic and tragic in experience and, finally, to remain uninvolved and indifferent. Again Miss Welty's characters learn that "nobody cares"—the discovery made by "Old Mr. Marblehall."

Cassie and Loch "care"—but "it was only we two," Cassie thinks. When she sees Virgie walking past Miss Eckhart, she anticipates a dramatic confrontation between the two.

> "She'll stop for Miss Eckhart," breathed Cassie.
> Virgie went by. There was a meeting of glances between the teacher and her old pupil, that Cassie knew. She could not be sure that Miss Eckhart's closed once in recall—they had looked so wide-open at everything alike. The meeting amounted only to Virgie Rainey's passing by, in plain fact. She clicked by Miss Eckhart and she clicked straight through the middle of the Rook party, without a word or the pause of a moment (80).

It is a painful, affecting scene—one of the most moving in all of Miss Welty's fiction—and Virgie would seem to have treated Miss Eckhart with a final and unnecessary cruelty. But later that night, after she has returned from the hayride, Cassie lies in bed and realizes that the "snub" had gone both ways—that Miss Eckhart and Virgie had each intuitively known that it was too late for communication, reconciliation, or "rescue":

> What she was certain of was the distance those two had gone, as if all along they had been making a trip (which the sailor was only starting). It had changed them. They were deliberately terrible. They looked at each other and neither wished to speak. They did not even horrify each other. No one could touch them now, either. . . . Both Miss Eckhart and Virgie Rainey were human beings terribly at large, roaming on the face of the earth. And there were others of them—human beings, roaming, like lost beasts.

Lines from Yeats's "Song of the Wandering Aengus" had earlier "tumbled in her ears" (31, 33), and now, as the story ends,

> Into her head flowed the whole of the poem she had found in that book. . . . All of it passed through her head, through her body. She slept, but sat up in bed once and said aloud, " *'Because a fire was in my head'* " [the second line in Yeats's poem]. Then she fell back un-

resisting. She did not see except in dreams that a face looked in; that it was the grave, unappeased, and radiant face, once more and always, the face that was in the poem (85).

The face is the "glimmering" vision that Yeats's Aengus had glimpsed only fleetingly and spent his life pursuing. Symbolically, all the wanderers in the book are searching for this "radiant face," for to possess it—to realize one's most passionate dream or ambition—is, in the terms of the poem, to gain access to the golden apples and to achieve fulfillment and happiness. The apples have been withheld from Miss Eckhart and her "roaming" is over. But for Virgie the search has only begun.

Cassie Morrison, however, is no wanderer. Unlike Virgie or Loch, "she could not see herself do an unknown thing. . . . She was Cassie in her room, seeing the knowledge and torment beyond her reach" (68). After returning from the hayride, Cassie remembers "the way she herself had let nobody touch even her hand." When Loch was a boy, she tried "to shield his innocence," and, in the final story, "The Wanderers," the reader discovers, not surprisingly, that she has never married, but has remained at home taking care of her father, who became psychotic after his wife's suicide. Like Snowdie MacLain and Nina Carmichael (in "Moon Lake"), Cassie is one of a group of characters who serve as foils to the rebellious, searching wanderers. They are the passive, protective, adoring, and sympathetic spectators who often simultaneously love, fear, and envy the wanderers for their free and vaunting ways—as a child Virgie is Cassie's "secret love, as well as her secret hate"—and it is to these stable, retiring, "unmysterious" characters that the wanderers return. Sensitive and perceptive, their powers of moral insight develop quietly. Even at twelve, Cassie perceived Miss Eckhart's suffering. As Cassie dyes the scarf, she wonders whether she might have been able to help Miss Eckhart.

. . . she thought that somewhere, even up to the last, there could have been for Miss Eckhart a little opening wedge—a crack in the door. . . .
But if I had been the one to see it open, she thought slowly, I might have slammed it tight for ever. I might (59).

In spite of her age, she recognizes that human motivations are by definition ambivalent, and that good intentions and sympathy notwithstanding, there is still no predicting the uses one will make of knowledge of another's inner being. Her perception is implicitly ironic. Shortly after Mr. Sissum's death, Miss Eckhart had asked Cassie for a definition of "pizzicato." She had replied,

> *"Pizzicato* is when Mr. Sissum played the cello before he got drowned."
> That was herself: Cassie heard her own words. She had tried—she was as determined as if she'd been dared—to see how that sounded, spoken out like that to Miss Eckhart's face. She remembered how Miss Eckhart listened to her and did nothing but sit still as a statue (48).

Although unaware of it, Cassie has justified her own skepticism.

Loch Morrison, in contrast to his sister, has an adventurous, restless, and independent spirit. In "June Recital" his mind is filled with heroic dreams, and, despite his youthful misogyny, there are veiled suggestions that he too may be another of King MacLain's "unknown" children. Mr. Morrison, the editor of the Morgana newspaper, has little time for his gay, seemingly happy wife—Cassie remembers how at the breakfast table "he turned to his paper like Douglas Fairbanks opening big gates" (43)—and it is conceivable that she may have turned to King for sexual fulfillment; "You're *my* child," she softly tells Loch (67). He has King's stiff, golden hair, and, when he feverishly dreams of the big fig tree outside his window, it "was many times a magic tree with golden fruit that shone in and among its branches like a cloud of lightning bugs—a tree twinkling all over, burning, on and off, off and on. The sweet golden juice to come—in his dream he put his tongue out" (23)—and in "The Wanderers" the reader discovers that Loch does get to taste the golden apples. He has left Morgana and found "a life of [his] own" in New York City.

In "June Recital," Loch is already distrustful of others and is living apart in a solitary world, where he looks out "all eyes like Argus, on guard everywhere" (25). His fearless, heroic bent is revealed when he dives out of the tree to rescue the metronome which Old Man Moody has thrown out the window. Oblivious to the possibility that the "time-bomb" may explode, he hides it in his night shirt and carries it back to his room. This incident foreshadows the central episode of the book's fourth story "Moon

Lake," when Loch dives into the lake to rescue the orphan Easter, whom he miraculously returns to life.

Moon Lake is the site of the girl's camp at which Loch serves a one-week "ordeal" as attendant Boy Scout and Life Saver. His "martyred presence" there is due to his mother's insistence, for the camp is the product of Christian magnanimity; while half the girls are from middle-class Morgana homes, the other half are county orphans, "wished on them by Mr. Nesbitt and the Men's Bible Class after Billy Sunday's visit to town" (99).

Easter is the unofficial "leader," the wanderer among the orphans. Wild and independent, she bites Deacon Nesbitt's "collection hand" on Opening Day (for too closely scrutinizing her front, where "she had started her breasts"), plays mumblety-peg instead of Cassino, and takes Nina Carmichael and Jinny Love Stark deep into the woods, where she smokes a piece of vine. Easter's dress is "stained green behind" and the Morgana girls elatedly stare at the ring of "pure dirt" around her neck. Her eyes

were neither brown nor green nor cat; they had something of metal, flat ancient metal, so that you could not see into them. Nina's grandfather had possessed a box of coins from Greece and Rome. Easter's eyes could have come from Greece or Rome that day. . . . The color in Easter's eyes could have been found somewhere, away—away, under lost leaves—strange as the painted color of the ants. Instead of round black holes in the center of her eyes, there might have been women's heads, ancient (106).

This mythic aura suggests that she too may be one of King MacLain's unclaimed children. She has the family crest—her "hair was a withstanding gold" and it "seemed to fly up at the temples, being cropped and wiry"—and a radiance that recalls King's "shower of gold": the Morgana girls like to walk behind her and "see her back, which seemed spectacular from crested gold head to hard, tough heel"; even the dark band of dirt on her neck looks "like the mark a gold bracelet leaves" (105). One remembers, finally, Katie Rainey's remark that there are "children of [King's] growing up in the County Orphan's" (4).

Easter has an almost mystical sense of self: she has chosen her own name, and Nina thinks that "even on being watched, Easter remained not answerable to a soul on earth. Nobody cared! And so, in this beatific state, something came out of *her"* (112). Whenever directly questioned, Easter answers with a standard refrain—"I should worry, I should cry."

Easter makes Nina aware of the world beyond safe and secure Morgana—a world of uncertainty, danger, and, finally, death. "To *have been* an orphan," Nina imagines; then she "sat up on the cot and stared passionately before her at the night—the pale dark roaring night with its secret step, the Indian night" (123). When Easter first sees Moon Lake, she comes to a "dead stop" and looks "at it squinting as though it floated really on the Moon. And mighn't it be on the Moon?—it was a strange place, Nina thought, unlikely—and three miles from Morgana, Mississippi, all the time" (102). It is here that Easter undergoes an ordeal which somehow makes the vagaries of chance less terrifying to Nina.

While Easter is standing high above the lake on the diving board, she is tickled on the heel by a child. She drops into the water like "one hit in the head by a stone from a sling." Only after many dives does Loch Morrison find Easter, and pull her almost dead, horribly transfigured body from the muddy lake bottom. As a thin stream of water oozes out of Easter's mouth, the little girls gather around to witness death for perhaps the first time.

Placing Easter on a picnic table, Loch mounts her and begins to administer artificial respiration. The strong rhythmical motions of his resuscitation are decidedly sexual—"by now the Boy Scout seemed for ever part of Easter and she part of him"—and at one point the skittish Miss Lizzie Stark shouts, "What's he *doing* to her? Stop that." After many exhausting hours, Loch revives Easter, and the resemblance between his life-saving technique and the sexual act symbolically intensifies the scene's effect. Not all of the children realize that they have witnessed a virtual death and resurrection—"If Easter's dead, I get her coat for winter," says one orphan (132), and later Gertrude Bowles says, "I'm so tired! . . . And hot. Ain't you tired of Easter, laying up there on that table?" (134)—but the incident is not lost on Nina: "At least what had happened to Easter was out in the world, like the table itself. There it remained—mystery, if only for being hard and cruel and, by something Nina felt inside her body, murderous"

(136). Death has been seen, recognized, perhaps even *defeated;* as such, it is less terrifying.

The mythic correspondences of the episode at Moon Lake strengthen the possible filial link between Loch and the Jovian King MacLain. When Zeus [King] visited Danaë [Snowdie] in a "shower of gold," the hero Perseus was begotten—and Loch can be identified with him. There is a picture of Perseus in Miss Eckhart's studio which fascinates both Cassie and Virgie, and, when Loch saves Easter, one may be reminded of Perseus' rescue of Andromeda from her impending watery death. Like King Mac-Lain, Loch is capable of the heroic gesture, but like King, he also assumes the comical and eminently human posture of the show-off. The night after the rescue Nina and Jinny Love wander near Loch's tent. They see him study "his sunburn in a Kress mirror like theirs" and when he comes naked to the open tent flap and looks out into the night one possibly recalls Mrs. Rainey's description of King MacLain's swaggering, uninvited participation in Governor Vardaman's inaugural parade ("Shower of Gold"):

> Hadn't he surely, just before they caught him, been pounding his chest with his fists? Bragging on himself? It seemed to them they could still hear in the beating air of night the wild tatoo of pride he must have struck off. His silly, brief, overriding little show they could well imagine there in his tent of separation in the middle of the woods, in the night. Minnowy thing that matched his candle flame, naked as he was with that, he thought he shone forth too. Didn't he? (138)

But success does not come so naturally to King's "known" children, Randall and Eugene MacLain, the twins whose careers are chronicled in "The Whole World Knows" and "Music from Spain"—stories in which the book's symbolic frame seems to expand beyond Yeats's golden apples to include the golden apples which, in the Greek myth, were rolled across Atalanta's path as she ran, causing her to stop and lose the race. Each of King's sons is, ironically enough, unsuccessful in love, and remembering their appearances in the earlier episodes of *The Golden Apples* as mischievous and irrepressible children—trotting together "like a pony pair that could keep time to music in the Ringling Brothers'" (87)—one is perhaps surprised to learn that their adult lives are filled with suffering and frustration.

"The Whole World Knows" is an extended soliloquy by Ran MacLain—a plea for help addressed to his errant father King. Ran's mother, Snowdie, has said to him, *"Son, you're walking around in a dream"* (145), and his anguished, confused, and confusing thoughts are appropriately presented as a kind of montage or collage in which his mother's italicized statements and his interpolations of remarks made about him by the townspeople are combined with his guilt-ridden exposition of events to form a first-person narration aimed helplessly at an unhearing, distant wanderer—"Father, I wish I could talk to you, wherever you are right now," are the story's opening words (139).

Ran is by disposition a wanderer but one who, by inclination, never "wanders" far. Although his mother has sold the family house and moved back home to MacLain, Ran has remained in Morgana, where he works as a teller in the bank. He has married resilient Jinny Love Stark, who was seen in "Moon Lake" (set some ten years earlier) as a carefree child to whom even the frightening swamp sounds were "a song of hilarity." When Jinny is unfaithful to Ran with Woody Spights, the other bank teller, Ran leaves her and moves back to the old MacLain house as a boarder. The title alludes to the central events which lie in back of Ran's narration: everybody in Morgana—"the whole world"—knows that Jinny Love has been unfaithful and that Ran, in return, has had a brief but tragic affair with an eighteen-year-old country girl, Maideen Sumrell.

Although "The Whole World Knows," no one can see the reasons for Jinny's infidelity. Her mother offers a clue. "You men. You got us beat in the end," she tells Ran. "We'd know you through and through except we never know what ails you. . . . Of course I see what Jinny's doing, the fool, but you ailed first. You just got her answer to it, Ran." But Ran doesn't understand the "question": "And what ails me I don't know, Father." What "ails" him is Jinny's joyousness and contentment. Like Marjorie in "Flowers for Marjorie," she is a person who remains untouched by frustration and whose gaiety and immunity to suffering may finally seem reproachful, thus becoming unbearable, even enraging. Ran remembers how she never acknowledged "sorrow and pain. When I couldn't give her something she wanted she would hum a little tune . . . her voice would go low and soft to complete disparagement." Ran's exasperation over this baffling imperturbability—"you ailed first," says Mrs. Stark—probably goaded Jinny into having her affair.

The "ailment" is most clearly seen when, during their separation, Ran visits Jinny to have her sew a button on his sleeve. While she sews, her face is only inches away from his, but the contrast between her invulnerable, untroubled look and his turbulent thoughts bring to his mind a vision of murder—the actual denouement of "Flowers for Marjorie"—and he imagines shooting her.

> I fired pointblank at Jinny—more than once. It was close range. . . .
> But Jinny didn't feel it. She threaded her needle. She made her little face of success. Her thread always went straight in the eye.
> "Will you hold still."
> . . . the little cheat. I waited on, while she darted the needle and pulled at my sleeve, the sleeve to my helpless hand. It was like counting my breaths. I let out my fury and breathed the pure disappointment in: that she was not dead on earth. She bit the thread—magnificently. When she took her mouth away I nearly fell. The cheat (152).

Because she refuses to suffer with him, she is a "cheat."

Ran forces himself into having a joyless affair with gentle and "country-prim" Maideen Sumrell in order to ease his loneliness and to reaffirm his sexuality with a girl who looks like "a child's copy of Jinny," uncontaminated by any "mockery." Ran takes Maideen to Vicksburg to seduce her, but his father's element is not Ran's and the affair ends disastrously. After getting Maideen mildly drunk at a tawdry bar, he takes her to a tourist cabin, where all of his suffering and self-laceration reach their culmination in an unsuccessful attempt at suicide with his father's old pistol. The gun jams, Maideen takes it from him and hides it, and a moment later Ran "had her so quick." Afterwards each feels a poignant sense of loss—Ran for Jinny, and Maideen over her realization of the vast gulf separating love from lovemaking. When Ran later awakens, "she lay there by the side of me, weeping for herself. The kind of soft, patient meditative sobs a child will venture long after punishment. So I slept. How was I to know she would go and hurt herself?" he desperately asks his father. "She cheated, she cheated too" (160).

How has Maideen "hurt herself" and "cheated," and why,

much earlier in the story, does Ran wail "Father! Dear God wipe it clean. Wipe it clean, wipe it out. Don't let it be" (152)? These obliquities seem to be clarified in the final story "The Wanderers," when one learns that soon after the hallucinated cabin episode Maideen commits suicide with Ran's gun—a disclosure which fully justifies Ran's grief, sense of guilt, and the almost confessional tone of his anguished outpouring. Maideen "cheated" because she didn't share Ran's assumption that "there was nothing between them but time." She was too vulnerable and took her experience too seriously; ironically and tragically, her "cheating" is the opposite of Jinny's. But there is another obliquity that remains tenuous, its very ambiguity adding a further tragic dimension to the story. There is a hint that Maideen may be another of King MacLain's "unknown" children—and Ran's half sister. One recalls how King seduces and most likely impregnates Mattie Will Sojourner in "Sir Rabbit," coming upon her after his two young sons have dallied with her. The adult Ran is distraught when he learns the maiden name of Maideen's mother: "God help me, the name Sojourner was laid on my head like the top teetering crown of a pile of things to remember. Not to forget, ever to forget the name of Sojourner" (153). "Sir Rabbit" implies that the MacLain twins may have seen their father with Mattie Will, and Ran would now seem to have a buried memory of that day, which he censors out of his conscious mind; after asking his unhearing father "what ails me," Ran adds, "maybe you know"—in other words, *was* Mattie Will Maideen's mother, were you the father, and if so, more the terrible need to "wipe it clean."

The story ends as Ran asks, "And where's Jinny?"—a plaintive question which is answered in "The Wanderers" some twelve or so years later. The reunited couple appear with their children at Mrs. Rainey's funeral—Jinny "in her thirties strangely childlike"— and Virgie smiles faintly as she realizes, "without warning, that two passionate people stood in this roomful, with their indifferent backs to each other" (225). Ran is now the mayor of Morgana, a justly "royal" reward for the son of King. Like his father, he has become a legend: "They had voted for him for that—for his glamour and his story . . . it had made their hearts faint, and they would assert it again. Ran knew that every minute, there in the door he stood it" (211).

Although "The Whole World Knows" is an inventive and affecting story, it is not—like "June Recital" or "Why I Live at the P.O."—one of Miss Welty's most successful experiments in point of view, and not because of its partial obscurities—"June Recital" also has a difficult "surface"—but rather because of a basic conceptual weakness: the story's first-person voice is not always convincingly "masculine." There are several waverings in point of view—as when Ran calls Maideen "dainty," an unlikely word for him to use—but whenever Ran interpolates any of the remarks made by Miss Perdita Mayo, Morgana's ranking old-maid gossip, who says, "I'm a woman that's been clear around the world in my rocking chair" (140), the story's "voice" becomes most believable—since Miss Perdita's is the kind of voice for which Miss Welty has so unerring an ear. It is not surprising that the male consciousness is not Miss Welty's forte, yet in "Music from Spain" she nevertheless demonstrates that it is not beyond the range of her imagination.

"Music from Spain" is about Ran's twin brother Eugene and is told from his point of view, but in the third person. It is one of Miss Welty's rare excursions out of Mississippi and the only story in *The Golden Apples* which is not set in or near Morgana. Its seven carefully structured sections record Eugene's one-day journey through San Francisco shortly after the Second World War. Eugene is not, figuratively, his father's son; although he has wandered as far as San Francisco, he works there as a decidedly unheroic watch repairman—he calls himself a "little drudge"— and he owes his gentle, sensitive temperament to Snowdie, his mother. Emma, for twelve years his wife, had been his landlady; a gossipy, self-indulgent woman, she is older than Eugene and, by his admission, outweighs him by nineteen pounds. His long-nurtured resentment of Emma suddenly erupts one morning at the breakfast table when "without the least idea of why he did it, when his wife said some innocent thing to him—'crumb on your chin' or the like—he leaned across the table and slapped her face" (161). He leaves the apartment and begins to wander through the city streets, pondering the reasons behind his inexplicable gesture of protest.

Emma's extreme self-solicitude has driven the love out of their marriage. The death, a year earlier, of their young daughter Fan has only increased the distance between them: "Mourning over the same thing she mourned, he was not to be let in. For letting in was something else. How cold to the living hour grief could make you!" (168). Her inviolable grief is thoroughly narcissistic, rendering her unapproachable, unassailable; when she doesn't get her own way, she cries. Although Emma's ability to love has died, Eugene's life is not over, and he realizes that *"he struck her because he wanted another love. The forties. Psychology"* (164).

As Eugene approaches the jewelry store where he works, the lift of fog reminds him of the past, of Mississippi winters and boyhood longings to "see the world," and he decides to take the day off. After bypassing the store he notices that "the line of movie houses fluttered streamers and flags as if they were going out to sea" (168)—or heralding Ulysses-MacLain's embarkation on his day-long odyssey. Eugene's wandering takes him through crowded, grotesque Market Street—"a street of trusses, pads, braces, false bosoms, false teeth, and glass eyes"—through inviting open-air markets, and eventually to the ocean. He is involved in some kind of search; as he walks through the city, nothing is lost upon him—he watches everything with interest, boldness, and almost recklessness, as if in preparation for a revelation.

Eugene then sees walking ahead of him the Spaniard whom he and Emma had heard play the guitar in solo recital at Aeolian Hall the evening before. When the Spaniard begins to step in front of a speeding car, Eugene runs forward and pulls him back, possibly saving his life. Then "rescuer and rescuee shook hands"— unaware that they will exchange their roles later in the story—and begin to stroll along together. Eugene is at first disappointed to learn that the Spaniard speaks no English, but "after a little it seemed something of a favor, a privilege, to be unable to communicate any more than by smiles and signs," for the imperturbable old guitarist is radiant with a fearlessness, a mysterious energy that transcends any vocabulary. "Now that [Eugene] thought back, the big fellow had walked out in front of the automobile almost tempting it to try and get him, with all the aplomb of—certainly, a bull fighter." The Spaniard is enormous and has long, thick, black hair "combed back to hang behind him almost to his shoulders, like an Indian." He is at once wild and tender, primitive and dignified—"serious as a doctor"—and when he performs, he is inscrutable—like Powerhouse, the jazz musician. Eugene remembers how

in love songs as in the rest, the artist himself remained remote, as a conscientious black cloud from a summer day. He only loomed. He ended the recital with a formal bow—as though it had been taken for granted by then that passion was the thing he had in hand, love was his servant, and even despair was a little tamed animal trotting about in plain view. The bow had been consummate with grace, and when he lifted up, he was so big he looked very close to the eyes (184).

Eugene takes the Spaniard to lunch. While the stranger devours his meal—pulling apart a chicken outrageously, then spitting out the bones—Eugene studies him in the way that Powerhouse's audience gazed up at that fabulous performer, hoping for insights into a secret, exciting mode of being. "Artists were chameleons," thinks Eugene, "what mightn't this Spaniard be capable of?" He imagines the Spaniard undergoing a series of protean transformations, "and always the one, dark face, though momently fire from his nostrils brimmed over, with that veritable *waste* of life!"

Eugene next takes the guitarist by streetcar to the edge of the city, and as they walk toward the ocean "the Spaniard rather unexpectedly lunged forward, swung his big body around, and gazed for himself at the world behind and below where they had come." In "The Wanderers," Virgie Rainey recalls a picture of Perseus holding aloft the head of the Medusa—"the vaunting was what she remembered, that lifted arm" (243)—and when the Spaniard makes this same heroic gesture—a gesture also associated with Loch Morrison and King MacLain—he seems to bring the city into being, to transform it into a glorious cityscape out of El Greco:

He tenderly swept an arm. The whole arena was alight with a fairness and blueness at this hour of afternoon; all the gray was blue and the white was blue—the laid-out city looked soft, brushed over with some sky-feather. Then he dropped his hand, as though the city might retire; and lifted it again, as though to bring it back for a second time. He was really wonderful, with his arm raised.
They walked on, until the sky ahead was brilliant enough to keep the eyes dazzled (187).

The Spaniard would seem to have subsisted on a steady diet of golden apples—"his large face overhead flowed over with commiseration and pleasure"—and Eugene is automatically drawn to him in the hope that the Spaniard will somehow be able to communicate or transfer to Eugene some of his almost God-like creative energy.

Eugene's day-long odyssey can partly be seen as his search for a father. In the restaurant he imagines himself in various daring, exotic roles; toward the end of his reverie he wonders what it would be like if, rather than someone exciting, he chanced to find himself "simply out looking: not for anyone in particular; on the track, say, of his old man? (God forbid he'd find him! . . .)" (178). While he is watching the guitarist, he remembers "the kneeling Man in the Wilderness in the engraving in his father's remnant geography book, who hacked . . . at the Traveler's Tree. . . . That engraving itself, he had once believed, represented his father, King MacLain, in the flesh, the one who had never seen him or wanted to see him" (180). Eugene describes his satyr-like father as an "old goat" (178), then imagines the protean "Spaniard with horns on his head" (179), and later notices that the buckles on the Spaniard's suspenders are trimmed "with little bearded animal faces" (188). These subtle connections are made explicit when Eugene watches the Spaniard's "great fatherly barrel of chest move" (188). Eugene's own father is indeed a fiery and alluring man, but because he is beyond his son's reach, Eugene looks to the Spaniard as a symbolic father. Viewing the old guitarist in these terms helps to explain the story's strange climax.

The unusual nature of the impending action is foreshadowed by Eugene's dream-sensations: the countless hills that they walk over, the increasing freshness of the air and warmth of the nearer sun, and the dreamlike silence between the men make Eugene feel like a somnambulist; the hills are to him "like those stairs he climbed in dreams" (185). As the sun sets the two men ascend treacherous rocks to the windy cliffs of "Land's End." When they get to the edge of the precipice, Eugene suddenly, ecstatically

thrust both hands forward and took hold of the other man, not half compassing the vast waist. . . . One more move and the man would go, drop out of sight. He would go down below and it took only a touch.

Eugene clung to the Spaniard now, almost as if he had waited for him a long time with longing, almost as if he loved him, and had found a lasting refuge. He could have caressed the side of the massive face with the great pores in the loose hanging cheek (195).

Rather than seeing Eugene's gesture as additional "proof" of Leslie Fiedler's thesis concerning homoerotic love in American fiction, one may prefer to interpret it as the culmination of Eugene's search for a father and as part of a ritual of spiritual rebirth analogous to Loch's "resurrection" of Easter in "Moon Lake." But having no symbolic imagination, the Spaniard emits "a bullish roar," followed by "a terrible recital" of ear-shattering oaths. "Eugene suddenly lost his balance and nearly fell, so that he had to pull himself back by helplessly seizing hold of the big man." When the wind blows off the Spaniard's broad-brimmed black hat, Eugene runs after it—"inspiration was with him now"—and puts it on his own head: "It stayed on, and at the same time it shadowed him. The band inside was warm and fragrant still. Elation ran all through his body." He returns to the Spaniard, who now grabs Eugene with "hard calloused fingers like prongs." The Spaniard lifts him, and Eugene feels a sudden weightlessness— "only the finest, frailest thread of his own body seemed to exist. . . . He was without a burden in the world. Pillowed on great strength, he was turned in the air" (197). As the Spaniard swings him over his head and near the edge of the cliff, the wheeling, spinning motion fills Eugene with a sensation akin to sexual euphoria, and he has a vision of an Emma freed of all her debilitating self-pity, "sinking upon him" with awesome passion. Minutes earlier Eugene had thought of his lifelong inability to express himself at crucial moments, and now he desperately wishes to express to Emma his vision of "some future" between them:

> If he could have spoken! It was out of this relentlessness, not out of the gush of tears, that there would be a child again. Could it be possible that everything now could wait? If he could have stopped everything, until that pulse, far back, far inside, far within now, could shake like the little hard red fist of the first spring leaf!
> He was brought over and held by the knees in the posture of a bird, his body almost upright and his forearms gently spread. In his nostrils and relaxing eyes and around his naked head he could feel the reach of fine spray or the breath of fog. He was upborne, open-armed. He was only thinking, My dear love comes (198).

Voices from below abruptly end this unique scene. "Aren't you ashamed of yourself, teasing a little fellow like that, scaring him?"

a girl yells up. "Put him down and pick up one your own size" (198). The Spaniard lowers him to the ground, and the absurd, comically anticlimactic interruption evokes our delight; it is Miss Welty's rare gift that she can make comedy appear at will, as it does in life, even at the most intense, personal, and solemn moments.

Eugene's experience has been one of transcendence ("the posture of a bird") and rebirth (his pulse like a "little hard red fist"). It is as though the guitarist—with his overabundant, "veritable *waste* of life"—had given the weaker man a kind of blood transfusion, for the Spaniard's limitless energy, boldness, and passion seem literally to have flowed from his powerful hands and "warm" hat and into Eugene—infusing him with the essence of the "Music from Spain," filling him with the possibilities of a new child and a new life with Emma.

Eugene races home, but finds Emma sitting in the kitchen, gossiping with her friend Mrs. Herring. "You've left your hat somewhere," Emma tells him. "I'll be burying you next from pneumonia." With a stamp of her foot, she then shows him where some hot grease has splattered on her hand during the day. Although she has forgotten the incident at the breakfast table, Emma remains unchanged. Eugene tells her about seeing the Spaniard in traffic, and Mrs. Herring wonders if he's the same Spaniard who earlier that morning in church had showed "bad taste" by laughing out loud with a woman and then slapping her leg. "That would be him," says Emma as the story ends, and one senses the depths of Eugene's misery as he quietly watches Emma pop some grapes in her mouth. In that one ecstatic moment on the cliff, Eugene had had a fleeting vision of happiness and fulfillment—of the golden apples—but Emma makes it impossible for him ever to pluck them. At the end of "The Whole World Knows," Ran MacLain imploringly asks, "Father, Eugene! What you went and found, was it better than this?" (160). "Music from Spain" provides Eugene's answer—*no*.

In "Sir Rabbit," the fifteen-year-old Eugene seemed to Mattie Will to be a gamboling young kangaroo, but in the final section one learns that it was a sad and thwarted wanderer who years later returned to Morgana to die soon afterwards of tuberculosis. Virgie Rainey recalls that Eugene's wife did not come to the funeral, although a telegram had been sent.

The action of the book's final story "The Wanderers" is initiated by the death of old Katie Rainey, whose monologue opened *The Golden Apples*. From her dairy stand on the MacLain road she has for forty years served as Morgana's unofficial chorus, watching and commenting on the passing and changing scene. A strong sense of community is felt in the last section, as it was in the first. Everyone turns out for Miss Katie's funeral, including most of the characters from earlier sections of *The Golden Apples*. Their presence points to the final episode's structural function as an epilogue: the careers of several of the wanderers are concluded here; the book's central thematic concern is underlined by Virgie Rainey's renewed search for the golden apples; and a sense of the immutable patterns of life and death is poignantly communicated.

"The Wanderers" is mainly the story of Virgie Rainey. The spirited sixteen-year-old of "June Recital" is now a woman past forty. At seventeen she had briefly run away to Memphis with the sailor; then she had returned to Morgana to live an oppressive life with her mother. The keyboard at the Bijou is abandoned for an office job as a typist, and at night she milks the cows and helps her mother with other domestic chores. The long years at home are perhaps a necessary ordeal for Virgie: the rebellious girl learns that while fulfillment cannot be achieved without a modicum of freedom, neither can it be made meaningful without discipline and control. But it is a painful discovery and Virgie's attempts to learn discipline often involve her in an agonizing process:

> Her fingers set, after coming back, set half-closed; the strength in her hands she used up to type in the office but most consciously to pull the udders of the succeeding cows, as if she would hunt, hunt, hunt daily for the blindness that lay inside the beast, inside where she could have a real and living wall for beating on, a solid prison to get out of, the most real stupidity of flesh, a mindless and careless and calling body, to respond flesh for flesh, anguish for anguish. And if, as she dreamed one winter night, a new piano she touched had turned, after the one pristine moment, into a calling cow, it was by her own desire (235).

Virgie and her mother share a mutual devotion and loyalty. Mrs. Rainey has never confronted Virgie with any of the gossip which she has overheard about the affairs which, over the years, Virgie has had with second-rate local men, and, in turn, Virgie's hard-won self-discipline has been the solace of her mother's old age:

The day Miss Katie died, Virgie was kneeling on the floor of her bedroom cutting out a dress from some plaid material. . . .

"There's nothing Virgie Rainey loves better than struggling against a real hard plaid," Miss Katie thought, with a thrust of pain from somewhere unexpected. . . . Her last clear feeling as she stood there, holding herself up, was that she wanted to be down and covered up, in, of all things, Virgie's hard-to-match-up plaid (207).

All of Morgana comes to the Rainey house for the "laying-out" of Mrs. Rainey—a richly described ritual at which large displays of flowers are arrayed and great amounts of food and drink consumed. Virgie disappoints the falsely solicitous Morgana old maids by failing to show her grief, and, when she does weep, after a brief but harrowing scene in which they force Virgie to gaze upon her mother's "layed-out" corpse, they fail to understand that her tears are for the passing of the old ways of life in and around Morgana.

Although Virgie's "confined" existence has not been as oppressive as Livvie's or Jenny Lockhart's ("At the Landing"), she is waiting to discover the changes that will now take place in her life. When the last guests leave that night, "they seemed to drag some mythical gates and barriers away from her view." Virgie walks down to the river, undresses, and lets herself into the water.

All was one warmth, air, water, and her own body. All seemed one weight, one matter. . . . She felt the sand, grains intricate as little cogged wheels, minute shells of old seas, and the many dark ribbons of grass and mud touch her and leave her, like suggestions and withdrawals of some bondage that might have been dear, now dismembering and losing itself (219).

She begins her process of emotional resurgence by experiencing a dreamlike sense of metamorphosis, reminiscent of Eugene's birdlike "flight" and the water's transfiguration of Easter into a "dead rabbit" with arms and legs like "unopen leaves": "Virgie had reached the point where in the next moment she might turn into something without feeling it shock her. She hung suspended in the Big Black River as she would know to hang suspended in felicity" (219). Her ablution in the river suggests that the only experiences that will have any real meaning to Virgie during her bereavement are those personal and spontaneous moments apart from the tribal piety of a small-town funeral.

Thus the next day at the sanctimonious funeral service she watches King MacLain as a child's singing of a hymn makes most of the guests cry:

> Every now and then Mr. King, his tender-looking old head cocked sidewise, his heels lifted, his right hand pricking the air, tip-toed down the hall to the table to pick at the ham—all as if nobody could see him. . . . Mr. King sucked a little marrow bone and lifted his wobbly head and looked arrogantly at Virgie . . . [he] pushed out his stained lip. Then he made a hideous face at Virgie, like a silent yell. It was a yell at everything—including death, not leaving it out—and he did not mind taking his present animosity out on Virgie Rainey; indeed, he chose her. Then he cracked the little bone in his teeth. She felt refreshed all of a sudden at that tiny but sharp sound. . . . looking out of the . . . window through which came the cries of the little Mac-Lains playing in the yard, she knew another moment of alliance. Was it Ran or King himself with whom she really felt it? (227).

But whomever it is with, she knows the kinship for what it is, something indelible, intruding in the middle of sorrow. She rightly looks to King, for with his little, pinkish white patch of hair under his lip (216) and his "fierce lapels alert as ears" (223), he is Morgana's own self-styled satyr-god—while the funeral choir sings "Nearer, My God, to Thee," King MacLain "with the blue sky at his back" sticks out his tongue and wags it like a child (227); he has butted his "hard little horns" against the "walls" of both life and death, and, by allying herself with King and his family, Virgie asserts her own "pure wish to live."

Returning from the cemetery later that day, Virgie feels an impulse of hope emerging through her sense of loss and despair; she decides to leave Morgana, and, after quickly giving away most of her mother's belongings, she departs in her run-down old car. But it is fitting that before Virgie goes "into the world" she should make one last stop—at the family seat of the legendary, wandering MacLains.

Virgie drives seven miles to the town of MacLain and stops her car in front of the courthouse. At her mother's grave that afternoon a cornucopia of flowers had fallen over but no one had bothered to pick them up because "already, tomorrow's rain pelted the grave with loudness . . . this was the past now" (232). This sense of mutability is sustained throughout "The Wanderers," reaching a crescendo effect in the final scene as Virgie—"bereaved, hatless, unhidden now, in the rain—all to herself" (242)—sits on a stile amid an "open shelter" of trees in the deserted, rain-soaked courthouse square: "the Confederate soldier on the shaft looked like a chewed-on candle, as if old gnashing teeth had made him. On past him, pale as a rainbow, the ancient circus posters clung to their sheds, they no longer the defacing but the defaced." She can see the cemetery where the MacLains bury their dead—the MacLain Hill is "bigger than the Courthouse"—and her mind fills with memories of that fabulous clan: of Eugene, and how, "for a long interval, [he] had lived in another part of the world, learning while he was away that people don't have to be answered just because they want to know"; and finally of Miss Eckhart, whom Miss Snowdie had buried in the MacLain lot, in a grave near Eugene's. Suddenly Virgie remembers and for the first time begins to understand the meaning of a "threatening" picture which Miss Eckhart had hanging on her wall—"it showed Perseus with the head of the Medusa."

> The vaunting was what she remembered, that lifted arm.
>
> Cutting off the Medusa's head was the heroic act, perhaps, that made visible a horror in life, that was at once the horror in love, Virgie thought—the separateness. She might have seen heroism prophetically when she was young and afraid of Miss Eckhart. She might be able to see it now prophetically, but she was never a prophet. Because Virgie saw things in their time, like hearing them—and perhaps because she must believe in the Medusa equally with Perseus—she saw the stroke of the sword in three moments, not one. In the three was damnation—no, only the secret, unhurting because not caring in itself—beyond the beauty and the sword's stroke and the terror lay their existence in time—far out and endless, a constellation which the heart could read over many a night (243).

Perseus is an obvious emblem of the hero, but the success of the dual symbolism depends on one's seeing the evil Medusa as the victim; the Medusa, one recalls, had been a beautiful Gorgon until Athena had transformed her into an ugly monster. But the symbolism is appropriately ambiguous, for heroes and victims, like lovers, find themselves involved in one another's fate in tenuous and unexpected ways. "How much might depend on people's being linked together?" Cassie wonders, thinking of Miss Eckhart and

Virgie (56). And now Virgie, the most intelligent and intuitive of all the wanderers, realizes that every "vaunting" or "heroic act" also involves a victim—"endless the Medusa, and Perseus endless." The transcending or destructive act—"the sword's stroke"—makes visible the hero's "separateness," as well as the victim's, for the sensitive "hero" recoils at seeing the cost of his success—"the horror in life" that is the victim's suffering. But from Virgie's new perspective she sees beyond the "hurt" to the "third moment" of "the sword's stroke"—a timeless realm in which both "the heroic act" and the pain of human separateness have been absorbed and transmuted into art and made available to the world at large— "endless, a constellation which the heart could read over many a night." With perhaps a subliminal recollection of that one time when Miss Eckhart had played Beethoven on the piano, Virgie understands how Beethoven had enabled Miss Eckhart to project herself into that timeless realm and how Miss Eckhart had provided Virgie with this knowledge:

Miss Eckhart, whom Virgie had not, after all, hated—had come near to loving, for she had taken Miss Eckhart's hate, and then her love, extracted them, the thorn and then the overflow—had hung the picture on the wall for herself. She had absorbed the hero and the victim and then, stoutly, could sit down to the piano with all Beethoven ahead of her. With her hate, with her love, and with the small gnawing feelings that ate them, she offered Virgie her Beethoven. She offered, offered, offered—and when Virgie was young, in the strange wisdom of youth that is accepting of more than is given, she had accepted *the* Beethoven. . . . That was the gift she had touched with her fingers that had drifted and left her.

In Virgie's reach of memory a melody softly lifted, lifted of itself. Every time Perseus struck off the Medusa's head, there was the beat of time, and the melody. Endless the Medusa, and Perseus endless (243).

This passage is crucial because it underlines the definite but almost imperceptible widening of scope that has taken place in Miss Welty's fiction, concurrent with the shift of emphasis in her comic writing (a shift from satiric, grotesque modes to more joyous, "open" forms of comedy). In many of the early stories, such as "Clytie," "A Curtain of Green," and "A Visit of Charity," isolation was seen as tragic and the innocent self was often shown in retreat from a world that seemed endlessly terrifying (in "A Memory," "Flowers for Marjorie"). But to Virgie and the other wanderers, isolation is not necessarily "tragic," for through apartness one may discover the essential nature of oneself or others. Loneliness is still a dominant theme in *The Golden Apples* and later stories, but it is now seen as one component of a broader and more complex attitude: "Virgie never saw it differently, never doubted that all the opposites on earth were close together, love close to hate, living to dying; but of them all, hope and despair were the closest blood—unrecognizable one from the other sometimes, making moments double upon themselves, and in the doubling double again, amending but never taking back" (234). Thus hope and despair, beauty and terror, love and separateness—irreconcilable to the girl in "A Memory"—are now coequal in the world of Miss Welty's fiction; the Medusa and Perseus are "endless" and inseparable.

The conclusion of "The Wanderers," and *The Golden Apples,* is for Virgie only a beginning. As an old Negro woman with a red hen under her arm comes and sits down by her, Virgie feels the cool rain on her face and arms. "October rain on Mississippi fields. The rain of fall, maybe on the whole South, for all she knew on the everywhere. She stared into its magnitude," feeling "the earth's fuming breath." Then she smiles once, seeing before her "the hideous and delectable face Mr. King MacLain had made at the funeral, and when they all knew he was next—even he." If not her actual, "unknown" parent, then King is certainly her spiritual father, and, although it may be too late for Virgie to recapture *"the* Beethoven," she is finally setting out on her own search, ready to "pluck till time and times are done/ The silver apples of the moon,/ The golden apples of the sun."

"The Wanderers" completes the book's sense of an epic cycle: *The Golden Apples* opens with Mrs. Rainey's monologue on King and ends with King dominating Virgie's thoughts; the reader learns of King's departure from Morgana in the first section, and of Virgie's in the last; and, when Mrs. Rainey dies, her daughter is "reborn." Thus the ending is a beginning; the epic search is eternal, and in the book's last paragraph it literally becomes timeless when Miss Welty suddenly withdraws the story's point of view and removes the "vectors" which have situated the action in time and space, in Morgana, Mississippi:

Then [Virgie] and the old beggar woman, the old black thief, were there alone and together in the shelter of the big public tree, listening to the magical percussion, the world beating in their ears. They heard through falling rain the running of the horse and bear, the stroke of the leopard, the dragon's crusty slither, and the glimmer and the trumpet of the swan (244).

With the movement from time into timelessness and an archaic, mythical world, the wanderers' search for the golden apples assumes an archetypal dimension: their search has been underway since creation, and there is no "end" to this story—which is why, in the book's final moments, there is in fact no "story."

8

THE
ELUSIVE
BRIDE

EUDORA WELTY has exhorted young writers to "take chances," to "go out on a limb and dare as much as you can."[1] Her most recent collection of stories *The Bride of the Innisfallen* demonstrates that Miss Welty herself has continued to take these risks in an effort to invest her art with surprise and freshness. Shortly after its publication, she told an interviewer, "I tried some stories laid in locations new and strange to me (result of a Guggenheim that let me go to Europe), and tackled with some pleasure the problems the stories set me of writing from the outside, where my honest viewpoint had to look in from."[2]

Thus four of the seven stories in *The Bride of the Innisfallen* are set outside Mississippi ("Flowers for Marjorie" and "Music from Spain" are her only previous stories without Southern settings). The title story is set on a boat train heading for Cork, Ireland, and "Going to Naples" is about Italian-Americans on a ship going to Italy. "Circe" is a retelling of the myth and is set on

Circe's legendary island. Although "No Place for You, My Love" takes place in the South, its setting is the bayou country south of New Orleans, a region Miss Welty has visited only once, and its main characters are a man from the East and a woman from the Midwest. And of the three stories that take place in Mississippi, only "Ladies in Spring" has a familiar setting, whereas "The Burning" is a Civil War story, and "Kin" is told from the point of view of an "outsider"—a young woman who as a child had left Mississippi and is only now returning home for her first visit in many years. With their experimentation and variety of moods and settings, the stories in *The Bride of the Innisfallen* make it evident that Miss Welty's work continues to elude categorization; yet some of these stories remain elusive in less happy ways, and this too should be commented upon.

"Ladies in Spring" is set in a tiny hamlet named Royals. Young Dewey Coker decides not to go to school one morning when he sees his father Blackie, heading down the road carrying two fishing poles. Ignoring his father's mild protestations, he accompanies him into the woods. The action is seen through the innocent eyes of the boy, and, although he matter-of-factly comments that the river is dry, he does not view his father's motives suspiciously. In the woods they come upon Miss Hattie Purcell, kneeling on the ground "bringing rain" (86). She serves Royals as both postmistress and rainmaker and is yet another addition to Miss Welty's gallery of amusing small-town eccentrics. Like Edna Earle in *The Ponder Heart,* she is a spinster-matriarch who continually proclaims her odd authority; at the end of the story, Dewey thinks of how Miss Hattie looked "when she stood in the door of the post office looking out at the rain she'd brought and remarking to the world at large: 'Well, I'd say that's right persnickety' " (101).

Miss Hattie's antics dominate the action, but the story is about *two* "Ladies in Spring," and the brief appearance of a second, unnamed lady suggests that beneath the humorous surface of events—and beyond Dewey's point of view—something more important has been happening. While the Cokers are fishing, a "mysterious lady" appears three times through the trees on the other side of the water and calls to Blackie. He ignores her and she disappears. Dewey has no idea that he has spoiled a liaison and the incident is seemingly forgotten in the excitement following

Dewey's catching of a fish and the arrival of a drenching rain. The father and son share Miss Hattie's umbrella on her triumphal return to town—"We're real proud of you, Miss Hattie!" "You're still a credit to Royals, Miss Hattie!" (94)—and when they get home, Mrs. Coker, surrounded by four other small children, inexplicably yells at Dewey and his father.

Although at the end of the story Dewey is delighted by and preoccupied with the loud sounds made by the rain on all the tin roofs in Royals, Miss Hattie's sorting of the mail, and the unknown bird who "makes the lonesomest sound in creation," there is a sense that the impressionable but naïve boy will in time understand what *really* had happened in the woods that day and why his mother had been so agitated—and that its meaning will some day have more than passing significance to him.

An opposite perspective is rendered in "Kin": an adult is shown in the process of meaningfully recollecting her childhood. The story is told in the first person by Dicey Hastings, who had moved North when she was eight and is now returning to visit her family in Mississippi. Dicey and her cousin Kate drive out to Mingo, the old family homestead—"it was miles from anywhere"—to visit their dying Uncle Felix, who is being cared for by Sister Anne, a crafty, "buzzard-like" old maid cousin who specializes in unexpectedly "claiming kin" on her most remote relatives and then moving in with them. When Dicey and Kate arrive at Mingo, they discover that Sister Anne has moved the old man into a storage room in the back of the house and, in exchange for a promised free picture, has loaned out the parlor and bedroom to an itinerant photographer for use as a "studio" ("he's of the Yankee persuasion," says Sister Anne). Mingo is filled with most of the countryside, all in their Sunday best; "everybody that can walk, and two that can't," says Sister (134).

The first two sections are delightfully comic, but beneath the humor in the third section, Miss Welty perceptively investigates the nature of memory. When Dicey enters Uncle Felix's room, she begins a movement out of time. Immediately after arriving at Mingo, Dicey "looked and saw the corner clock was wrong" (128). As she approaches her Uncle's room, she notices "a banjo hung like a stopped clock" (134). "What must have been a Civil War musket stood like a forgotten broom in the corner" (137), and the delirious old man—who can only speak after his tongue has been moistened—rants incoherently about the Civil War:

"Hide," gasped the old man. . . . "And I'll go in. Kill 'em all. I'm old enough I swear you Bob. Told you. Will for sure if you don't hold me, hold me."
Sister Anne winked at me.
"Surrounded. . . . They're inside" (138).

Then Dicey notices a stereoptican lying on a barrel, the "once mysterious contraption" which years before had transported Dicey, the child, and her beloved Uncle to fabulous and faraway places. The sight of the old stereoptican returns her to the past—to "the real Uncle Felix," to "the real house . . . then cypressy and sweet, cool, reflecting, dustless" (141), and to the Sunday dinners at Mingo with her parents and all the other "kin" who are now dead. For a moment, the past is recaptured. But Dicey's is not the only memory which has been stirred. Uncle Felix asks her for a piece of paper on which he laboriously writes a message: "River—Daisy—Midnight—Please" (148). Seeing Dicey and hearing her name (Dicey equals Daisy), the old man has himself been transported in time and reminded of an early love, a tryst of long ago. But the note confuses the literal-minded Kate: "You must mean Beck, that was his wife. . . . His mind has wandered, the poor old man." For Dicey, however, the experience has underlined her own deep sense of loss—"it was the 'please' that had hurt me" (152)—and her knowledge that what was once taken "so for granted" has now spun far away out of time, never to be recaptured again—"and when I had left for ever I wondered at that moment, the old soft airs of Mingo as I knew them" (150). As the story ends, Dicey is driving away from Mingo, back into "time." She thinks about her fiancé in the North.

However unusual its form, "Circe" is not so far from "Kin" as it might seem. Based on the Circe episode in the *Odyssey,* the story is Miss Welty's most explicit use of mythology. It is narrated by Circe, whose syntax and language are suitably formal and vaguely archaic. The sorceress' curse, ironically enough, is immortality and foreknowledge. When she thinks of her "father the Sun, who went on his divine way untroubled, ambitionless—unconsumed; suffering no loss, no heroic fear of corruption through his constant shedding of light, needing no story, no retinue to vouch for where he has been" (105), she senses that by being exempt from all human pain and tragedy, she has also been denied access to what Miss Welty calls the endlessly new, "pervading and changing mystery" of relationship. Circe wishes for grief and tries to "find the dusty mouth of grief," for "it has no heavenly course; it is like mystery"— but "it would not come" (111). When Odysseus tells her about the Cyclops, she says, "I had heard it all before. . . . I didn't want his story, I wanted his secret" (105). After seducing Odysseus, she watches him sleep, hoping—like Rosamond in *The Robber Bridegroom*—that the mystery of identity will somehow be revealed in this unguarded moment. But her magic is useless, and she is as helpless as any of those human lovers who despair over their inability to fathom the inner life of another (William Wallace in "The Wide Net," Ellie Morgan in "The Key," and Ran Mac-Lain in "The Whole World Knows"). Thus the immortal Circe envies human beings for their frailty:

> Yet I know they keep something from me, asleep and awake. There exists a mortal mystery, that, if I knew where it was, I could crush like an island grape. Only frailty, it seems, can divine it—and I was not endowed with that property. They live by frailty! By the moment! I tell myself that it is only a mystery, and mystery is only uncertainty. (There is no mystery in magic! Men are swine: let it be said, and no sooner said than done.) Yet mortals alone can divine where it lies in each other, *can find it and prick it in all its peril, with an instrument made of air.* I swear that only to possess that one, trifling secret, I would willingly turn myself into a harmless dove for the rest of eternity [italics mine] (106).

The "instrument made of air" is perhaps a metaphor for the "weapons" beyond Circe's grasp—such as sensitivity, tenderness, and imagination—which human beings use to apprehend the mysteries of reality. The story may be from Homer, but thematically it is very much a piece with several of the stories set on Mississippi ground. Circe's is the penultimate version of the lost innocence for which so many of Miss Welty's characters long.

In *The Bride of the Innisfallen,* Miss Welty continues to focus on the themes which occur throughout her fiction. But the elusive and perhaps obscure nature of Circe's "instrument of air" metaphor draws attention to the dominant qualities of *The Bride of the Innisfallen* and to some of the changes which have taken place in Miss Welty's fiction. The elliptical and inconclusive form of several of the stories in this volume bears witness to her considerable admiration for Elizabeth Bowen and especially for Henry Green, whom she considers "the most interesting and vital imagination in English fiction in our time." [3] The stories have less plot than ever before and it is often difficult to tell what "happens" in a given story; several defy paraphrase, and the reader may find himself "lost in a void" and "all at sea," which is how Henry Green, in his autobiography, *Pack My Bag* (1940), describes the impact of his own fiction. The style is more complex and the metaphors are sometimes perplexing or teasing. In most of Miss Welty's earlier stories, the opening sentences were direct and lucid and served to subtly foreshadow the impending action. But many of the first sentences in *The Bride of the Innisfallen* are elaborately indirect. The lyric impulse which informs Miss Welty's best work now asserts itself obliquely; the denouements of her most recent stories are more tenuous than ever before because she views many of the characters from a distance, and the weighty burden of communication falls fully on the telling, external gesture, on the significant moment. And in the stories set outside Mississippi, the characters become subordinate to place, mood, and atmosphere; in two of the stories, the characters do not even have names. *The Bride of the Innisfallen* is thus characterized by an acute, impressionistic rendering of the visible world; the book is appropriately dedicated to Miss Bowen.

Louis D. Rubin comments that "in a sense, each of the stories in *The Bride of the Innisfallen* is about time—a moment, an afternoon, a day. The search for the meaning of the moment of time provides the structure of the story, and each has this for its progression"; "the moment" is "the goal, the key" to each story. [4] But in trying to glimpse each moment, many readers may—like Circe—find themselves wishing for an "instrument of air"—some kind of exegetical tweezers with which to pluck elusive moments out of a story's shimmering atmosphere. Most elusive of all are the stories told from an "outsider's" point of view; the most successful of these is "No Place for You, My Love."

"No Place for You, My Love" is the most experimental and interesting story in *The Bride of the Innisfallen*. A man and woman find themselves seated next to one another at a luncheon in New Orleans; they are strangers to each other and to the place. He is a married, middle-aged eastern businessman, she is about thirty-two and from Ohio; neither is ever named and both are vaguely unhappy. The moment he sees her face, he thinks that she is a woman who is having an affair, most likely with a married man (he does not notice the bruise on her temple, suggestive of a recent "scene"). After a few casual words, they embark on a long drive south from New Orleans in an effort to unburden themselves of "the formidable third"—"the one who didn't—couldn't—understand the two [of them]" (12)—and to achieve anonymity and "immunity from the world" (22). When they first get into the car, the woman says of the heat, "it's out of this world" (6), and as they race through a "universe" of mosquitoes and gnats into the sweltering, steamy bayou country, with its "crawling hides you could not penetrate with bullets or quite believe [and] grins that had come down from the primeval mud" (8), there is a sense of their speeding back and out of time. Miss Welty has said that the story's plot is "the vain courting of imperviousness in the face of exposure." [5]

Because the man and woman ride mostly in silence, the reader gradually realizes that the story's point of view belongs to *neither* of them, but rather to what Miss Welty calls a "third character." In "How I Write," she describes the genesis of "No Place for You, My Love" and how, in rewriting it, she discovered "where the real point of view belonged":

I saw it was outside—suspended, hung in the air between the two people, fished alive from the surrounding scene, where as it carried the story along it revealed itself (I hoped) as more real, more essential, than the characters were or had any cause to be. In effect there'd come to be a sort of third character present—an identity, rather: the relationship between the two and between the two and the world. It was what grew up between them meeting as strangers, went on the trip with them. . . . I wanted to suggest that its being took shape as the strange, compulsive journey itself, was palpable as its climate and mood, the heat of the day—but was its spirit too, a spirit that held territory—what's seen fleeting past by two vulnerable people who might seize hands on the run. . . .

I wanted to make it seen and believed what was to me, in my story's grip, literally apparent—that secret and shadow are taken away in this country by the merciless light that prevails there, by the river that is like an exposed vein of ore, the road that descends as one with the heat —its nerve (these are all terms in the story), and that the heat is also a visual illusion, shimmering and dancing over the waste that stretches ahead. I was writing of a real place; but doing so in order to write about my subject. I was writing of exposure, and the shock of the world; *in the end I tried to make the story's inside outside and then throw away the shell* [italics mine].[6]

The story is thus essentially visual:

> On this side of the river, the road ran beneath the brow of the levee and followed it. Here was a heat that ran deeper and brighter and more intense than all the rest—its nerve. The road grew one with the heat as it was one with the unseen river. Dead snakes stretched across the concrete like markers—inlaid mossaic bands, dry as feathers, which their tires licked at intervals that began to seem clocklike.
>
> No, the heat faced them—it was ahead. They could see it waving at them, shaken in the air above the white of the road, always at a certain distance ahead, shimmering finely as a cloth, with running edges of green and gold, fire and azure.
>
> "It's never anything like this in Syracuse," he said.
>
> "Or in Toledo, either," she replied with dry lips (12–13).

It is only fitting that the formidable presence of the heat should be *seen,* because their anxieties seem to dissolve in it. The abstract and the concrete are brilliantly merged: their feelings of estrangement are invested in the landscape, and it becomes the hallucinatory third character—"he had the feeling that they had been riding for a long time across a face—great, wide, and upturned. . . . A whole giant body sprawled downward" (25)—which frees them from their distracting concerns.

Their day's journey takes them to what literally seems to be the end of the world: the pavement gives way to a roadbed made of shells, and as darkness comes they arrive at the end of the road; stepping out of the car, she can not remember ever having seen a road simply end. "We're at the jumping-off place," he says (16). They enter "Baba's Place," an almost deserted cajun beer shack that later becomes crowded. The setting and atmosphere are carefully delineated: the slap of cards, the distant yell of Baba, and the bubbling of shrimp seem "to come in fits and starts." As the evening approaches, a "battalion" of little boys takes over the half-dozen slot machines, and Baba's Place comes to life. The scene is rich in simile and metaphor. The "functional" analogies are appropriately linked with the place and the region. Electric lights are strung over the room "from a kind of spider web of old wires," the slap of cards is "like the beating of moths on the screens" (18), the boys are "brushed away from the [card] table like mosquitoes," and a vivid sense of the heavy, hot bayou air is rendered by the image of the large, rough dog sleeping in front of the juke box, "his ribs working fast as a concertina's" (20). Not reading the story on its own terms, one critic complains that the place is far more vivid than the two characters,[7] which is precisely Miss Welty's aim, for the sense of place *is* the story. While they are dancing to music from the juke box, they each separately sense that if they were ever going to "overstep themselves" and fall victim to an easy, ignorant sympathy, "it would be now as he held her closer and turned her, when she became aware that he could not help but see the bruise at her temple" (22). But looking past his shoulder into the room, she whispers, "and all the time, it's real. It's a real place—away off down here." They dance gratefully to a song delivered in the local patois, sensing that the crowd in the room is an insulating presence and that their desired state of imperviousness is made possible by the strangeness of Baba's Place: "their bodies circling the odorous, just-nailed-down floor, they were, at last, imperviousness in motion. They had found it, and had almost missed it. . . . They were what their separate hearts desired that day, for themselves and each other" (22). Here, there is "No Place for You, My Love."

They drive back to New Orleans, but on the way to her hotel they get lost in the city streets. Finally recognizing a street sign, he mutters, "We're all right now," which describes the effect of their journey on each of them; in "How I Write," Miss Welty quotes an appropriate line from Richard Wilbur, "So strangeness gently steels us." The denouement is ephemeral and internal, but it *is* communicated. For a day they have been suspended outside of time, beyond their "worlds." Their lives have not changed, but they return to them refreshed. The woman gets out at her hotel "and he thought a figure in the lobby strolled to meet her" (26). He thinks of his wife, now back home entertaining some old, unmarried college friends, and, as the story ends, he drives his rented car into its garage, remembering "for the first time in years when he was young and brash, a student in New York, and the shriek and horror and unholy smother of the subway had its original meaning for him as the lilt and expectation of love" (27).

Although they granted "No Place for You, My Love" its impressionistic brilliance, a few critics were troubled by the vagueness surrounding the characters' motivations. "Above all I had no wish to sound mystical," says Miss Welty, "but I did expect to sound mysterious now and then, if I could: this was a circumstantial, realistic story in which the reality *was* mystery." [8] By trying to write about the tenuous mysteries of the inner life without writing stories which are themselves *mysteries,* Miss Welty has in most of her fiction been performing a hazardous balancing act. Perhaps only in "Going to Naples" and "The Bride of the Innisfallen" does she falter and stumble by burying each story's "meaning" too far behind its rich and shimmering impressionistic surface. "The Purple Hat" and "The Whole World Knows" also have their obliquities—which are surmountable—and in "The Burning," one never does find out whether Phinny, the child who is burned to death, is Miss Myra's, Miss Theo's, or the Negro slave's. Miss Welty has pushed her method to its extreme in "No Place for You, My Love" by "making the story's inside outside," but she succeeds—almost miraculously—in communicating what seems all but incommunicable; the transitory and the intuitive are made discernible through art. Yet the story has its obscure moments, which is perhaps inevitable, given its theme. Near the end, when the couple are about to part, "something that must have been with them all along suddenly, then, was not. In a moment, tall as panic, it rose, cried like a human, and dropped back" (26). The metaphor is elusive, perhaps incomprehensible; without Miss Welty's explanation, the impatient reader might never realize that

the cry that rose up at the story's end was, I hope unmistakably, the cry of the fading relationship—personal, individual, psychic—admitted in order to be denied, a cry that the characters were first able (and prone) to listen to, and then able in part to ignore. The cry was authentic to my story and so I didn't care if it did seem a little odd; the end of a journey *can* set up a cry, the shallowest provocation to sympathy and love does hate to give up the ghost. A relationship of the most fleeting kind has the power inherent to loom like a genie. . . .[9]

However "odd" the metaphor, it is a brilliantly apt summary image for a story in which the line between the exterior and the interior world is never drawn. The pulse of life that is felt throughout the story does not recognize this distinction, either; landscape, heat, insects, people, and the cry of the fading relationship all share a joint "metabolism." "No Place for You, My Love" is by far the finest of the stories which, in Miss Welty's words, were "written from the outside, where my honest view point had to look in." It succeeds where "Going to Naples" and "The Bride of the Innisfallen" do not.

"Going to Naples" humorously describes the shipboard activities of a large group of Italian-Americans bound for Italy during Holy Year. The principal characters are enthusiastic Mama Serto and her fat eighteen-year-old daughter Gabriella—the class clown of the St. Cecilia Sodality and the Sacred Heart typewriting class, Buffalo, New York. Whenever the opportunity arises, the ebullient Gabriella gives vent to her overabundant spirits by screaming: "but there were also screams that seemed offered through the day for their own sake, endeavors of pure anguish or joy that youth and strength seemed able to put out faster than the steady, pounding quiet of the voyage could ever overtake and heal" (161).

The story is leisurely told and its several single-faceted comic types are delightfully presented: there is Papa, an outrageous, somewhat grimy, twice-married old man who at each meal fights for the whole carafe of wine for himself and then sends the waiter for another and who has a tin whistle which he triumphantly blows *"Tweeeeet!"* whenever he feels like it—whether on the deck or in the lounge or dining room—signaling "life's most precious moments" (162); Mr. Ugone, the only passenger bound for Genoa, who is forever recommending his native city ("for one thing, is in Genoa most beautiful cemetery in world" [177]); La Zingara, a third-rate "actress" who infuriates the black-shawled mothers by seducing a spectacled youth "marked for the priesthood"; Poldy, a Polish-American who does nothing but talk about the girl in Italy whom it has been arranged for him to marry ("We've never seen each other. But do we love each other? Oh boy!" [167]); and the hovering, solicitous Mama Serto—telling clumsy Gabriella, "You saw! Every girl on ship is fat" (157), pairing her off with the equally awkward and good-natured Aldo Scampo, and giving her daughter an "incredibly quick little slap" during the shipboard church service when she notices the burgeoning curlers under Gabriella's kerchief ("You stay after Mass and confess sloth, you hear?" whispers Mama [169]).

"Going to Naples" is almost plotless, and most of what "happens" in the story happens to Gabriella. At the outset of the journey, while describing the character known only as Papa, Miss Welty asks, "Was it on every boat that tried to cross the ocean that some old fellow and his ten-cent whistle alerted the whole assembly at life's most precious moments?" (162). However entertaining its surface may be, the story's success finally depends on the reader's perceiving each "precious moment," and the impact it may have on the characters. Aldo and Gabriella romp together on the deck like overgrown puppies; she bites his arm, he pecks at her neck and she screams; when he buries his face in her blouse she smiles quietly. Watching Aldo and Gabriella, the old people sitting in the sun contemplate "the weakness and the mystery of the flesh." Her "smile was as rare as her silence, and as vulnerable—it was meant for everybody."

And it lifted the soul. . . . Looking, dreaming, down at Gabriella [the old people] felt something of an old, pure loneliness come back to them—like a bird sent out over the waters long ago, when they were young. . . . Only the long of memory, the brave and experienced of heart, could bear such a stirring, an awakening—first to have listened to that screaming, and in a flash to remember what it was (166).

The next important "moment" occurs at the Gala Night. Aldo's seasickness sends Gabriella to the Gala unaccompanied (except for Mama Serto). But the disappointment—and it is mainly her mother's—disappears when Gabriella is asked to dance:

. . . as Gabriella went swinging in the arms of Joe Monteoliveto the whole round of the room, a gentle breath of wonder started after her. . . . Dancing, poor Mrs. Serto's daughter was filled with grace.
The whole company—mothers banked around the walls, card players trapped at the tables, and the shadowy old—all looked her way. *Indisposti* or not, of course they knew what was in front of their eyes. Once more, slipping the way it liked to do through one of life's weak moments, illusion had got in, and they were glad to see it. . . (186).

Although La Zingara takes Joe Monteoliveto away in the middle of a waltz, Gabriella goes on dancing by herself. She ends it with a dozen whirling turns—"the stunt Gabriella was famous for in the St. Cecilia Sodality"—and receives a joyous acclamation. But as debarkation nears, she wonders, "was now the time to look forward to the doom of parting, and stop looking back at the doom of meeting?" (192). When they land, she is surprised to see that the seemingly joyous old man with the whistle is not met by anyone and that he is coming home to die. On the dock she meets Aldo carrying a cumbersome piece of luggage: "Hey! What you got in that thing, a dead body?" she cries out. Incongruously enough, it turns out to be a cello case—and as she says good-bye to Aldo, she finds out for the first time why he has come to Italy: to study cello in Rome under the G.I. Bill. Aldo leaves, and, as he walks through the crowd of acrobatic porters, his back grows less and less familiar with each step. Gabriella follows her Mama and grandmother out of the dock area. The random movements of the voyage are now realized as experience:

. . . all seemed caught up and held in something: the golden moment of touch, just given, just taken, in saying good-by. The moment—bright and effortless of making, in the end, as a bubble—seemed to go ahead of them as they walked, to tap without sound across the dust of the emptying courtyard, and alight in the grandmother's homely buggy, filling it (207).

In spite of the story's many delights, one may justifiably wonder whether these "moments" are substantial enough to sustain a fifty-one page narrative.

The paucity of characterization in "Going to Naples" and "The Bride of the Innisfallen" reminds us that the short story is seldom, if ever, used for the analysis or development of character, which is the novelist's task. The modern short story should aim instead for what Elizabeth Bowen calls a "central, single effect." [10] It is remarkable that Miss Welty often achieves this "central, single effect" while at the same time managing to reveal so much about her characters, including a sense of their development—witness Jenny Lockhart in "At The Landing" and Virgie Rainey in "June Recital" and "The Wanderers." If *The Golden Apples* is Miss Welty's finest achievement, it is because of the conjunction between character portrayal and "single effects" which is sustained throughout the book. Miss Welty has said, "when [plot] is identifiable in every motion and progression of its own with the motions and progressions of simple revelation, then it's at its highest use" [11]—this describes the excellence of *The Golden Apples* and stories such as "Death of a Traveling Salesman" and "A Still Moment" and the reasons for the comparative failure of "Going to

Naples" and "The Bride of the Innisfallen." Both stories are virtually plotless, and the "progressions" of each are not adequate to the story's length. Thus for most readers the revelatory moments—the "central, single effects"—remain submerged beneath the attenuated surface of the prose, elusive or out of sight. But this may not be just criticism. Perhaps "Going to Naples" demands a different critical vocabulary: its intermediate length makes it something more than a short story, its narrow scope and distance from its characters make it something less than a *novella;* talking about "central, single effects" may be irrelevant, like criticizing a tone poem for not being either a song or a symphony. With their tenuous interaction of character and event and their abundance of casually observed details pregnant with meanings that are never fully revealed, "No Place for You, My Love," "Going to Naples," and "The Bride of the Innisfallen" bring to mind the work of Elizabeth Bowen and Henry Green, and, as with, say, Green's *Party Going* (1939) or *Loving* (1945), one would do best not to read these stories with any hopes for an "exposition" of the action. Yet even granting them their special mode, "Going to Naples" and "The Bride of the Innisfallen" are still unsuccessful; the reasons for this are most apparent in the latter.

The title story records the all-night journey of a group of nameless travelers on a boat train taking them from Paddington to Fishguard, where they continue to Cork on a boat named the *Innisfallen.* Except for a young American woman who is leaving her husband in England, the characters are Irish or Welsh, and most of the story's "action" takes place in the train compartment and consists of their leisurely, irrelevant, sometimes comical conversations.

"The Bride of the Innisfallen" makes many demands on its readers. It opens with an oblique, "rococco" metaphor: "There was something of the pavilion about one raincoat, the way—for some little time out there in the crowd—it stood flowing in its salmony-pink and yellow stripes down toward the wet floor of the platform, expanding as it went" (47). In the train compartment, the lady in the raincoat says, " 'Four minutes to four' . . . those fours sounding fated. . . . Her gaze was almost forgiving. . . . Even yet, somewhere, sometime, the owner of those eyes might expect to rise to a tragic occasion. . . . Her raincoat gave off a peppermint smell that might have been stored up for this moment" (49–50), and then she says good-bye to a man who has accompanied her to the train. She keeps her raincoat on, and Miss Welty parenthetically adds, "what she had on under her raincoat was her own business and remained so" (51). The careful reader's mystification may be satisfied at the end of the story when the woman is met at Cork by another man—her husband?—and several children; one assumes that she has been having an affair in England, and her brightly colored raincoat is the symbol of this "other" life. The woman has of course never been developed as a character. As in a fiction of Henry Green or Elizabeth Bowen, she is there as a kind of symbol, intended to project wordlessly some resonant truth about human plight. But the tenuousness and portent with which she is described is gratuitous not because she mysteriously remains a stranger, but, paradoxically, because she is finally not that mysterious; in spite of the web of insinuations, she does not suggest fully the nameless sorrows she seems intended to suggest.

Not surprisingly, many readers and reviewers were perplexed by the story. William Peden's was a typical reaction. He found it "richly allusive, lavishly embroidered . . . evoking a sense of place so real as to be almost magical," but "unnecessarily indirect and self-consciously elliptical"; he finally admitted that "even after several readings I could neither accept it on a realistic level nor understand it on any other level." [12] For its "meaning," one has to look to the young American wife, and a full understanding of the story depends on one's seeing *her* as "The Bride of the Innisfallen."

The American girl remains silent and aloof throughout most of the trip. Only near the end of the story does Miss Welty focus on her. In the *Innisfallen* lounge, one of the travelers stares at her, "as if he saw somebody desperate who had left her husband once, endangered herself among strangers, been turned back, and was here for the second go-round, asking again for a place to stay in Cork" (77). "What was always her trouble? 'You hope for too much,' her husband said" (82). The young wife suffers—if that is the word—from an excess of joy and hope. "Love with the joy being drawn out of it . . . was loneliness . . . *I* was nearly destroyed, she thought, and again was threatened with a light head, a rush of laughter" (81). She has left her husband and is "desperate" because she is unable to share or communicate her boundless joy:

If she could never tell her husband her secret, perhaps she would never tell it at all. You must never betray pure joy—the kind you were born and began with—either by hiding it or by parading it in front of people's eyes; they didn't want to be shown it. And still you must tell it. Is there no way? she thought—for here I am, this far. I see Cork's streets take off from the waterside and rise lifting their houses and towers like note above note on a page of music, with arpeggios running over it of green and galleries and belvederes, and the bright sun raining at the top. Out of the joy I hide for fear it is promiscuous, I may walk for ever at the fall of evening by the river, and find this river street by the red rock, this first, last house, that's perhaps a boarding house now, standing fullface to the tide, and look up to that window—that upper window, from which the mystery will never go (82).

There are only two fleeting glimpses of the ostensible bride of the title; she is elusive as both fact *and* symbol—or as elusive as the story itself. Wearing a white spring hat, she makes her first appearance on deck as the boat enters Cork: "The boat whistle thundered like a hundred organ notes. . . . 'There's a bride on board!' called somebody. 'Look at her, look!' . . . She stood there all ready to be met. . . . Delight gathered all around, singing began on board. . . . The bride smiled but did not look up; she was looking down at her dazzling little fur muff" (79). The bride symbolizes all the hope and wonder with which the American girl radiates. The estranged young wife walks through Cork, crossing "swan-bright bridges," passing dozens of little girls who, in their confirmation dresses, look "like miniature and more conscious brides," and luxuriating in the spring weather: "the trees had almost rushed with light and blossom; they nearly had sound, as the bells did" (81). The world is her wedding and, symbolically, *she* is "The Bride of the Innisfallen." She tries to write a telegraph message to her husband, but "all she could bear this evening to know . . . was light and rain, light and rain, dark, light, and rain" (82). Passing by a pub, she hears "a glad cry" being called out "like the signal for a song." The story ends as "the girl let her message go into the stream of the street, and opening the door walked into the lovely room full of strangers."

Having found its "meaning," one may be disappointed to discover that the American girl's "trouble" is similar to the excess of joy experienced by Marjorie ("Flowers for Marjorie"), Hazel ("The Wide Net"), and Jinny Love ("The Whole World Knows"). Miss Welty has only modulated the theme in new surroundings. Moreover, the stasis which the American girls seeks on the boat train and the self-preserving anonymity which she is about to enjoy at the end of the story both recall "No Place for You, My Love." In addition to repeating herself, Miss Welty has perhaps been overscrupulous in maintaining the "outsider's" vantage point: the story may be about strangers, but even the American wife, who is ostensibly the main character, is only briefly seen; and her husband, the cause of her flight, is never seen. To be sure, the very inconclusiveness of this action expresses a firmly held idea about reality, but what one surmises to be behind the association of hints is not complex enough to justify all the complicated indirections. Thus both "The Bride of the Innisfallen" and "Going to Naples" represent a falling off in Miss Welty's fiction that may in part be the result of her having experimented with a mode more congenial to Henry Green or Elizabeth Bowen.

Miss Welty has always wanted her readers to perceive that smallest gesture, and in so doing she has continually run the risk of pushing her method too far, which would lead to decorative elaboration. This tendency is sometimes present in *The Wide Net,* and it emerges most fully in "Going to Naples" and "The Bride of the Innisfallen." "No Place for You, My Love" is successful because the form and style are appropriate to the subject and situation, but in "Going to Naples" and "The Bride of the Innisfallen," the subject matter is subordinate to the style and, in the absence of any fully realized characters, the fine style is forced to carry the main burden of the fiction.

The rich, varied impressionism and acute visual apprehension of atmosphere and scene in the stories in *The Bride of the Innisfallen* may recall the analogies between Miss Welty and the French Impressionist painter Monet, which were made early in this study. Reading "Going to Naples" and "The Bride of the Innisfallen" is, in a sense, like approaching a canvas by Monet. Viewing it at close range, one appreciates the brush strokes, but having lost the *Gestalt,* must step back until the myriad of individual touches coalesces again, and the picture once more has its subject. In these two stories one has the sense of wanting to step back to see all the shimmering "touches"—the brilliant moments and vivid single effects—fall into place. Although this never happens satisfactorily and Miss Welty falls victim to her impressionism, one can still express qualified admiration and, borrowing Cézanne's judgment of Monet, say that in these two stories Miss Welty is "only an eye, but what an eye!"

What is most remarkable about Miss Welty's fiction is that, given her methods, they have not failed her more often. As for "The Bride of the Innisfallen" and "Going to Naples"—the matter of "influences" aside—one might simply say that Miss Welty's fiction is best set on home ground, where she can deal with the kinds of environment and characters she knows so well—a fact underlined by *The Ponder Heart,* which was published at about the same time that "Going to Naples" appeared in magazine form and two years after "The Bride of the Innisfallen." Speaking to an interviewer about her use of the "outsider's" vantage point in *The Bride of the Innisfallen,* Miss Welty said: "The inside kind of story, where the outside world is given, I'll always come back to, as I do in a number of stories in the new book; for the interior world is endlessly new, mysterious, and alluring"; [13] the words have an unhappy ring for Miss Welty's admirers, for, excepting occasional articles and reviews, only one very brief story has appeared since that 1955 interview.

It is a commonplace to say that the short story has become the lyric poetry of our time; it follows, then, that the careers of many short story writers are characterized by a youthful burst of creative energy followed by a reduced productivity. It would be presumptuous, however, to comment on Miss Welty's relative silence; for she is currently at work on a long story, and the seven books she published between 1941 and 1954 represent a major contribution to modern American literature. She is clearly the outstanding short story writer of the 1940's. Moreover, "Powerhouse," "A Curtain of Green," "Petrified Man," "Why I Live at the P.O.," "A Worn Path," and "Death of a Traveling Salesman" are masterpieces of the short story, and, along with *The Golden Apples,* should guarantee her a secure place in our literature. But it is too early to predict her eventual place in American literature, although one can focus briefly on the nature of her considerable achievement.

With her wide range in style, point of view, subject matter, and fictional modes, Miss Welty has thoroughly investigated the possibilities inherent in the short story form, enriching and extending the potential of this demanding genre. Through her constant experimentation she has literally defied the genre's limitations and boundaries, and in exploring the mysteries of the inner life she has used dream and fantasy in a manner that has enabled her to produce a heightened realism. Her vision of relationship as a "changing and pervading" mystery is consistent throughout her fiction, and her characters are continually probing into these mysteries, trying to surmount the separateness existing between themselves and others, and undergoing experiences in which they are "initiated" or "reborn" into the world.

In "June Recital," Cassie Morrison thinks that "both Miss Eckhart and Virgie Rainey were human beings terribly at large, roaming on the face of the earth. And there were others of them— human beings, roaming like lost beasts" (85). The "lost beasts" appear throughout Miss Welty's fiction—Clytie, the deaf-mutes in "The Key," the traveling salesmen, Steve in "Keela, the Outcast Indian Maiden," the sharecroppers in "The Whistle," the old ladies in "A Visit of Charity," Howard in "Flowers for Marjorie," Mrs. Larkin in "A Curtain of Green," and Eugene MacLain in "Music from Spain"—but they are predominant in the early stories, where human isolation is seen most starkly. But like King MacLain in *The Golden Apples,* Miss Welty has also celebrated the "pure wish to live."

In addition to the primal loneliness, her characters have discovered, like the American girl in "The Bride of the Innisfallen," "the pure joy . . . you were born and began with" (81). And like William Wallace dancing with a catfish on his belt ("The Wide Net") or fat Gabriella doing her solo dance while "Going to Naples," they have illustrated the possibility of joyous self-perpetuation. Through the years the scope of Miss Welty's fiction has expanded until, in *The Golden Apples,* "hope and despair [are] the closest blood—unrecognizable one from the other sometimes" (234). The conception of her fiction is highly original,

and, although she has been concerned with loneliness and isolation, her work is anything but another predictable assertion of
modern *angst*. She continually celebrates the phenomenon of life.
Her characters are "at large" in an indifferent, unregenerate universe, and the burden falls completely on the self. But characters
such as Virgie Rainey and Powerhouse and Phoenix Jackson demonstrate that psychic survival is not impossible, that resistance,
resourcefulness, and the redemptive powers of the imagination can
sustain the individual. The world may be overwhelming to many
of her characters—the husband in "The Key," Sister in "Why I
Live at the P.O.," Miss Eckhart, and the narrator of "Old Mr.
Marblehall," if not the old man himself—but they are still *alive*,
in the fullest sense, even if they are rendered grotesque by isolation
and adversity and live so inwardly in delusory, protective "seasons
of dreams." Just when one is perhaps most ready to describe them
in clinical terms, these much put-upon characters will suddenly
and unexpectedly manage to find some pleasure in their lives,
thereby mitigating their situation, fleetingly, but long enough to
establish a sense of self that movingly reasserts their humanity and
asserts too the truth that they are part of us, that we share their
fate. These are the radiant moments in Eudora Welty's fiction,
when the inner voice is raised, evoking poetry, hope, or laughter
amidst the circumscribing absurdity and terror.

But perhaps generalizations deny Eudora Welty's work its basic
virtue—that it eludes categorization. In each of her stories, Miss
Welty has created a unique world which can be approached and
appreciated on its own terms. She has created a body of fiction
which abounds in those qualities which she ascribes to the "interior world"—it "is endlessly new, mysterious, and alluring."

NOTES

Introduction

1   Welty, "How I Write," in Cleanth Brooks and Robert Penn Warren (eds.), *Understanding Fiction* (2nd ed.; New York, 1959), 552.
2   In 1942 and 1943 Eudora Welty won first prize in the annual O. Henry Memorial Contest for "The Wide Net" and "Livvie," and second prize in 1941 for "A Worn Path" and in 1951 for "The Burning." She has twice held Guggenheim Fellowships, and in 1952 was elected to membership in the National Institute of Arts and Letters. She received that society's William Dean Howells Medal for "the most distinguished work of American fiction" of the period from 1950–55 (*The Ponder Heart*). She lectured at the 1954 Conference on American Studies held for six weeks at Cambridge University, was an honorary consultant of the Library of Congress (1958–61), and has received honorary LL.D. degrees from the University of Wisconsin (1954), Western College for Women (1955), and Smith College (1956) where in 1962 she was the William Allan Neilson Professor.
3   See William Bleifuss, "The Short Story in Text and Intact," *College English*, XXIII (February, 1962), 402–408, a survey of short story texts published from 1957 through 1961.

Chapter 1

1   See Robert Penn Warren, "The Love and Separateness in Miss Welty," *Kenyon Review,* VI (Spring, 1944), 253.

2 Eudora Welty, *Place in Fiction* (New York, 1957). Because it is un-paged, subsequent references to this work will not be footnoted.
3 Robert Van Gelder, "An Interview with Eudora Welty," in *Writers and Writing* (New York, 1946), 289.
4 The original title of the story when it was first published in the *Southern Review* (Spring, 1938) was "Old Mr. Grenada." Renaming him Mr. Marblehall enriched the story symbolically.
5 See Robert B. Heilman, "The Southern Temper," in Louis D. Rubin, Jr., and Robert D. Jacobs (eds.) *South: Modern Southern Literature in Its Cultural Setting* (Garden City, 1961), 56.

Chapter 2

1 Welty, "In Yoknapatawpha," *Hudson Review,* I (Winter, 1949), 597.
2 Quoted by Wylie Sypher in his *Comedy* (Garden City, 1956), 200.
3 See Lodwick Hartley, "Proserpina and the Old Ladies," *Modern Fiction Studies,* III (Winter, 1957–58), 350–54.
4 The diagnosis is Katherine Anne Porter's, in her Introduction to *Selected Stories of Eudora Welty* (New York, 1954), xx.
5 See Ruth M. Vande Kieft, *Eudora Welty* (New York, 1962), 65. My line of analysis in "The Wide Net" owes much to Miss Vande Kieft.
6 He is perhaps also a re-creation of what F. M. Cornford, in his discussion of "The Stock Masks," calls the "Learned Doctor." See his *The Origin of Attic Comedy,* ed. Theodor H. Gaster (Garden City, 1961), 136–41.
7 See Warren, "The Love and Separateness in Miss Welty," 254.
8 Welty, "A Touch That's Magic," *New York Times Book Review* (November 3, 1957), 5.
9 Van Gelder, "An Interview with Eudora Welty," 288.

Chapter 3

1 I am presently undertaking a full-length study of the grotesque in modern literature. The remarks I will have to limit myself to here are intended only as working definitions appropriate to the subject at hand.
2 Classic nineteenth-century American writing abounds in Gothic trap-pings: the obsessive image of the mirror in Hawthorne's work, the letter *A* written in the heavens in *The Scarlet Letter,* and Chillingworth, who is among other things a version of that Gothic staple, the mad medico; all the supernatural portents of the river world in *Huckleberry Finn,* and the grave robberies throughout Twain's work; the ghosts and gloomy interiors of James's *The Jolly Corner* and *The Turn of the Screw;* in *Moby Dick,* the baptism in blood, the mysterious appearance of the Parsee, Queequeg's coffin, and the flames in the try-works.
3 The most withering pejorative which Vladimir Nabokov can direct at an earlier master of the grotesque, Dostoevsky, is that of "Gothic novelist."
4 Louise Bogan, "The Gothic South," *Nation,* CLIII (December 6, 1941), 572.
5 "New Writer," *Time,* XXXVIII (November 24, 1941), 110.
6 Rose Feld, "New Novels and Short Stories of America," New York *Herald Tribune Books,* November 16, 1941, p. 10.
7 A notably confused passage in Robert E. Spiller, *et al.,* (eds.), *The Literary History of the United States* (New York, 1953), furthers the

assumption that all contemporary Southern writers are working in the same "Gothic" vein. See the remarks on the "Mississippi Delta School" in "Postscript at Mid-Century," 1401.

8   Vande Kieft, *Eudora Welty*, 89–90.
9   Welty, "The Reading and Writing of Short Stories," in William Van O'Connor (ed.), *Modern Prose: Form and Style* (New York, 1959), 437.
10 *Ibid.*, 441.
11 Warren, "The Love and Separateness in Miss Welty," 258.
12 Margaret Mitchell, "Notes by the Way," *Nation,* CLXIX (September 10, 1949), 256.
13 Welty, "The Abode of Summer," *Harper's Bazaar,* No. 2887 (June, 1952), 115.
14 "Eudora Welty," *Wilson Library Bulletin,* XVI (February, 1942), 410.
15 See Homer *The Odyssey* xi. 1. 543; trans. Robert Fitzgerald (Garden City, 1961), 214.
16 The bottled twins recall Sherwood Anderson's story "The Egg." As symbols, the twins are analogous to the malformed baby chicks which are similarly bottled and displayed for all to see on a shelf in the restaurant run by the narrator's parents. In both stories, the grotesqueness of the main characters is mirrored in the bottled specimens. Another parallel to "Petrified Man" is found in the macabre comedy of life and death in Charles Dickens' *Martin Chuzzlewit:* " 'Which Mr. Chuzzlewit,' said Mrs. Gamp,' 'is well-known to Mrs. Harris as has one sweet infant (tho she do not wish it known) in her own family by the mother's side, kep in spirits in a bottle; and that sweet babe she see at Greenwich Fair, a travelling in company with the pink eyed lady Prooshan dwarf, and livin skelinton, which judge her feeling when the barrel organ played and she was showed her own dear sister's child . . .' " (chap. LII). Like Dickens, Miss Welty cannot abide egregious piety toward the dead and toward children; witness Billy Boy and Shirley T. ("Why I Live at the P. O."), and the comedy of Bonnie Dee's death and funeral (*The Ponder Heart*).
17 Porter, Introduction, *Selected Stories of Eudora Welty,* xxi.
18 For a similar usage in literature, see Milton on the Garden of Eden, *Paradise Lost* IV.1.136. Mrs. Larkin's frantic planting may perhaps be seen as a terrifying attempt to duplicate that first garden.
19 See illustrations in William S. Lieberman (ed.), *Max Ernst* (New York, 1961), 32, 38, 39, 40.
20 See the reproductions of paintings by Bacon, de Kooning, and Dubuffet in Peter Selz, *New Images of Man* (New York, 1959).

Chapter 4

1   Eudora Welty, "Literature and the Lens," *Vogue,* CIV (August 1, 1944), 102. Included are three photographs taken by Miss Welty; five more appeared in "Welty Country," *New York Times Book Review* (January 10, 1954), 10, and three others can be seen in *Mississippi: A Guide to the Magnolia State,* comp. Federal Writers' Project of the Works Progress Administration (New York, 1938).
2   Mark Schorer suggests that all the events are perhaps hallucinatory and take place in Bowman's mind while he lies in a hospital; see *The Story* (New York, 1950), 354–55.

3 William M. Jones, "Growth of a Symbol: The Sun in Lawrence and Eudora Welty," *University of Kansas City Review,* XXVI (Autumn, 1959), 68–73, examines Lawrence's possible influence on Miss Welty and decides that she has improved upon Lawrence's use of the sun symbol "in a manner that Lawrence himself had recommended."

4 Thus, while Beulah brings to mind the Bible, *Pilgrim's Progress,* and the gospel hymns, it is also an *actual* place: Beulah, population 342, Boliver County, N.W. Mississippi.

5 In the Old Testament (Isa. 62:1), a burning lamp is used as an image of salvation. The analogy is of course ironic.

6 In "The Whistle," the images of the ebbing fire are identified with the fatigued man, and the sun that warms his wife's dream has definite sexual connotations. The Dionysian triumph of Mr. Don and the goats in "Asphodel" takes place beneath the brilliant noon sun, while Mrs. Larkin, in "A Curtain of Green," conducts her furious researches under the harsh glare of a seemingly malignant sun. Phoenix Jackson, the aged woman in "A Worn Path," is named after the legendary bird which was the embodiment of the Egyptian sun god, and as in "First Love," "Death of a Traveling Salesman," and throughout *The Golden Apples,* the sun is used to establish the characters' relationship with the natural world, ultimately defining the quality of their lives.

7 A comparison of this scene as it appears in the two versions of the story shows how Miss Welty deliberately strengthened these effects through rewriting. In the first version, *Southern Review,* V (Fall, 1939), 293–307, the scene is more clearly articulated: the unnamed girl in a white dress has a name (Mrs. Pettibone) and has just done a Beatrice Lillie imitation; the mysterious piano players are rendering a skating song; the girls cook some eggs; these details are dropped from the *Curtain of Green* version. "The phone rang and rang, and he caught himself jumping" (*Southern Review,* 301) is changed to "somewhere in the house the phone rang and rang. . ." (CG, 135). Miss Welty makes several similar changes. The most important *addition* to the story is the surrealistic sequence in which they pick up Carol and stop at the bridge. This did not appear in the *Southern Review* version, in which Carol is already at the party and is introduced by a straight-forward, " 'My name's Carol,' said a blonde" (*Southern Review,* 301). An even more detailed comparison of the two texts would provide a kind of laboratory example of how Miss Welty creates a dream-perspective.

Chapter 5

1 Welty, "Where Is the Voice Coming From?" *The New Yorker,* XXXIX (July 6, 1963), 24–25.

2 Ralph Ellison, "Change the Joke and Slip the Yoke," *Partisan Review,* XXV (Spring, 1958), 222.

3 This is not to say that all the Negroes in Miss Welty's fiction are of a heroic dimension. Some of the minor characters who are Negro may "keep their place," but their conception is consistent with the time and place of the fiction and its point of view; witness the Negro servants on the plantation in *Delta Wedding,* the action of which is set in 1923.

4 I am using the first and, I think, the most successful version of the story (*Harper's Bazaar,* No. 2872 [March, 1951]). It is reprinted in

Robert Gorham Davis (ed.), *Ten Modern Masters* (New York, 1953), 462–76; the page references in parentheses are to this text. Miss Welty rewrote this story considerably after its magazine and anthology publication; the altered version of "The Burning" is in *The Bride of the Innisfallen.*

5 Van Gelder, "An Interview with Eudora Welty," 290.
6 Stanley Edgar Hyman, "The Folk Tradition," *Partisan Review,* XXV (Spring, 1958), 201.
7 Ralph Ellison, "Richard Wright's Blues," *Antioch Review,* V (Summer, 1945), 199.
8 *Ibid.,* 219–20.
9 Ray B. West, Jr., "Analysis: Form Through Theme," in West and R. W. Stallman (eds.), *The Art of Modern Fiction* (New York, 1955), 404–405.
10 See Hyman, "The Folk Tradition," 202–203.
11 Constance Rourke, *American Humor* (Garden City, 1952), 234–35.
12 Welty, "Pageant of Birds," *New Republic,* CIX (October 25, 1943), 565–67.
13 Welty, "Ida M'Toy," *Accent,* II (Summer, 1942), 214–22.
14 Welty, "Some Notes on River Country," *Harper's Bazaar,* No. 2786 (February, 1944), 156.

Chapter 6

1 Van Gelder, "An Interview with Eudora Welty," 290.
2 Welty, "Some Notes on River Country," 85.
3 Bruno Snell, "Arcadia: The Discovery of A Spiritual Landscape," in his *The Discovery of the Mind; The Greek Origins of European Thought,* trans. T. G. Rosenmeyer (London, 1953), 283.
4 Northrop Frye's term, "analogue of innocence," used in his *Anatomy of Criticism* (Princeton, 1957), is perhaps more suitable, since it does not recall a specific genre.
5 Diana Trilling, "Fiction in Review," *Nation,* CLVII (October 2, 1943), 386–87.
6 Jean Stafford, "The Empty Net," *Partisan Review,* XI (Winter, 1944), 114.
7 Isaac Rosenfeld, "Consolations of Poetry," *New Republic,* CIX (October 18, 1943), 526.
8 Warren, "The Love and Separateness in Miss Welty," 256.
9 Hawthorne, "The Artist of the Beautiful," in *The Complete Novels and Selected Tales of Nathaniel Hawthorne,* ed. Norman Holmes Pearson (New York, 1937), 1,151.
10 Warren, "The Love and Separateness in Miss Welty," 255.
11 *Ibid.,* 254.
12 Diana Trilling, "Fiction in Review," *Nation,* CLXII (May 11, 1946), 578; Isaac Rosenfeld, "Southern Fiction and Social Reality," reprinted in his *An Age of Enormity,* ed. Theodore Solotaroff (Cleveland, 1962), 104–107.

Chapter 7

1 Yeats, "Song of the Wandering Aengus," in *The Collected Poems of W. B. Yeats* (New York, 1954), 58.

2   Welty, "The Reading and Writing of Short Stories," in O'Connor (ed.), *Modern Prose,* 437.

Chapter 8

1   Welty, "The Teaching and Study of Writing," *Western Review,* XIV (Spring, 1950), 168.
2   Bernard Kalb, "The Author," *Saturday Review,* XXXVIII (April 9, 1955), 18.
3   Welty, "Henry Green. A Novelist of the Imagination," *Texas Quarterly,* IV (Autumn, 1961), 247.
4   Louis D. Rubin, Jr., "Two Ladies of the South," *Sewanee Review,* XLIII (Autumn, 1955), 676–77.
5   Welty, "How I Write," in Brooks and Warren (eds.), *Understanding Fiction,* 551.
6   *Ibid.,* 550–51.
7   Thomas H. Carter, "Rhetoric and Southern Landscapes," *Accent,* XV (Autumn, 1955), 293.
8   Welty, "How I Write," in Brooks and Warren (eds.), *Understanding Fiction,* 552.
9   *Ibid.*
10 Elizabeth Bowen, *Stories* (New York, 1959), ix.
11 Welty, "The Reading and Writing of Short Stories," in O'Connor (ed.), *Modern Prose,* 437.
12 William Peden, "The Incomparable Welty," *Saturday Review,* XXXVIII (April 9, 1955), 18.
13 Kalb, "The Author," 18.

SELECTED BIBLIOGRAPHY

BY EUDORA WELTY

Books

The Bride of the Innisfallen. New York: Harcourt, Brace, 1955.
A Curtain of Green and Other Stories. Introduction by Katherine Anne Porter. New York: Doubleday, Doran, 1941.
Delta Wedding. New York: Harcourt, Brace, 1946.
The Golden Apples. New York: Harcourt, Brace, 1949.
Music From Spain. Greenville, Miss.: The Levee Press, 1948.
Place in Fiction. New York: House of Books, 1957. Unpaged. An edition limited to three hundred copies signed by the author. Originally published in *South Atlantic Quarterly,* LV (January, 1956), 57–72.
The Ponder Heart. New York: Harcourt, Brace, 1954.
The Robber Bridegroom. New York: Doubleday, Doran, 1942.
The Wide Net and Other Stories. New York: Harcourt, Brace, 1943.

Uncollected Work

"The Abode of Summer," *Harper's Bazaar,* No. 2887 (June, 1952), 50, 115.

"The Burning" [first version], in Robert Gorham Davis (ed.), *Ten Modern Masters*. New York: Harcourt, Brace, 1953. Pp. 462–76.

"The Doll," *The Tanager* (Grinnell College, Grinnell, Iowa), XI (June, 1936), 11–14.

"A Flock of Guinea Hens Seen From a Car," *The New Yorker*, XXXIII (April 20, 1957), 35.

"Hello and Good-Bye," *Atlantic Monthly*, CLXXX (July, 1947), 37–40.

"Henry Green. A Novelist of the Imagination," *Texas Quarterly*, IV (Autumn, 1961), 246–56.

"How I Write," *Virginia Quarterly Review*, XXXI (Spring, 1955), 240–51. Reprinted in Cleanth Brooks and Robert Penn Warren (eds.). *Understanding Fiction*. 2nd. ed. New York: Appleton-Century-Crofts, 1959. Pp. 545–53.

"Ida M'Toy," Accent, II (Summer, 1942), 214–22. Reprinted in Joshua McClennen (ed.). *Masters and Masterpieces of the Short Story*. New York: Holt, 1957. Pp. 221–25.

"In Yoknapatawpha," *Hudson Review*, I (Winter, 1949), 596–98. Review of William Faulkner's *Intruder in the Dust*.

"José de Creeft," *Magazine of Art*, XXXVII (February, 1944), 42–47.

"Life's Impact is Oblique," *New York Times Book Review* (April 2, 1961), 5. Review of book on Henry Green.

"Literature and the Lens," *Vogue*, CIV (August 1, 1944), 102–103.

"Pageant of Birds," *New Republic*, CIX (October 25, 1943), 565–67.

"The Reading and Writing of Short Stories," *Atlantic Monthly*, CLXXXII (February, 1949), 54–58, and (March, 1949), 46–49. Reprinted in William Van O'Connor (ed.). *Modern Prose: Form and Style*. New York: Crowell, 1959. Pp. 427–43.

"Retreat," *River*, I (March, 1937), 10–12.

"A Sketching Trip," *Atlantic Monthly*, CLXXV (June, 1945), 62–70.

"Some Notes on River Country," *Harper's Bazaar*, No. 2786 (February, 1944), 85–87, 150–56.

"A Sweet Devouring," *Mademoiselle*, XLVI (December, 1957), 49, 114–16.

"The Teaching and Study of Writing," *Western Review*, XIV (Spring, 1950), 167–68.

"Time and Place—and Suspense," *New York Times Book Review* (June 30, 1963), 5, 27. Review of *The Stories of William Sansom*.

"A Touch That's Magic," *New York Times Book Review* (November 3, 1957), 5. Review of Isak Dinesen's *Last Tales*.

"Where Is the Voice Coming From?" *The New Yorker*, XXXIX (July 6, 1963), 24–25.

ABOUT EUDORA WELTY

For useful bibliographical references, see my notes; only the most suggestive criticism of Eudora Welty's fiction is included below. For an extensive bibliography, see Seymour L. Gross, "Eudora Welty: A Bibliography of Criticism and Comment," *Secretary's News Sheet,* Bibliographical Society, University of Virginia, No. 45 (April, 1960), 1–32.

Daniel, Robert. "Eudora Welty: The Sense of Place," in Louis D. Rubin, Jr., and Robert D. Jacobs (eds.). *South: Modern Southern Literature in Its Cultural Setting.* Garden City: Dolphin, 1961. Pp. 276–86.

Glenn, Eunice. "Fantasy in the Fiction of Eudora Welty," in John W. Aldridge (ed.). *Critiques and Essays on Modern Fiction, 1920–51.* New York: Ronald Press, 1952. Pp. 506–17.

Hardy, John E. *"Delta Wedding* as Region and Symbol," *Sewanee Review,* LX (Summer, 1952), 397–417.

Hicks, Granville. "Eudora Welty," *College English,* XIV (November, 1952), 69–76.

Morris, H. C. "Eudora Welty's Use of Mythology," *Shenandoah,* VI (Spring, 1955), 34–40.

Porter, Katherine Anne. Introduction to *Selected Stories of Eudora Welty.* New York: The Modern Library, 1954. Pp. xi–xxiii.

Ransom, John Crowe. "Delta Fiction," *Kenyon Review,* VIII (Summer, 1946), 503–507.

Rubin, Louis D., Jr. "The Golden Apples of the Sun," in *The Faraway Country.* Seattle: University of Washington Press, 1963.

Vande Kieft, Ruth M. *Eudora Welty.* New York: Twayne, 1962.

Warren, Robert Penn. "The Love and Separateness in Miss Welty," *Kenyon Review,* VI (Spring, 1944), 246–59. Reprinted in his *Selected Essays.* New York: Random House, 1958. Pp. 156–69.

INDEX

269